MW00824611

HASHAMAYIM 1B
Adonijah O. Ogbonnaya, PhD
Copyright © 2017 Adonijah O. Ogbonnaya, PhD

All rights reserved. No part of this publication may be reproduced, distributed, or transmitted in any form or by any means, including photocopying, recording, or other electronic or mechanical methods, without the prior written permission of the publisher, except in the case of brief quotations embodied in critical reviews and certain other non-commercial uses permitted by copyright law. For permission requests, write to the publisher, addressed "Attention: Permissions Coordinator," at the address below.

King James Version (KJV): Scripture quotations marked "KJV" are taken from the Holy Bible, King James Version (Public Domain).

New American Standard Bible (NAS): Scripture taken from the NEW AMERICAN STANDARD BIBLE®, Copyright © 1960,1962,1963,1968,1971,1972,1973,1975,1977,1995 by The Lockman Foundation. Used by permission.

New King James Version (NKJV): Scripture taken from the New King James Version®. Copyright © 1982 by Thomas Nelson. Used by permission. All rights reserved.

The Greek New Testament by Henry Alford (ALF): Scripture quotations marked "ALF" are taken from The Greek New Testament by Henry Alford (Public Domain).

William Tyndale Translation (WTT): Scripture quotations marked "WTT" are taken from the Holy Bible, William Tyndale Translation (Public Domain).

All verses are New King James Version unless otherwise stated.

Front Cover Illustration by Taylor Remington

Published by Seraph Creative in 2017
United States / United Kingdom / South Africa / Australia
www.seraphcreative.org

Typesetting, Illustration & Layout by Feline
www.felinegraphics.com

Aactev8
1020 Victoria Ave, Venice, California
www.aactev8.com

First printed in South Africa.

ISBN: 978-0-620-77237-2

HASHAMAYIM 1B

THE ROLE OF THE SONS OF GOD IN STRUCTURES OF THE NESTED HEAVENS

By

ADONIJAH O. OGBONNAYA, PHD

Published by Seraph Creative

CONTENTS

FOREWORD

For any of us to have access to and to navigate within the Heavenly realm, engaging it for the transformation of our life in creation, we must first know Jesus Christ as the way, the truth and the life. We must be certain within our heart that we have been crucified with Christ (Rom. 6:6). We must hold firmly to the testimony of the shed blood of Jesus Christ. It is only by the shedding of the blood of the Son of God that we have salvation.

To begin to enter these Heavenly dimensions we must overcome the disease of restlessness, sit still and know and practice engaging His presence (from the scriptures, the inner experience of the Spirit and even early Christian tradition). It is the practice of the presence and inward looking, informed by the revelation of the Word, which will allow you to enter into certain places and gates depicted by the book of Revelation.

When God reveals the 12 Lower Kingdom Dimensions, He is saying: "I am going to give it to you in the names of the sons of Jacob, so that you can understand what I am doing in the Heavens." We should not just see things from an Earthly perspective. God has given us a pattern to access what He is doing in Heaven so that, when we get transported or carried in our soul to Heaven, we know what to look for. God shows us the pattern so we see the footprints that God has laid out. He has done this by laying out the dimensions in the 12 tribes.

When we can get into these dimensions and our heart's desires are pure, God will begin to manifest different aspects for us because of His great love. God deliberately does this because He wants to have intimacy with us based on our heart's desires. It is important to understand why God speaks a lot about our heart's desires being pure. God wants to create and manifest for us what is in our heart so we can have intimate fellowship with Him. That is what Jesus meant by "For indeed, the kingdom of God is within you" (Luke 17:21). That which is within is what the Father manifests. The Lord already has what He has built, the things He's created, but oftentimes He wants to manifest for us our heart's desire. God will grant the desires of our hearts, not just on Earth, but in the Heavenly dimensions!

Dr. Adonijah Ogbonnaya

PUBLISHER'S NOTE

Welcome to Hashamayim 1B. This book is part two of a four book series: Hashamayim 1A, 1B, 2A & 2B.

Hashamayim 1A "Angels, Heavenly Structures & The Sons Of God" introduced us to the reality of the Heavens, the structures of the Heavens and the Father's desire to give you access through Jesus Christ. It is highly recommended that you read 1A before commencing this book. However, we will be recapping and reintroducing some of the content of 1A to retain understanding and context. If you have read the first book, you will find it an invaluable reminder.

Hashamayim 1B is the amazing continuation of the study of the twelve lower dimensions of the City of God, revealed to John in Revelation 21.

It is a great honor to help facilitate bringing this revelation to Earth. It is part of the life work of Dr. Adonijah Ogbonnaya (Dr. O). Dr. O is an essential component of the reformation of the church on Earth today. With a deep love and understanding of the scriptures, a life long knowledge of the Hebrew language and Jewish culture, a continual insistence on academic excellence and a genuine Christo-centric mystic - there is no one like him.

To Dr. O and the AACTEV8 family, we thank you for trusting us with your message and for being a true living epistle and letter of recommendation for this message.

HOW TO USE THIS BOOK

In your hands you are holding a man's life. The HaShamayim series is the result of decades of intimacy and pursuit of a man for his Creator.

From years spent with God and the scriptures, Dr. O has accessed dimensions of the Heavenly realms through the work of Christ. With clarity and vulnerability, Dr. O has opened his understanding for the hungry. Accordingly, may what cost him 30 years take you 3, as God opens your heart to the great things he has prepared for you.

Hashamayim 1B is not a book to be intellectually understood and categorized. It is a doorway to experiencing the person God and His Kingdom (and thus yourself) in greater and greater truth. Please take your time in marinating and meditating on the scriptures and revelation contained in this book. Ask Holy Spirit to reveal to you the deep realities behind the printed words. He surely will.

Also, we have produced illustrations to help the reader gain an accurate grid for what is being presented - but even the best diagram will not come close to conveying the wonder of encountering the multi faceted wisdom of God and His created dimensions for yourself. All glory to Him!

Go higher. Go deeper. Enjoy. It is the Father's delight to give you the Kingdom - so let us go boldly through the New and Living Way, Jesus Christ.

Great Peace,

The Seraph Creative Team

ACKNOWLEDGEMENTS

I asked God for the words to share with you the vision I have when I look at you:

You hold within your frame a divine purpose. When I interact with you, I am shown a marvelous mystery. I am graced with a glimpse of revelation.

You are the form of mystery. You are the reason for revelation. You are the wonder of worlds. You are the image of the Creator – a visible image of the unseen.

I especially want to thank my wife Benedicta Ogbonnaya, who has walked this path with me for 37 years. Her patience, love, strength and wisdom have touched the lives of many and she has most profoundly blessed my life.

I want to thank all my students in AACTEV8 and worldwide for your support over the years, especially those who have contributed directly to this book series. Also, to those who have co-ordinated conferences in South Africa. Nigeria, Jamaica, Uganda, The Caribbean, United Kingdom, Singapore, Malaysia and the Philippines, I am deeply grateful. I am honored to call you my friends and co-laborers.

Thank you, Helen Stanley, who transcribed the lectures and made this book possible.

May God richly bless you all.

PREFACE

JESUS IS THE LIVING DOOR TO THE HEAVENS

Then Jesus said to them again, "Most assuredly, I say to you, I am the door of the sheep. "All who ever came before Me are thieves and robbers, but the sheep did not hear them. "I am the door. If anyone enters by Me, he will be saved, and will go in and out and find pasture. "The thief does not come except to steal, and to kill, and to destroy. I have come that they may have life, and that they may have it more abundantly. "I am the good shepherd. The good shepherd gives His life for the sheep". (John 10:7-11).

For most of modern Christianity, Heaven is the place where God lives, and the Christian will go to live there after they die. The truth is "the Heavens" are a dimension opened through Christ to all His believer's. They are available right now and it is the Father's delight that you understand and mature in them.

Jesus was from Heaven and invites us there; "I have come down from Heaven" (John 6:38 NAS).

Jesus was in Heaven while being on the Earth; "No one has ascended into Heaven, but He who descended from Heaven: the Son of Man." (John 3:13 NAS)

The Christian is in the Heavens with Christ right now; "and

raised us up with Him, and seated us with Him in the Heavenly places in Christ Jesus" (Eph 2:6 NAS)

The message of Christianity is that the door to the Heavens has opened to all who, by their free will, choose to believe the Messiah whom God has sent in the Person of Yeshua (Jesus) HaMashiach (The Christ).

Jesus said, "I am the way, the truth and the life. No one comes to the Father but through Me." (John 14:6 NAS). Entering Heaven is a gift given freely through grace by God the Father through the Son Jesus Christ. It cannot be achieved by our own power or righteousness.

Christ, through his sacrifice, came to grant man the opportunity to enter, or rather re-enter, into paradise and therefore have access into the Heavens again.

"Since therefore, brethren, we have confidence to enter the holy place by the blood of Jesus, for He has given us a new and living way which He inaugurated for us through the veil, that is, His flesh and since we have a great priest over the House of God, let us draw near with a sincere heart in full assurance of faith, having our hearts sprinkled clean from an evil conscience and our bodies washed with pure water." (Heb 10:19-22 NAS)

We can only enter the Heavens, and especially the place where the throne of the LORD dwells, through this "new and living way" and not by the old and dead way of the flesh. Three things define this new and living way; the blood of Jesus Christ, the veil of His flesh, His priesthood.

On our part, we must come with a heart full of assurance of faith. Our hearts must be sprinkled by the blood, resulting in the removal of an evil conscience. Our bodies must be washed with pure water, which is the Word of God.

Jesus was our apostle, blazing a new path, and our High Priest, making a permanent way through his torn body for us to go beyond the veil (Heb 3).

ACCESSING BY THE NAME OF GOD

| HEH | VAV | HEH | YOD |

"Praise the Lord! Praise the Lord from the Heavens; Praise Him in the heights!" (Psa 148:1 NAS)

Let us revisit a powerful tool for accessing the Heavens and their dimensions.

When we see the term "the Lord" in the Old Testament, it is always the Hebrew "YHVH" (Yod-Heh-Vav-Heh). The name of the Lord can be chanted. By voice and sound you can access the various Heavens. When scripture says, "Praise Him in the heights!" it is not talking about physical mountains.

Chanting the name of God is a powerful tool. For more understanding, please visit our website www.aactev8.com

Another exercise is to sit in a quiet place, with your hands stretched half way open in front of you. Take a deep breath and exhale slowly. You may want to breathe in the first syllable of the name of Jesus, "Jeeeee...," then exhale with "suuuuus," inhale "Jeeeee....," exhale "suuuuuuuus."

Do this as many times as you need to. Listen to the sound of the name of the Lord Jesus Christ as it vibrates through your body. Call upon His name until you feel His presence through the Holy Spirit. Proclaim the Lordship of Jesus Christ and make sure that Jesus is in the center of your space. Time and space cohere in him.

THE HEART-MIND

"He has made everything beautiful in its time. Also He has put eternity in their hearts" (Ecclesiastes 3:11).

The best way to access spiritual mysteries is to use your heart-mind, not just your rational-mind. This heart-mind is able to remember large amounts of information and revelations.

The heart has the revelation of eternity - things that go back to the beginning of creation. The very principle of eternity is embedded within the heart by God at the moment of conception. One can even say that God has locked within the human heart the mystery of the universe!

One way to help unlock this eternity locked in the heart is to follow the biblical encouragement "Be still, and know that I am God" (Psa 46:10).

As we begin examining the Heavens, we must learn the protocol of reverence through prayer and deal with areas in our lives that might cause problems for us as we navigate the mystery of the Heavens. The first order of the protocol is acknowledging the Lordship of Jesus Christ, followed by an attentive listening to the Holy Spirit, while maintaining a meditative attitude and self-immersion in the Scriptures.

HASHAMAYIM 1B

Preface

SECTION 1

Section 1: Hashamayim

HASHAMAYIM

"In the beginning God created the Heavens and the earth" (Gen 1:1)

The Hebrew word for Heaven is 'HaShamayim'. The word always occurs in plural form, so it should be translated 'the Heavens' or 'the Heavenlies'. We are speaking about more than one Heaven, connected to a single source.

The plurality of the Heavens is seen in the revelation of "the Heaven of Heavens" or "the highest Heaven".

"Behold, the Heaven and the Heaven of Heavens is the LORD'S thy God, the earth also, with all that therein is." (Deut 10:14 KJV)

"Behold, to the LORD your God belong Heaven and the highest Heavens, the earth and all that is in it" (Deut 10:14 NASB)

"But will God indeed dwell on the earth? Behold, Heaven and the Heaven of Heavens cannot contain You. How much less this temple which I have built!" (1 Kin 8:27).

The idea of the plurality of Heaven continues in the New Testament. After being baptized, Jesus came up immediately from the water; and behold, the Heavens were opened, and he saw the Spirit of God descending as a dove and lighting on Him, further Matthew 17 and behold, a voice out of the Heavens said, "This is My beloved Son, in whom I am well-pleased." (Matthew 3:17)

"the powers of the Heavens shall be shaken." (Matthew 24:29) "you will see the Heavens opened and the angels of God ascending and descending on the Son of Man." (John 1:51)

"he said, 'Behold, I see the Heavens opened up, and the Son of Man standing at the right hand of God' (Acts 7:56)

"He who descended is also the One who ascended far above all the Heavens, that He might fill all things" (Eph 4:10)

We will revisit the structure of the Heavens in the chapter "Israel as a pattern of Heaven"

WHAT ARE THE HEAVENS?

When I think of Heaven, biblically there are Heavens of Heavens of Heavens. The Kingdom of God includes all the Heavens. The Heavens include the planets and everything else you can think of - all the 100 billion galaxies all are part of the Heavens!

Moreover, Heaven is a series of interconnected dimensions - more accurately described as 'the Heavens' (Hashamayim) - that God wants you to discover right now. God created the Heavens for the very reason that you could experience Him, know Him and become like Him. The Heavens were made for you!

These Heavenly dimensions are your home, the place you

were born. Understanding the nature of these Heavens and how they relate to each other, and to yourself, is key to starting your journey of discovering all God has for you and revealing who you truly are.

We will re-examine the structure of the Heavens before continuing our understanding of the Lower 12 Houses.

"Be exalted, O God, above the Heavens; Let Your glory be above all the earth" (Psa 57:5).

Heaven sits in God, as there is nothing outside Him. God is greater than the Heavens.

"Sing unto God, sing praises to his name: extol him that rideth upon the Heavens by his name Yah, and rejoice before him" (Psa 68:4 KJV).

"Who humbles Himself to behold the things that are in the Heavens and in the earth?." (Psa 113:6)

God is so much greater than his created realms He needs to stoop down to view them (although He is already in them!)

As believers it is essential we understand the pattern of the Heavens. Such understanding will:

- affect how you see, grasp, and understand the structures of Heaven and the New Jerusalem.

- radically transform the way we see God, the world, ourselves, matter, reality and the way we operate in our day-to-day lives.

- help you to grasp your body, soul and spirit and give you a glimpse of the inter-relationship of everything.

- aid in the understanding that everything spoken of in Scripture - cherubim, seraphim, angels, Heaven and hell, soul, spirit and even demons - are connected in a special way.

- help you co-work with God that the principalities and powers that are in the Heavenlies, who have occupied the places rightly belonging to man created in the image and likeness of God, might learn wisdom because of our fall (Eph 3:10).

TYPES OF HEAVENS

There are different types of Heaven described in scripture that we can experience.

Mobile Heaven: that which God moves about in / rides upon and sets up sometimes to interact with His creatures. In Ezekiel and Daniel we see God move to engage creation. Where ever God is, is Heaven. Heaven moves with Him. So this is a mobile Heaven.

Malleable Heaven: You are a child of God. The Father builds a house according to the desires and needs of His child. He forms it based on your experiences and what you need. The more you mature, the more He opens this Heaven up and redesigns it.

"Now if anyone builds on this foundation with gold, silver, precious stones, wood, hay, straw, each one's work will become clear; for the Day will declare it, because it will be revealed by fire; and the fire will test each one's work, of what sort it is" (1 Cor 3:12-13).

Everything you create will be tried by fire. Most of the Heavens you create will be destroyed. This destruction is fine - as you are learning so you can create a universe! God is a patient and loving Father!

Set Heaven: This Heaven is not malleable. It does not change.

How it is experienced may differ between people and depend on their maturity. However, this actual Heaven did not change, just people's perception of it.

HOW DO THE HEAVENS AFFECT US?

Heaven is concerned for the Earth;

"The Lord is in His holy temple, The Lord's throne is in Heaven; His eyes behold, His eyelids test the sons of men" (Psa 11:4).

Heaven is directly connected to the earth. God has a particular interest in the Earth. Only here on Earth does there exist a record of God's life and spirit in the form of a human being which can be transferred to other dimensions.

Heaven wars on behalf of Earth;

"And it happened, as they fled before Israel and were on the descent of Beth Horon, that the Lord cast down large hailstones from Heaven on them as far as Azekah, and they died. There were more who died from the hailstones than the children of Israel killed with the sword" (Jos 10:11).

"The adversaries of the Lord shall be broken in pieces; From Heaven He will thunder against them. The Lord will judge the ends of the earth. He will give strength to His king, And exalt the horn of His anointed." (1 Sam 2:10).

Deborah tells us that the stars in their movements around the Heavens fought for Israel.

"They fought from the Heavens; The stars from their courses fought against Sisera." (Jud 5:20)

The movement of Heaven affects the Earth;

"Then the earth shook and trembled; The foundations of the hills also quaked and were shaken, because He was angry." (Psa 18:7)

Heaven reveals iniquity;

"The Heavens will reveal his iniquity, And the earth will rise up against him." (Job 20:27)

Wisdom is a gift from Heaven. James tells us to ask of God who gives wisdom. The book of Job asks;

"Do you know the ordinances of the Heavens? Can you set their dominion over the earth? ... Who can number the clouds by wisdom? Or who can pour out the bottles of Heaven?" (Job 38:33 and 37)

Heaven is where covenant is kept and mercy flows;

"and he said: "Lord God of Israel, there is no God in Heaven above or on earth below like You, who keep Your covenant and mercy with Your servants who walk before You with all their hearts." (1 Kin 8:23)

Or similarly promises are kept and blessing flows;

"Look down from Your holy habitation, from Heaven, and bless Your people Israel and the land which You have given us, just as You swore to our fathers, a land flowing with milk and honey." (Deut 26:15).

Prayer is heard and forgiveness flows from Heaven;

"And may You hear the supplication of Your servant and of Your people Israel, when they pray toward this place. Hear in Heaven Your dwelling place; and when You hear, forgive." (1 Kin 8:30)

Natural and Spiritual blessings are controlled from Heaven;

1 Kings 8: 35 says "When the Heavens are shut up and there is no rain..."

Heaven is also where the thrones of God and Angels reside. Let's look at that in more detail.

THE THRONES AND OF THE HEAVENS

"The Lord has established His throne in Heaven, And His kingdom rules over all. Bless the Lord, you His angels, who excel in strength, who do His word, heeding the voice of His word. Bless the Lord, all you His hosts, You ministers of His, who do His pleasure. Bless the Lord, all His works, In all places of His dominion. Bless the Lord, O my soul!" (Psa 103:19-22)

In the Heavens is where the ultimate throne of God is. It is where everything starts and everything finds its end. This dimension is above the Heavens. "There is no one like the God of Jeshurun, Who rides the Heavens to help you, And in His excellency on the clouds." (Deut 33:26)

Isaiah reveals the whole of the Heavens as God's throne. "Heaven is My throne, And earth is My footstool. Where is the house that you will build Me? And where is the place of My rest?" (Isa 66:1).

In every Heaven or Heavenly dimension there is a throne

that serves as God's seat of rest. From these thrones God's representatives direct that particular dimension. Every being, in every dimension, must deal with the fact that God's "Kingdom rules over all."

The Throne (singular) of God sits above all other thrones, far above all the Heavens. From this Ultimate Throne emerge all other thrones.

> "In the year that King Uzziah died, I saw the Lord sitting on a throne, high and lifted up, and the train of His robe filled the temple. Above it stood seraphim; each one had six wings: with two he covered his face, with two he covered his feet, and with two he flew. And one cried to another and said: "Holy, holy, holy is the Lord of hosts; The whole earth is full of His glory!" And the posts of the door were shaken by the voice of him who cried out, and the house was filled with smoke." (Isa 6:1-4)

> "Your throne, O God, is forever and ever; A scepter of righteousness is the scepter of Your kingdom. You love righteousness and hate wickedness; Therefore God, Your God, has anointed You with the oil of gladness more than Your companions. All Your garments are scented with myrrh and aloes and cassia, out of the ivory palaces, by which they have made You glad." (Psa 45:6-8).

Scripture also refers to man as the dwelling place of God. Therefore the earth, as the abode of humanity, now comes to serve as God's resting place. In a sense, man is the final extension of the divine being and the place of God coming to rest.

Of all the things that God has made, it is man whom God looks to as His divine resting place. Man is then the throne of God on the earth!

THE THRONE IN MAN

Whatever God is in macrocosm, man is in microcosm. The human being himself is a throne surrounded by a constellation of thrones - in the midst of which God the Three-in-One sits! If a human has been washed by the blood, the redeemed individual's structure corresponds to that which was written in the book of God for their lives from the foundation of the world.

Israel carries a type. Israel is in her constellation around the tabernacle and the whole earth is in a constellation around Israel. The constellations of various galaxies surround their sun. So the heart of man, who is inhabited by God through the blood of Jesus Christ, is constellated by thrones over which he serves as vice-regent for God Almighty! He vibrates the rulership frequencies of the twenty-four dimensions of the Heavenly city as he matures and manifests the intertwining spiral of his divine sonship!

Those who become the throne of the Most High (the dwelling place or the seat of God's rest) upon which constellations of lower thrones revolve, all directed to the glory of God the Father, must carry themselves as King. He must know that it is an abomination for kings to commit wickedness (Pro 16:12). Every constellation of thrones around him must be established by righteousness and must be committed to the divine essence in him, not to mere personality projections.

This person must also develop 'eyes' (allowing all the eyes within the body, soul and spirit to be cleansed and focused), for every throne must be a seeing device. Thus, "A king who sits on the throne of judgment, scatters all evil with his eyes" (Pro 20:8).

This person must remember that every throne in his or her constellation must flow in "mercy and truth." They must answer by the center of his/her essence, which is the image and likeness of God. It is mercy and truth that preserve one as king, ruler, prophet and priest and uphold the throne upon which God the

Almighty has placed them.

This understanding is the reason for the Hashamayim series - to make one a throne in all dimensions to bring the rule of the Kingdom.

There are twelve glories of man in the lower Heavens upon which man must practice kingship until he comes into the City and receives the other twelve. These 24 dimensions complete him as the City of the Living God, combining the Patriarchal (Lower 12) and the Apostolic (Upper 12). "He raises the poor from the dust, and lifts the beggar from the ash heap, to set them among princes and make them inherit the throne of glory" (1 Sam 2:8). We will continue to deal with these twelve dimensions of the Lower Heavens in the second part of this book.

The Kingdom of God, though manifesting on the Earth, is not confined to the little portion of the universe called Earth, especially if we consider Earth in its current state. The current Earth is only as the transitional note to a new Earth. It is the training ground for the human being who bears the record of the DNA of God in the created universe.

The Earth, as it is currently, is not the Kingdom of God. It must pass through the fire so that it will be able to handle the imposition of the schematics of Heaven upon it. In order to reconnect it to the Heavens, this old Earth must give way to a new one. As His kingdom rules over all (Psa 103), we can infer that He sets His throne in the Heavens in all the dimensions of time and space and in every dimension of the Heavens. He sets thrones for those whom He has appointed kings and priests.

ANGELS

The term 'angels', as Dionysius of Areopagus states, is a general term used for beings that are diverse and distinctly designed in their being and their functions.

Every dimension and every Heaven have angelic structures. Angels are assigned to particular aspects of the universe - even on Earth.

Angels do not cross dimensions of duty unless by the direct command of a higher authority. (The demonic function and cater to the whims and lusts of man, in opposition to God. The demonic are mimickers. So if you can manipulate an angel to do what you want it to do when it comes to give you a message, you are not dealing with an angel from God. Angels from God are answerable to the Master).

Angles can refer to beings that may be called beasts and other strange looking creatures who do the will of God, ministering to God and ministering to humanity as angels.

There are angelic beings that are legions by nature. Remember, Jesus said, "What is your name?" He said, "I am legion, for we are many." He did not say, "we are legions" in plural but "I am legion" (Remember, whatever you find in the dark world, there is always the original counterpart in the world of light). Angels have the capacity in themselves. There are myriads and myriads of beings put together who can release all kinds of realities. Usually, these are creatures used for warfare by God.

"Bless the Lord, all you His hosts, You ministers of His, who do His pleasure?" (Psa 103:21). A minister is someone who serves directly - a servant. Many of the beings you see that come and do things for you are servants; they are ministers that God sends. Angels are meant to operate with us in certain ways as tutors (Gal 4:1-2) until we come to the fullness of what God created us to operate in.

So, understand that my use of the word angels does not mainly refer to angels in the Western tradition - beings that look like men but differ only in the strange protrusion of wings and feathers growing from their shoulder blades.

(For greater discussion on angels I refer you to the series on angels and their function at www.aactev8.com or you can purchase the book on angelic structures).

THE NEW JERUSALEM

[1] "The first Heaven and the first earth passed away, and there is no longer any sea.

[2] And I saw the holy city, New Jerusalem, coming down out of Heaven from God, made ready as a bride adorned for her husband.

[3] And I heard a loud voice from the throne, saying, "Behold, the tabernacle of God is among men, and He shall dwell among them, and they shall be His people, and God Himself shall be among them,

[4] and He shall wipe away every tear from their eyes; and there shall no longer be any death; there shall no longer be any mourning, or crying, or pain; the first things have passed away."

[5] And He who sits on the throne said, "Behold, I am making all things new." And He said, "Write, for these words are faithful and true."

[6] And He said to me, "It is done. I am the Alpha and the Omega, the beginning and the end. I will give to the one who thirsts from the spring of the water of life without cost.

[7] "He who overcomes shall inherit these things, and I will be his God and he will be My son.

8 "But for the cowardly and unbelieving and abominable and murderers and immoral persons and sorcerers and idolaters and all liars, their part will be in the lake that burns with fire and brimstone, which is the second death."

9 And one of the seven angels who had the seven bowls full of the seven last plagues, came and spoke with me, saying, "Come here, I shall show you the bride, the wife of the Lamb."

10 And he carried me away in the Spirit to a great and high mountain, and showed me the holy city, Jerusalem, coming down out of Heaven from God,

11 having the glory of God. Her brilliance was like a very costly stone, as a stone of crystal-clear jasper.

12 It had a great and high wall, with twelve gates, and at the gates twelve angels; and names were written on them, which are those of the twelve tribes of the sons of Israel.

13 There were three gates on the East and three gates on the North and three gates on the South and three gates on the West.

14 And the wall of the city had twelve foundation stones, and on them were the twelve names of the twelve apostles of the Lamb.

15 And the one who spoke with me had a gold measuring rod to measure the city, and its gates and its wall.

16 And the city is laid out as a square, and its length is as great as the width; and he measured the city with the rod, fifteen hundred miles; its length and width and height are equal.

17 And he measured its wall, seventy-two yards, according to human measurements, which are also angelic measurements.

18 And the material of the wall was jasper; and the city was pure gold, like clear glass.

19 The foundation stones of the city wall were adorned with every kind of precious stone. The first foundation stone was jasper; the second, sapphire; the third, chalcedony; the fourth, emerald;

20 the fifth, sardonyx; the sixth, sardius; the seventh, chrysolite; the eighth, beryl; the ninth, topaz; the tenth, chrysoprase; the eleventh, jacinth; the twelfth, amethyst.

21 And the twelve gates were twelve pearls; each one of the gates was a single pearl. And the street of the city was pure gold, like transparent glass.

22 And I saw no temple in it, for the Lord God, the Almighty, and the Lamb, are its temple.

23 And the city has no need of the sun or of the moon to shine upon it, for the glory of God has illumined it, and its lamp is the Lamb.

24 And the nations shall walk by its light, and the kings of the earth shall bring their glory into it.

25 And in the daytime (for there shall be no night there) its gates shall never be closed;

26 and they shall bring the glory and the honor of the nations into it;

27 and nothing unclean and no one who practices abomination and lying, shall ever come into it, but only

those whose names are written in the Lamb's book of life.
(Rev 21:1-27 NAS)

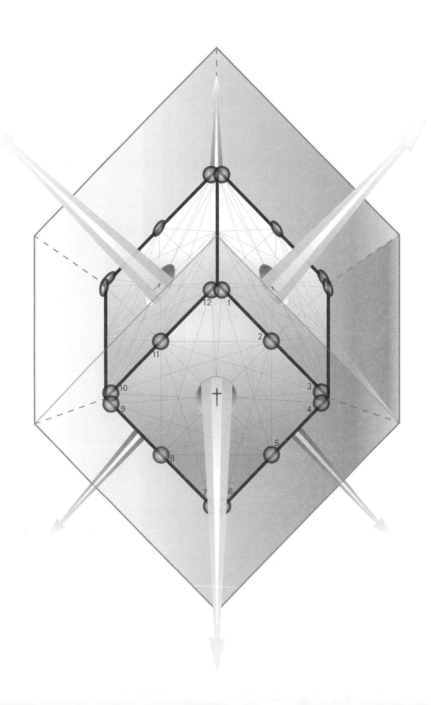

ISRAEL AS A PATTERN OF THE HEAVENS, PERFECTED BY CHRIST

"Who serve the copy and shadow of the Heavenly things, as Moses was divinely instructed when he was about to make the tabernacle. For He said, "See that you make all things according to the pattern shown you on the mountain." But now He has obtained a more excellent ministry, inasmuch as He is also Mediator of a better covenant, which was established on better promises." (Heb 8:5-6)

The experiences of those who call themselves by the name of Christ must be examined to determine if they correlate with the revelation that the LORD has given in the various images, structures and processes used in Scripture.

I focused my attention on how God structured His interaction with the people of Israel, knowing that this relationship serves as an interpretive archetype for making sense of the secret things of God on Earth.

"Therefore it was necessary that the copies of the things in the Heavens should be purified with these, but the Heavenly things themselves with better sacrifices than these." (Heb 9:23)

The sacrifice of the LORD Jesus Christ was to make tainted

dimensions of the Heavens pure again, to open its gateways and pathways and to purify us so that we can again navigate the Heavens as washed beings.

All of Israel's religious activities were patterns of things in Heaven. The sacrifices were done so that through all of the feasts, rituals, garments, gates of the temple and city and the structures of the Heavenlies could be clearly envisioned and followed until the Heavenly things were purified by the better sacrifice.

Moreover, the way God organized the tribes of Israel in their encampment reveals (as a mystery!) the earthly pattern of the Heavenly reality. See Numbers 2:25-31 for a full description.

THE ENCAMPMENT OF THE OLD SYSTEM OF NUMBERS CHAPTER 2

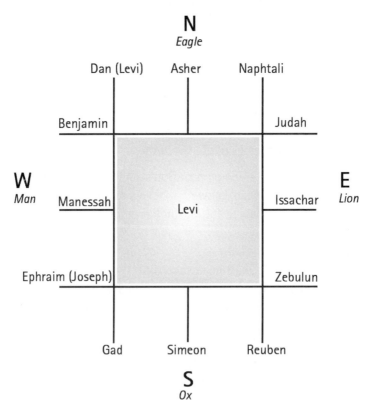

This is the Old Testament encampment as described in Numbers Chapter 2.

THE ENCAMPMENT OF THE NEW SYSTEM OF REVELATION

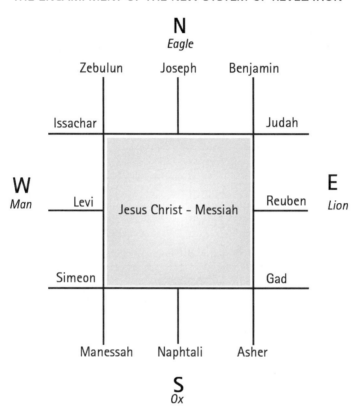

This the New Testament encampment as described in Revelation.

Genesis 29–30	Numbers 1	Revelation 7
Reuben	Reuben	Reuben
Simeon	Simeon	Simeon
Levi	Judah	Judah
Judah	Dan	Dan
Dan	Naphtali	Naphtali
Naphtali	Gad	Gad
Gad	Asher	Asher
Asher	Issachar	Issachar
Issachar	Zebulun	Zebulun
Zebulun	Ephraim	Ephraim
Joseph	Manasseh	Manasseh
Benjamin	Benjamin	Benjamin

Above is a table showing how the scriptures change the tribes included in the 12, and their order of mention. There are no mistakes. This a deliberate mystery to be uncovered.

WHY ARE THE CAMPS DIFFERENT ON THE OLD AND NEW TESTAMENTS?

Genesis 49 is Jacob blessing his sons, and thus their tribes, in birth order. There are 12, and one unnumbered, Dinah. Dinah is the 13th, the Messianic Principle.

In Numbers, over 400 hundred years later, Levi has become the priest and is not counted among the tribes. "But the Levites were not numbered among them by their fathers' tribe; for the Lord had spoken to Moses, saying: "Only the tribe of Levi you shall not number, nor take a census of them among the children of Israel" (Num 1: 47-49).

Levi becomes the 13th, the Messianic Principle. The tribe of Joseph has been split up between his two sons Ephraim and Manasseh, maintaining the 12 tribes. This was made legal when Jacob owned them as his own sons. "And now your two sons, Ephraim and Manasseh, who were born to you in the land of Egypt before I came to you in Egypt, are mine; as Reuben and Simeon, they shall be mine." (Gen 48:5)

In Revelation 7, written about 1300 years after Numbers, we see Levi has been restored to the tribe list. Levi has fulfilled his role as a prophetic metaphor as the Messiah has come and the Levitical priesthood completed. Two tribes are now missing that had been present in the previous lists - Dan and Ephraim. They have both been removed because of their trading with idols and can now only be brought back in by the door of Christ, like a gentile.

Ephraim: "Ephraim is joined to idols, let him alone." (Hos 4:17)

Dan: "The sons of Dan set up for themselves the graven image; and Jonathan, the son of Gershom, the son of Manasseh, he and his sons were priests to the tribe of the Danites until the day of the captivity of the land." (Judg 18:30 NAS)

"So the king consulted, and made two golden calves, and he said to them, "It is too much for you to go up to Jerusalem; behold your gods, O Israel, that brought you up from the land of Egypt." He set one in Bethel, and the other he put in Dan. Now this thing became a sin, for the people went to worship before the one as far as Dan." (1 Kin 12:28-30 NAS)

Note, the "king" mentioned here is Jeroboam, of the tribe of Ephraim!

We will deal with both Dan in Section 2 of this book.

THE ECOLOGY OF THE NESTED HEAVENS

Now let us revisit the diagram. The highest dimension is the Echad '1' Dimension. This is the very person of God. Next is the Trinitas '3' Dimension which is God in 3 persons. The "Trinitas Dimension" and the "Echud Dimension" equal four parts - "Yod-Heh-Vav-Heh."

These dimensions are not 'Heavens' as they are not created. They are dimensions of the person of God Himself. The Heavens are a created reality to help man know and experience the loving, infinite God.

Next is The Divinity / Human Intersection '6' Dimension. This Heaven is the first of the created Heavens. Its six dimensions are the embodiment of God (3 dimensions) in man (3 dimensions). This '6' Dimension is where God wants man to be. However, human beings will never get there while they're alive because this means that they have become the 'Heavenly man'. It is what Paul meant when he wrote: "but when the perfect comes, the partial will be done away." (1 Cor 13:10 NAS)

I know we say a lot of the time, "We are already like Him." True, we have His nature in us, but we have not been able to break through to this level because we are not yet glorified. It's because we still have flesh and blood.

There is a demarcation here between the '6' and the '12' Dimensions. The Divinity / Human Intersection '6' Dimension is Adam in the Garden of Eden. When man fell, God did not begin man again at the '6'. He began with man at the Lower 12, and this

Section 1: The Ecology of the Nested Heavens

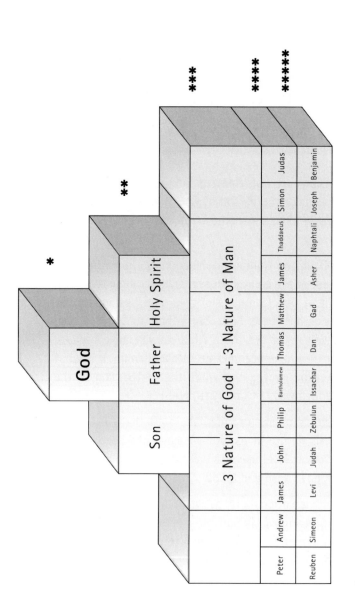

*   1   – The Echad Dimension: The Person of God (not a heaven) Deut 6:4

**   3   – The Trinitias Dimension: God in 3 Persons (not a heaven)

***   6   – The Divinity / Human Intersection Dimension: The Embodiment of God in Man (a created heaven of 6 dimensions)

****   12   – The Upper Kingdom Intersection Dimension: The Sons Of God (a created heaven of 12 dimensions)

*****   12   – The Lower Kingdom Intersection Dimension: The Sons of Israel (a created heaven of 12 dimensions) is where you can go right now! The two '12' Dimensions are the highest you can go. Unfortunately, 90% of the people who know God will never get there. To be clear, we are not saying that no living human being can access the '6', rather when a living human operates in manifest and matured Sonship all that belongs to the father is open to them.

The Upper Kingdom Intersection '12' Dimension (The Apostles) is where God is revealed in ever expanding space - this becomes the cubic city of the New Jerusalem, a living organism. This is not creation as we would currently understand it, but it is created all the same. This Heaven and all its dimensions are intended for you to explore. However, we must concentrate on the Lower '12' Dimension of the Patriarchs first in order to access the upper dimensions. We have not yet come to the Upper 12 Dimension. (Just know it is there for future reference, as 12 above plus 12 below is 24 - and there are 24 in the Kingdom of Heaven and in the Kingdom of God).

The Lower Kingdom Intersection '12' Dimension is where a Christian will first find themselves. This is where God is revealed in static material creation - creation as we traditionally know it. There are 12 dimensions in this Heaven that you have access to. Even though you are (subconsciously) everywhere because you are in God, this is the first level you can consciously interact with. As you intentionally engage with these 12 dimensions you will mature and be able to consciously access higher Heavenly dimensions.

THE LOWER KINGDOM INTERSECTION '12' DIMENSION

"Also she had a great and high wall with twelve gates, and twelve angels at the gates, and names written on them, which are the names of the twelve tribes of the children of Israel: three gates on the East, three gates on the North, three gates on the South, and three gates on the West. Now the wall of the city had twelve foundations, and on them were the names[a] of the twelve apostles of the Lamb. And he who talked with me had a gold reed to measure the city, its gates, and its wall. The city is laid out as a square; its length is as great as its breadth. And he measured the city with the reed: twelve thousand furlongs. Its length, breadth, and height are equal. Then he measured its wall: one hundred and forty-four cubits, according to the measure of a man, that is, of an angel. The construction of its wall was of jasper; and the city was pure gold, like clear glass. The foundations of the wall of the city were adorned with all kinds of precious stones: the first foundation was jasper, the second sapphire, the third chalcedony, the fourth emerald, the fifth sardonyx, the sixth sardius, the seventh chrysolite, the eighth beryl, the ninth topaz, the tenth chrysoprase, the eleventh jacinth, and the twelfth amethyst. The twelve gates were twelve pearls: each individual gate was of one pearl. And the street of the city was pure gold, like transparent glass." (Rev 21:12-21)

The City of God in the Book of Revelation has 12 foundations. God has shown us that the Heaven that we can access, the "Lower Kingdom 12", has patterns which deal with 12 dimensions of relating to God.

The nature of "Lower Kingdom 12" dimensions are revealed when Jacob blesses his son in Genesis 49. As we understand and process these 12 dimensions with God, it will deal with our fallen nature, allowing us to rule as kings and sons! As we understand the nature of the twelve sons, we will understand the nature of these dimensions of Heaven and thus the elements we will need to address in our lives.

The reason God reveals Israel this way is to teach you about

Heaven. Israel is the revelation of what God is doing in the supernatural realm.

In my experience, the Heavens that God reveals to us, whether they are infinite or not, are always divisible by three and four (based on the nature of God and the name of God). The "Lower Kingdom 12" dimensional Heaven is set out in four sets of three 'nested Heavens'.

Below is the same camp diagram set out linearly. You can clearly see the four sets of three. Moving through these dimensions is not a hierarchy or process of enlightenment, like an Eastern religion, or a system of works and achievements. It is a working with the Holy Spirit to remove the fallen DNA nature from your life to reveal your true nature. Many steps can be worked on simultaneously, but some are more foundational than others. To not address them will cause them to appear later in your life. The order follows the birth/camp order of the sons and was set by the wisdom of God.

THE PROGRESSION OF MATURITY

When you start to mature in the first dimension, which is represented by Reuben, you can move to the next dimension, Simeon, then to Levi and onwards through all 12. After you can consciously engage the Upper 12 Dimension, based on the apostles. We will deal more with this in Hashamayim 2A.

Remember, we need 3's, and we need 4's. So, in the first three dimensions, we have Reuben, Simeon and Levi. They are like a trinity. Three separate entities, yet the trinity is still one.

MOVING FROM ONE HEAVEN TO ANOTHER

The structures and dimensions of Heaven are revealed in

how God sets patterns in Scripture. Dimensions are intertwined, interwoven and interconnected. Dimensions are non-intersecting streams - either in consciousness or space.

People rarely move from one dimension to another without a crisis. We tend to sleep in every dimension we find ourselves. You want to go to sleep there, just like Peter. He says "Let us build a tent up here." God responds, "No, not on this mountain. This is not yours. You cannot build a tent here."

Some people find the gates themselves. That is what I am trying to help you do - to find the gates to get in a new dimension. It is not always through suffering. It is possible to purposely move from dimension to dimension, through the gates.

The gate is in your body, in your feelings, in all your emotions. The gates must be opened and the gates are opened by suffering. "Take up your cross and follow Me," says Jesus. God has so orchestrated life that the cycle of your life brings you pain and suffering. At every moment that you come into the context of suffering, you choose a response. When you respond to that suffering in the way you're supposed to, then a gate opens for you to move to the next place. If you are engaged in daily life and in relating to people, you are going to be tested - in the daily work of your life, in your workplace.

Christianity demands that you live life with thoughtfulness and intentionality and that you pay attention to everything. You are not to go through the world as a zombie. "Awake thou that sleepest, and arise from the dead, and Christ shall give thee light" (Eph 5:14 KJV)

The reason the two '12' Dimensions, Upper and Lower, are divided into triad nested Heavens is so you can navigate them easier. God uses these two '12' Dimensions, Upper and Lower, to train you. Remember, the first Heaven that man can grasp in this fallen state is the Lower '12' dimension. You go through the Lower 12 in order to go up to the Upper 12. There are 24 dimensions in this Heaven. As you process through, you understand how the 12 is related to the 24, and how the 24 is related to the rest of the higher Heavens - God in his fullness.

When you begin to master the various dimensions, you will find yourself beginning to move into your oneness with God. However, if you strive in your own efforts to become one with God, you end up going backward.

To talk about your oneness with God without dealing with your issues in these dimensions is to become like Lucifer. God teaches you so that when you become one, and your consciousness gets tied into the divine, you don't get yourself into hubris.

The person who has salvation, who knows God, can access the 24 dimensions in the Heavenly realm. That is precisely why you were given 24 hours in a day. It is an ecology of nested Heavens - Heavens within Heavens within Heavens within Heavens - that are relating to one another and allowing you to experience the different dimensions of God. You have been born again. You have been born into God. Now you need to start experiencing the different dimensions of God as you come into the fullness of who you are. As Christ gets formed in you, you get filled with the fullness of God.

Christians do not realize salvation is just the beginning. It is like a child that is born and stays as a one-day old baby. He can never really walk on his own, he cannot eat and enjoy an apple. You must enjoy the different dimensions of life to be a full human being.

The same thing is true with the Kingdom of God. God wants you to enjoy the different dimensions of His being. That is why the Bible says, "Oh, taste and see that the Lord is good." (Psa 34:8)

Remember in the Book of Leviticus and the Book of Numbers, where the ephod is put upon the priest. It represents the dimensional movement of God in the lower realm. It takes both the upper realm and the lower realm to make one Heaven. Above and below unify to make one Heaven. The lower realm of the Heavens is accessible to the human souls who have disciplined themselves. In every awakened consciousness, if it is a body consciousness, or if it is an emotional consciousness, or if its just a mere feeling consciousness, you need to pay attention. To move through the gates, we need to be aware and intentional about our lives.

The fullness of God and His Kingdom has been made available to us. Let us not fall asleep on the mount of transfiguration!

SUMMARY

This book is meant to give you a kind of technology for navigating the Heavenly region and for really understanding how it functions. An understanding based on the Bible, the objective provision that is hidden within Scripture itself. God's patterns are in Scripture.

The Scriptures were not written by any private interpretation. They were written as the Spirit of God moved upon man. In other words, they have a divine principle within them. They carry within them the structures and patterns of God.

We have been speaking of the Heaven as paradigmatic of self-construction, self-creation, self-constituting, self-alteration, self-transformation. We are talking about affirming the self in its divine nature. Not the self that you have created, that you are pretending to be. We're talking about your Christ nature transcending all the illusionary selves that you have created.

Heaven is seeing God as He is, standing before Him naked and not ashamed. That is what the Garden of Eden is. Until then, you are using activity to cover yourself.

We need to understand that in every Heaven there is a hell embedded in it. If you don't like that reality, you are not going to be able to deal with yourself. Whichever dimension of Heaven you go into, if you have this glorious experience, but it never raises the issue of you dealing with yourself, then you have a problem. Every dimension of Heaven calls attention to something in your humanity that you must deal with to effectively manifest the truth of that dimension.

Just because you are shown revelation does not mean you have the capacity to manifest. You have to ask yourself, "What keeps me from manifesting?" Every time a dimension of Heaven is shown to you, you need to ask yourself the question, "What hell do I need to walk through to have it manifest?" What hell did God have to walk through to create the Earth? Genesis 1:1-3. Chaos, death, non-productivity.

We are going to look in-depth into the Heaven and hell of each of the 12 dimensions. The first six were contained in Hashamayim 1A. We will summarize them next. It is certainly worth reading these again. This will be followed by the next six dimensions (2 triads). Reading carefully and applying it to your life, as opposed to getting purely an intellectual understanding, will help you identify and overcome troublesome areas of your life. These are the areas preventing you from moving through the dimensions and revealing your true self as a Son of God. I promise you, it will be challenging and very, very rewarding.

Section 1: The Ecology of the Nested Heavens

NAVIGATING 1ST TWO TRIADS

Let us revisit what we have studied so far. This is essential. Remember, this book is not information to be learned but a deep changing of your very being so you can be like your Creator - His very desire. Each dimension is for life application, not purely for understanding. God will take you through daily Christian life, giving you opportunity to confront these issues in your life and DNA. He will give you opportunity to walk through a hell as to establish these dimensions in your life. Revelation is not for information but to be lived, to become.

The 12 dimensions of the Lower 12 are split into groupings of 3, or 'triads'. So we have four triads, giving us the 3, 4 and 12. Each dimension follows the sons of Jacob as he blesses them in Genesis 49 and the Israelite camp layout in Numbers 2. Let us remember the first two triads of the Lower 12 Dimension and their natures as they are revealed in the blessing of Jacob.

THE PRIESTHOOD TRIAD

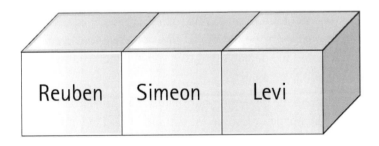

Progressing through this first triad forces you to deal with your elemental issues. Your feelings and emotions. It can be a difficult thing, facing up and owning your true self. However, it qualifies you for great things, to hear and judge clearly and to experience the secrets of God. Not many Christians make this journey through the first triad. They remain asleep.

In this first triad you are dealing with your feeling aspect - all that in you that makes you form attachments. It's where you act just because it feels good. You like it so much but you'll never manifest anything on earth because it's all about you.

This triad is in ascending order. Reuben, then Simeon, then Levi. When you get to the Levi dimension, there is a formation that happens. You have completed a cycle and now you are a priest. You're able to stand for other people because you have dealt with the inside of you that says, "hear me."

In this dimension, your feelings become more purified and more subtle and now you no longer react in anger. When you have dealt with a lot of issues and you're not attached to them any longer, you're able to begin to walk in manifestation. Again, if you're not trained in these three levels you're going to see a lot of things but you won't manifest them in your life.

What's important is self-transformation. When you're transformed - your feelings are transmuted in Reuben, your emotions are transmuted in Simeon and your priestly instincts are transmuted in Levi - you move to actual priesthood. Now we are talking about terra formation, physically changing creation! Whatever you terra form, you do so in your own image. If we still need to deal with the old us (all this nonsense that we have in ourselves and the damage that is in you and me) what we create will contain these issues.

You cannot be unified in your singular soul, which was created to bear the image of God unless you are unified in your feelings, your emotions and your thoughts. So what is God working on in these Heavenly dimensions of Reuben, Simeon and Levi? It is your will. His intent is to unify your will. "Your will be done on earth, as it is in Heaven." The earth is you.

Without going through this dimension you cannot get into the other Heavens and have the kind of experience that John is having in the Book of Revelation. John's whole life was the testing of these three dimensions.

In progressing through these first three dimensions of the Priesthood Triad, God begins to reveal secrets to you. This is where God teaches you how to keep secrets. In dealing with your issues in these dimensions He humbles you enough so that your mouth is not always open, like a leaky pump pouring out everything you hear. What you do with this understanding is your choice. You are free to choose and there is no wrong answer - just the option of staying asleep, or waking up and going higher!

Let's recap the individual dimensions. (See overleaf)

THE PRIESTHOOD TRIAD

Son: Reuben

Meaning: Excited/Excellent

Dimension: Sonship

Personsa: Judgement

Son: Simeon

Meaning: Heard

Dimension: Judgement / Severity

Persona: Wisdom

Son: Levi

Meaning: Joined

Dimension: Priesthood

Persona: Understanding

REUBEN - THE DIMENSION OF SONSHIP AND JUDGEMENT

"Reuben, you are my firstborn; My might and the beginning of my strength, Preeminent in dignity and preeminent in power. Uncontrolled as water, you shall not have preeminence, because you went up to your father's bed; Then you defiled it—he went up to my couch." (Gen 49:3-4)

Reuben means excited, excellent, dignity. These very qualities create hubris. In the 'Reuben dimension' you are navigating a Heaven of sonship. If you are the firstborn, you have the birthright. In this Heaven you have a right to provision. You have a relationship where God gives you access to inheritance because of your birth position.

Reuben sleeps with his father's wife. His problem is Lust. Reuben needs to learn how to respect boundaries. In this dimension, the issue is not the devil. The issue is you.

"He who is slow to anger is better than the mighty, and he who rules his spirit, than he who captures a city." (Pro 16:32).

Reuben issues are tied to your physical body - your physical desires, your physical feelings. This is the dimension where you begin to deal with that mess regarding the physical, actual behaviors that you are doing.

The key then is to find a place of intimacy with God where you are naked before Him and yourself, with nothing to hide. We need to be honest with ourselves and how we lie to ourselves.

It is in this place that God sends you people you don't like and He tells you to love them. However, 'like' is your god. You ask, "God, what did I ever do? Why are you sending me all these jerks?" It is because you need the jerk in you to be dealt with! You are being influenced by your feelings and can not follow the perfect will of the Father.

Pray instead; "Father - I want to move beyond what I'm feeling. I want something that I have never experienced, that has nothing to do with my feelings, even if it is painful. Take me to a new threshold. Take me to the crucible."

A good protocol to deal with these issues is vibrating and singing the name of God "Yod, Heh, Vav, Heh". You build your house with the name of the Lord. The house that you build with the four-letter name of God is also the source of the four rivers that strengthen your water. It gets your water balanced. Then you read the Word of the Lord and eat it. Chanting the name of

God begins to balance your water. It turns your bitter water into sweet water.

Then the next protocol is to ask for those angels who deal with the moving of waters, with the dividing of waters and the bringing back of waters.

It is not a simple thing to free yourself from your feelings but the rewards are great. You become like your Father in Heaven.

SIMEON: THE DIMENSION OF JUDGEMENT AND WISDOM

"Simeon and Levi are brothers; Instruments of cruelty are in their dwelling place. Let not my soul enter their council; Let not my honor be united to their assembly; For in their anger they slew a man, And in their self-will they hamstrung an ox. Cursed be their anger, for it is fierce; And their wrath, for it is cruel! I will divide them in Jacob and scatter them in Israel." (Gen 49:5-7)

Simeon means "heard." Simeon is somebody that always gets an answer. Either he has been heard by God or he wants to be heard by any means necessary.

Simeon is where your emotions are. These emotions are not the 'feelings' discussed above in Reuben. Emotions are not feelings. You can be very angry and yet feel nothing. Emotions are embedded realities in your body that have potentialities. Your emotions also reflect things that are of God. God gets angry - but not out of passion or feelings. God is love. We need to love the way God loves, not based on feelings or 'eros'.

The kind of love that God is asking for is too much for most of us. God says, love your enemies. What are your enemies trying to do? They are trying to kill you. Most of the people you love are people who love you. You have never really loved your enemy.

Therefore, to move from Reuben to Simeon, you have to face your emotions. Simeon is the one who, out of anger along with his brother, wiped out a whole village. They were offended at what was done to their sister. This is the negative side of the judgment and the severity of Simeon.

When dealing with this realm you want to be heard - even when you are not right. This means you begin to talk too much. You find yourself developing a spirit of offense when you feel people are not hearing what you are saying. This is the weakness of Simeon.

Emotions are more powerful than feelings because they are embedded in your body. This is why you need to develop your sound - your own unique, personal sound that unlocks this area for you. This is why chanting the name of God is so important in what we do - the vibrating of "Yod Heh Vav Heh."

LEVI: THE DIMENSION OF PRIESTHOOD AND UNDERSTANDING

Levi means "joined". Levi is a priest - a being of two worlds.

The down side of his nature is he joins his twin Simeon to go and kill. Aaron, being a Levite, joined with the people and said: "Tear off the gold rings which are in the ears of your wives, your sons, and your daughters, and bring them to me." (Exo 32:2) It is intrinsic to him. The way Levi experiences his own dimension is by joining other people. This can be positive or negative.

Levi doesn't get an inheritance in the land but by attaching himself to other people. It is not a bad thing. It is part of his character. It is part of how he functions as a priest. There are some people who struggle to enter the Heavens unless they are working with someone. They cannot walk alone. "How come when I'm at home I cannot experience the Heavens?" It is because they are operating in the Levi dimension.

You cannot experience this dimension of Heaven unless you understand forgiveness. Unforgiveness produces a sound in the Heavens and you cannot hear the voice of God clearly. If you hear the voice of God, sometimes it is your voice. God will teach you to make a distinction between your wishful thinking, your anger, your complaints about people and this Heavenly sound.

When you master this Levi dimension of Heaven, you can hear things that are not allowed for human beings to hear. You become an inheritance of God.

In Levi, you may meet cherubim for the first time. Not everybody gets to meet cherubim, e.g., Lion, Ox, Eagle, Man. You are going to have new experiences and this is where the temptation to get into witchcraft comes. Every true priest who comes to the consciousness of their priesthood goes through this.

It is what happened to Jesus when he first was in the desert. If Jesus had turned the stone into bread, where would the bread have come from - Heaven or hell? If you listen to Satan, you pull from that which is below. This is why it is so important to train yourself to hear God.

If you have not dealt with this witchy issue, you're going to want people to acknowledge you - that you are the "master" who delivered them - especially when you start successful priestly intercession. If you're interceding, you're the one in the middle and you get to bear the burden of the people. Once you can get into this place, you find yourself carrying other people's burdens. This is between you and God and not for recognition of the people.

It is clear to see why Reuben (feelings) and Simeon (emotions) come before Levi!

KINGSHIP TRIAD

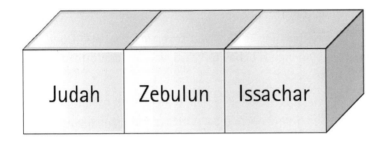

Let us look at the next three nested Heavens of the 12 and their natures as they are revealed in the blessing of Jacob (Gen 49). You are making the transition from Priesthood to Kingship. You are taking that big leap from your animalistic self into being a human! These three Heavens deal with our Kingship so you can judge and handle wealth, like your Father in Heaven.

Son: Judah

Meaning: Rulership

Dimension: Kingship

Personsa: Mercy

Son: Zebulun

Meaning: Exalted / Enthroned

Dimension: Adventurer

Persona: Power

Son: Issachar

Meaning: Heard

Dimension: Time & Eternity

Persona: Beauty

The reason God wants to give you wealth is to train you to get to where you can release it out of your hand, but you are independent of it.

The key question is "Are you sovereign over it?" Do you get agitated by people's behavior? If so, you are conformed to them and not sovereign.

Kingship has that Luciferian principle of trying to rise up against God. Remember, in every Heaven, there is a possibility of hell. There are no shortcuts to being a king like Jesus, the King of Kings. You keep going to the cross of Jesus Christ. You keep allowing the blood of Jesus Christ to cleanse and deal with your flesh.

This is where you have communion daily. You operate under the blood of Jesus Christ. This is where your DNA is being transformed.

JUDAH: THE DIMENSION OF KINGSHIP AND MERCY

"Judah, you are he whom your brothers shall praise; Your hand shall be on the neck of your enemies; Your father's children shall bow down before you. Judah is a lion's whelp; From the prey, my son, you have gone up. He bows down, he lies down as a lion; And as a lion, who shall rouse him? The scepter shall not depart from Judah, Nor a lawgiver from between his feet, until Shiloh comes; And to Him shall be the obedience of the people. Binding his donkey to the vine, And his donkey's colt to the choice vine, He washed his garments in wine, And his clothes in the blood of grapes. His eyes are darker than wine, and his teeth whiter than milk. (Gen 49:8-12)

In Judah is where you become a judge. When kingship comes

you must also stand as a judge.

Only a person with a clear identity can be a king and rule in their region. In Judah, God begins to show you hidden truths and starts teaching you how to form things and terraform domains. Remember, God created you in His image. God desires that when you create something, it reflects both you and Him. The Priesthood Triad deals with the fallen nature of man. The Kingship Triad deals with the capacity of a human being to create.

If you start to use the Kingship dimensions without going through the Priesthood dimensions you experience kingship without the independent will. You will see beauty but not be able to create things that last. Part of David's problem was that one aspect of his life was never dealt with - Reuben. David's sexuality is tied to his violence. David could not build the temple because he was a man of blood (Chr 28:3).

In kingship, you now have to deal with your sovereign self. Your 'I'. You do not act unless you have thought about it and your will is committed. It is better to argue with God, even say "no," than to just be a slave. You submit to God freely. Only a king has a right to submit to a king. At that point, you can enter into covenant and the devil gets scared of you.

You need to have sovereign choice. This is how Adam could choose. He chose to relate to somebody that he could be enslaved with rather than choosing to be the free person God desired.

In Judah is the test of hubris. People will say all kinds of nice things about you. Jesus said to be careful when men say wonderful things about you! (Luke 6:26). You want praise because God receives praise and you are in His image. However, your fallen nature wants to take whatever belongs to God and point it to itself. Your brethren will praise you, but that is not the issue. It is what you do with this praise!

The throne of kingship here is not the throne of God. It is the first place where you, as a man, reign over yourself and others.

"Judah is a lion's whelp." This is where your lion nature is formed. You are crouching under the Great Lion as a little lion. You are learning to be a son. A king does not go to court. He goes and takes vengeance. You have to develop the four faces that sit on that throne - Lion, Ox, Eagle, Man - reflecting the glory of the Father. Now you roar. You roar over an area. This is where your mountain is formed. The dragons you have to deal with in this region are the facets of pride and worship. You open your mouth and angels are there. You move and there they are. However, you have to keep your heart, because out of it are the issues of life.

Until you come to the place of rest, nothing belongs to you. The law of the Sabbath is also the foundational principle of kingship. So control your energy. Just because you are not committing fornication does not mean you're not wasting your sexual energy. You're wasting it in all that agitation - the anger and the unnecessary activity you do that uses up your emotions so that your energy is not directed towards your creativity. This means you're not bringing forth the new.

God also wants to teach you how to handle wealth, how to make wealth and how to transmute into actual wealth. This level is where you begin to ask to take things from the Heavens and manifest them on earth.

"Binding his foal unto the vine." That is a 'Jack and the Beanstalk' concept - it is all in the story. You go up into the Heavens and you come down the vine with the golden treasure. The vine becomes a pathway between Heaven and earth, between the spiritual realm and the physical realm.

ZEBULUN: THE DIMENSION OF THE ADVENTURER AND POWER

"Zebulun shall dwell by the haven of the sea; He shall

become a haven for ships, And his border shall adjoin Sidon" (Gen 49:13)

Zebulun's name means "exalted."

Operating at this level means you go in as a king and you sit in the Heavens, in your authority. People who experience this sovereignty, by this sea, and have the power to go to the other side and set people free. So ships come and they can go to the other side, release what has been taken and kept captive, put it on ships and bring it back to the shore. That is what the king does.

The reason you are being made into kings is that you are being given a certain royal authority to go and set the captives free. You bring them over and you hand them over to the King of Kings. This is not priestly intercession. You are facing down the enemy like a king. (Until you are a king you can't face down the enemy and you get into spiritual warfare at your peril). Therefore, you go and you set the captive free, but you do not stay there. You go, you do, and you come back.

This is strategic in nature. Do not just do an activity because you feel like doing it. If you operate in feelings as king, you will die. When you operate in feelings, you get yourself involved in issues just because you feel sorry for someone. You get into that troubled sea and the person drags you down with him. In this kingly place you have to understand your specific assignment because now you are dealing with a particular kind of angelic ministration.

Part of Zebulun's issues that you need to deal with is being a vagabond and wandering on the sea from one position to another, never landing in the Heavens so that your kingship never comes to fruition. You do not stay in anything long enough for it to give birth. That's why Zebulun needs Isaachar, to know the times and the seasons and to stay put.

ISSACHAR: THE DIMENSION OF TIME / ETERNITY AND BEAUTY

"Issachar is a strong donkey, Lying down between two burdens; He saw that rest was good, And that the land was pleasant; He bowed his shoulder to bear a burden, And became a band of slaves." (Gen 49:14-15)

The Issachar dimension is where you become the master of time. A king must understand times and seasons and be able to master them. His operation must come from his impact upon eternity.

Issachar can be a burden bearer but also the experience of rest made him lazy. The experience of pleasure made Issachar become a slave.

"Rejoice, Zebulun, in your going out, And Issachar in your tents! They shall call the peoples to the mountain; There they shall offer sacrifices of righteousness; For they shall partake of the abundance of the seas and of treasures hidden in the sand" (Deut 33:18-19)

Again, everything in this second triad deals with kingship issues of wealth, treasure and victory. It is about allowing the flow and releasing people who have the gifting from the world of darkness to come into this kingdom, bringing their gift with them. It is about releasing the captured wealth back and then trading at a higher level in terms of the mountain. Not trading based on your emotion but on discerning times and seasons.

If you always trade with an emotional attachment, it brings your trading down to the level of Reuben and your first level issues. It is not easy. Nobody said it was easy!

A king must know the times. Dealing with the Issachar dimension is the principle of the mastering of time. A king must master time. The Bible says Issachar, "shall call the people unto the mountain; there they shall offer sacrifices of righteousness" (Deut 33:19).

The Bible says, "The sons of Issachar understood the times" (1 Chr 12:32).

The Lower 12 Dimension level of Heavens are time oriented because they deal with you going through your life cycles and dealing with things inside of you. You have limited time on Earth to 'do'. Therefore, when you get to Issachar and kingship, you must understand how time functions and be able to do things in their right time and their right place. Creating wealth is based on understanding times and seasons. I cannot over-emphasize this.

When the Father decides to release His new works on the earth, He doesn't give it to Christians. He gives it into the atmosphere. However, if you train yourself, you can know when these things are coming and prepare yourself to receive and to attract them to yourself. If you are still operating in anger, in your lust for recognition or your self-definition based on identity and association, then you really cannot see this opportunity.

You become addicted to your experience of Heaven without production - like taking recreational drugs. God's fruit is the creation of the Earth and the universe. Fruit is a concrete creation of something new.

To understand the relationship between the Kingdom of God and the Kingdom of Heaven is to understand how to align things. The Lower 12 Dimension of the sons of Jacob are the Kingdom of God. Until you deal with the human body in the Israel paradigm, you really cannot truly experience the Upper 12 Dimension / Kingdom of Heaven and above.

Remember, when you are born again you're engrafted to the tree called Israel. There is a reason you are engrafted. It is so that your DNA can be transformed and you can deal with all that damage. God wants you to move through the triads to walk in your true nature. He wants you to be tested in the flames of the Seven Spirits of God and come back.

TRANSITIONING BETWEEN THE TRIADS

The transition between two triads is truly a quantum leap. The test of the quantum leap between 2 triads is how you deal with the Seven Spirits of God. Isaiah 11:2 names the Seven Spirits of God; The Spirit of the Lord, wisdom, understanding, counsel, might, knowledge, and the fear of the Lord.

The Seven Spirits of God are not the Holy Spirit. They are individual personalities created by God. Their role in the lives of humans is to tutor us into being fully mature sons. They work by relationship. To engage them is to start a relationship, based on honor. The Seven Spirits have always been interested in you. Your part is to consciously respond with intentionality.

You have to deal with each of these spirits individually. It is these 7 spirits that act as "governors and tutors" (Gal 4) to test whether you are ready to move (you may go in limping, like Jacob!).

How do I engage the Seven Spirits of God in my life and make this quantum leap from one set of triads to the next? My answer is "acquire knowledge." Learn something new every day. Really learn. This is for a purpose. You should learn a simple practical application every day.

The way you engage is to continue to be intimate with God and do the ordinary activities because the Seven Spirits will engage you in practical, everyday happenings. Engaging them in Heaven alone is not going to do you any good because they need to come down and help you manifest in this realm.

TRANSITIONING BETWEEN THE TRIADS

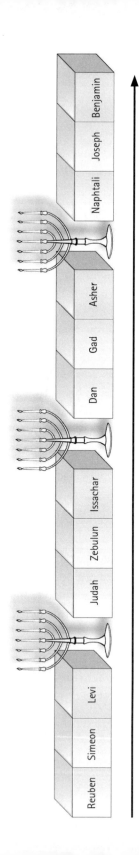

SECTION 2

Section 2

THE THIRD TRIAD.

THE TRIAD OF WARRIORSHIP

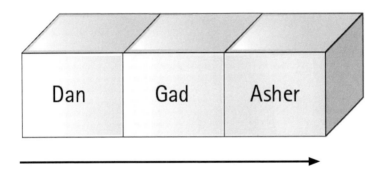

Section 2: The Third Triad. The Triad of Warriorship

DAN: THE DIMENSION OF JUSTICE

"Dan shall be a serpent by the way, a viper by the path, that bites the horse's heels so that its rider shall fall backward. I have waited for your salvation, O Lord!" (Gen 49:17-18)

DAN BECAME SERPENTINE

Dan is not mentioned in the Book of Revelation. This is significant. He was infected by the serpent seed. The tribe of Dan will not be among Israel, unless the Danites are purified. The Scripture says Dan went up North and took over Europe (Judg18). The kingship of Europe is from the tribe of Dan. They were the first tribe to embrace idols. This affected them genetically and is one of the reasons Dan is not mentioned in Revelation. He was removed completely and can only become a part of the kingdom by redemption through the blood of Jesus, but he cannot be a part of Israel anymore. The only one who can deal with the serpent is the Messiah.

BECOMING A JUDGE

"Dan shall be a serpent by the way ... I have waited for your salvation, O Lord!".

It is important to notice that Dan is the judge. It is easy to become serpentine in the process of judgment.

Jesus says, "Judge not, that you be not judged" (Matthew 7:1). The principle behind this command is like a reptile biting its tail. It poisons our genes. For example, demons are known to struggle and fight with one another. Two demons cannot occupy a common territory without fighting and trying to destroy each other, even though they cannot.

God gives the command not to judge because He does not like strife among His people. In addition, it is to reveal that the world is infected, even when the world decides they want peace. A good example of this is having one sect who wants to have peace and harmony and another sect determined to go to war. To have peace, the one with the peaceful desire must go to war and kill those who want war. The result of our desire for good is to do the same thing the other sect is doing. The action of the one desiring good is justified by the idea that their position is right. Such things lead to idolatry and self-perpetuating praise that says, "I am the one that defends everybody." The one who judges everybody else fails to judge himself and the poison grows and suffocates them.

BITTERNESS

Dan was bitter because he could not conquer the people that were given to him (Judg 1:34). His brothers and sisters did not come to help him.

On their way to look at the promised land they found a Levite praying in the house of Micah using an ephod (Judg 17 and 18). Micah had an idol that his mother had made of silver. They went in, took the idol and bound themselves to it. They defeated and took over much of the North and ultimately Europe - but they could not find their way back.

When we live in bitterness, it poisons our genes.

moving in dan

When we step into the dimension of Dan, there is this opening from the dimension of Issachar where the angel of time "Ayin Tau" stands.

There are intersecting foundations in Dan, enabling one to go up or down. If we move down, we will find the serpent. The serpent is inner bitterness. This dimension should be entered with humility and a clean heart.

David says, "Create in me a clean heart" (Psa 51:10). David did not sin as a king but as a judge. He killed Uriah because he was not an Israelite and David thought he would not be missed. What would God care about a Hittite, whom God had already said to wipe out? The more we focus on the negative, the more we act exactly how we don't want others to act. In this dimension, seek carefully for where God's light is shining. Vibrate your whole being in that light to expose whatever is not good, not to judge it, but to focus on it. The more the light exposes it, the more the undesired leaves on its own accord.

God created Israel for a reason. The Bible says the law was given to make sin appear very sinful. The law did not come out of man but from Heaven. It was given based on man's fallen nature. The law trains us to see better. Some have the experience of seeing spiritually for only a fleeting moment. This appearing and disappearing is to train our eyes to focus.

Dan is a realm where our capacity for harmony is trained by disharmony. Harmonization is messed up by a divine dissonance. For example, the capacity to love is tested by the feelings of hate that arise for things we don't like. God sees everything, but He doesn't respond to everything. He doesn't feel the need to change everybody, not even at our request.

It would serve a greater purpose to be conscious of this

dimension to know exactly what we are dealing with. Demons will come to us in this realm. (After dealing with the tribe of Judah demons are no longer a problem for you. However, when dealing with Dan in your life you will come up against the human propensity to engage with idols and thus the demonic).

SHAPES AND SYMBOLS

These four symbols are found all over the world. They reveal a hidden mystery about the foundation of the universe. There are not that many mysteries in the world. A circle, square or triangle up or down all point to something. The name of God, YHVH, is revealed through ancient prints. The symbols will be seen in different places but they are always near one another. Most foundations are that way.

These symbols are seen mostly in elevators. It is not coincidental.

Human beings have the capacity to move in different dimensions. In the dimension of Dan, we have this exact "Yod, Heh, Vav, Heh"; the key of all the names of God. The name is the symbolic principle of moving through dimensions, to understand what things look like when they come through a square or a triangle facing downward. A triangle facing down is female in its nature, the triangle facing up is male.

Twelve disciples and one Messiah equals thirteen. Thirteen is the female principle. Jacob had twelve sons and one daughter,

Dinah. There are twelve permanent star systems, plus one that is a moving and unstable. There are twelve apostles plus one, Paul, who cannot stay in one place.

A triangle is the base of 'Father, Son and Holy Spirit'. However, God is not facing up. He is facing us.

PASSING JUDGEMENT AND THE SERPENT LINE

When Jesus is talking to the Pharisees, He warns to not judge by appearance. If we do not deal with Dan, we will judge with unrighteous judgment. Judges can sentence or free people. The one who judges unrighteously will destroy someone who is weak in spirit. The people who suffer most from Dan's mishap are the weak because Dan is forceful in the way he judges.

In Judges 17 there is a Levite boy who has a weakness. He is looking for something to eat. As he is passing by, Micah convinces him to come and serve the idol in his house. The boy agrees. In this way, the Levi who serves God, by Micah's persuasion, comes and serves a silver god. When the tribe of Dan arrived, they persuaded the young Levite to be their priest. They took the idol of Micah, persuaded the priest to follow them and threatened to kill Micah if he went after them. They dealt with him based on the serpent, which activated a principle. Nobody could save Micah from their hands. By negotiation they made the Levite become their priest, shifting him from what he was called to do, to the worst and greatest sin.

The intrinsic judgment of God comes from a place of righteousness. This is a place in the heavenlies where the thrones of judgments are.

Dan is the judgment principle which can either increase or diminish. Dan is not part of Israel and will never be part of Israel, unless it is through the blood of Jesus Christ. It is one thing to be a judge. It is another thing to be able to stand in righteousness and not be a serpent in our judgment. We must judge from a place of righteousness, not from a place of bitterness, jealousy or greed.

Dan's judgment ended up destroying him because he was not only judging Israel; he was judging God! Dan took the place of Satan in putting God under judgment. Going to idols is to say God will not help us. Its an accusation against His character (see final chapters of Judges). Dan chose to bind himself to idols because he didn't believe the God of Israel. He thereby became part of the serpent seed, the demon seed.

All the religions of Greece were started by the Danites. The tribe of Dan attached itself to the Nephilim seed and became part of that group. That's where Alexander the Great and others like him came from. The whole royal European dynasty of leadership are all part of that lineage. They have Israelite blood mixed with the Nephilim seed. Now they have spread to other areas of the world and now, like Dan, these groups are against Israel.

Dan is not mentioned in the Book of Revelation because Dan is attached to the serpent. It is Dan that has done Israel more damage throughout history than any other group. It is that serpent nature that has made the Europeans enemies of Israel from the beginning. It has always been there from the time the Europeans began to form kingdoms. The lineage of the Greeks and the Romans is Danite. The bloodline runs through them. It is an attachment to idolatry that then changes the DNA to be in opposition to God. Idol worship affects DNA!

Why are the Danites so strong about eating pork? Everywhere they find Jewish or Israelite people they introduce pork to them. That is what they did in the temple - they sacrificed a pig in the temple! They had an instinctual hatred for God and God's people, even though they were supposed to be part of it. The people of Dan rejected their patrimony. They rejected the land that God gave them in Israel and decided to go and look for their own place. They made a covenant with the serpent. In Homer's epic, Zeus is the serpent god of the Danites. Zeus is not Yahweh.

Jacob, said, "Dan is a serpent on the way. He is an adder who bites the horse so that his rider may fall backward." So Dan is an attacker. His whole job is to cause destruction. In this dimension, we are dealing with destructive behavior.

THE ANTICHRIST AND THE CONTINUED FIGHT AGAINST ISRAEL

The Antichrist is not going to be a Muslim. The antichrist must come out of the Greco-Roman Empire - the children of Dan. The Antichrist should have Jewish blood, the blood of Israel. He cannot be someone without Israelite blood. The Antichrist must come from an Israelite tribe, but it is most likely the Danites as they are the ones who have that intrinsic hatred. They are willing to destroy everything.

The Danites were a mixture of Dan and Edom. Herod was an Edomite, but by that time Edomites had been mixed with Danites. These were two groups that hated Israel, based on the bloodline. Now days, the Dome of the Rock is the temple that is the issue. They don't want the site to be taken over by Arabs, so it is going to be destroyed. Solomon's temple is going to be destroyed. Then the Judeans are going to rebuild the temple, but the Danites will come. The Antichrist, who may be from the tribe of Dan, from this European lost tribe who do not want God anymore, will come and occupy it. Then Jesus will come and destroy them. So, Dan will be destroyed.

The Greco-Roman Empire is a result of the lost tribe of Dan. They are not tribes who are lost because they left Israel, but a tribe lost to Satan. It is in the bloodline. Jesus is the light to the Gentiles; His blood will redeem. The only way back for these tribes is through Jesus Christ. Christ is a pure Judean who is the only one who can handle Dan. Only the king can bring the judge into judgment because the King is a three-fold lion and even the serpent knows not to get around an old lion. Scripture says "Judah is a lion's whelp. Judah is a lion crouching" (Gen 49:9). Then it says, "Judah is an old lion. Who shall rouse him out?" So, Judah is a three-fold lion, while Dan is a two-fold serpent.

The story is told in Greek history that Phillip, who was a Spartan, went to Rome and had Remus and Romulus. They are descendants of Spartans, who are Danites. Their father went and started a colony in Italy. That whole lineage comes from that Phillip the Great (Phillip II of Macedon), the father of Alexander the Great. The legend says Phillip the Great came home and his wife was inside the bedroom. He could hear her moaning and groaning, so he looked through the door and saw a huge serpent lying by his wife. The Oracle of Delphi told Phillip that it was Zeus, the god of the Danites. In fact, the mother of Alexander the Great told Alexander that Phillip was not his real father. This fueled Alexander's rampage, the blood he had shed before he was 33 years old and all the Merovingian bloodletting around the world.

Dan is not mentioned later in the book of Revelation because, at the end of the Book of Revelation, there is no more judgment. There is no need for it. Dan has been chosen and separated from the tribe and separated forever to become the judgment of Israel. God uses them as a rod to challenge and chastise Israel through history.

In the Bible, the Hittites and all who keep coming down from the North to deal with Israel are still the Danites trying to destroy Israel, except for Nebuchadnezzar who was deliberately chosen by God to discipline Israel. In the Book of Daniel, Nebuchadnezzar's DNA was changed by God. He was of Nephilim seed but God transformed him and changed him to become a servant of God. Remember, Nebuchadnezzar had visions of God that no other person had. He fell, but later acknowledged the God of Heaven as the only true God in the world and died a righteous man (Daniel 4).

NAVIGATING THE DIMENSION OF DAN

The third triad is a dimension where we can fall because our capacity for self-righteousness is enhanced. Every human being has a propensity, especially the more gifted individuals, to judge others. The Word teaches us not to raise our self so high. Allow people to think whatever they want. If we choose to stand up for our self while condemning others, we are destroying ourselves while concurrently thinking we are doing work for God.

JUDGING OTHERS

Everybody is a judge. The question is, do we judge as a lion or a serpent? The judgment of a king (the lion) is based on justice and righteousness, for the foundations of His throne are justice and righteousness (Psa 97:2; Psa 89:14). Scripture also says the foundations of his throne are truth and mercy (Psa 89:14). In contrast, we condemn people and hound them, even when we know we cannot do ourselves what we are expecting them to do.

A good judge knows when somebody is incapable or not equipped to do what is asked of them. Therefore, if we are a king, figure out a way to train them, not a way to condemn. Alternatively, figure out where their strength is and give it to them.

No human being can change another human being. Any attempt will result in self-poisoning of both our self and the one we are trying to change. The subsequent result is a buildup of anger and self-righteousness. The serpentine nature within will come to the fore and the people we love will not be transformed. We become the "serpent in the way, biting the horse and making the rider fall." This is where kings get in trouble.

In this Heavenly region of ruling we will know the times and wealth is already prepared for us. God will say, "Let me see how you function in dealing with this region." Self-judgment is not the same as judging other people. Self-judgment never destroys if done the right way.

The first thing we need to do in this dimension is to identify which is our real self and pick out what is not us, set it against our true self as a reflection, deal with it as an idol and kill it. However, we cannot do this in other people.

It is one thing to judge those who are not human beings. It is another thing to judge human beings who are created in the image of God. There is a certain point when, in judging a human being you sit in judgment over God. It is difficult to make a good distinction between when people function from a place of malice or ignorance. Whenever we judge another human being, we put our self above them, making it difficult to see what they are struggling with. No one can look at another from above, as the same inherent nature in them is also in us.

God will open the area of judgment when we walk into this dimension. We will see judges in the court of judgment, but too many people remain in the place of the court.

KINGSHIP AND JUDGMENT

There are other courts in heaven. In a king's palace, for example, there is a court of the princes, a court of the concubines and courts of judgment. There are courts of the lords, which is the courts of the foreign kings. There are different courts in the palace for different groups of people.

God will expose us to the capacity of judgment. If in our kingship we develop greed, when we go to heaven we will judge from that place of greed or self-righteousness. Jesus says we are going to judge angels. Then He tells us, "Judge nothing before its time" (1 Cor 4:5). There is timing in everything. Traveling in the heavens is always a test to see which part of us has been developed and how closely our image is reflecting the Father's image. Everything we see in Heaven has a purpose. One purpose is to see how we reflect God and how much power, insight and revelation is to be released to us.

When God releases these things, there is a tendency to be puffed up with the intention to prove how righteous we are. However the more we try to prove our self to people, the more judgmental we become. It never fails. Every time someone tries to prove they have something from heaven, they deal with other people from a place of judgment.

It is here in judgment where we might end up making an idol of our self, embracing the ephemeral or the vanishing aspect of who we really are. We begin to believe in our own propaganda, rather than constantly looking beyond the mirage to know exactly what is there.

Satan loves to come to this court. It is in this court that the brethren get accused with constant complaining lodged against them. This is where most people who go to Heaven stumble. The downside to spending too much time in this court is that time will be spent trying to fix people who don't need fixing. It becomes a familiar spirit behind us, whispering in our ear. This is where the past is brought up. The past does not exist, but it is brought up so that we can give people life.

When we accept Christ, we receive our authority of kingship and are inducted into the priesthood. The firstborn inheritance has been restored and the firstborn angel is standing by us. We have subdued Simeon (emotions) and are now attached to the Lord. The only way the enemy can resuscitate that which has died is to point at somebody else.

When we first get into this dimension of Dan, we may discover that something is wrong with everybody. It can be interpreted as great discernment. However, the truth is, we become great discerners of other people's faults and get stuck in Dan, going around in circles and bitterness will keep coming up.

"But if your eye is bad, your whole body will be full of darkness. If therefore the light that is in you is darkness, how great is that darkness!" (Matthew 6:23)

What we see in other people is what is in us. Therefore, it is better to keep quiet! It is Dan on the road, striking the horse so that the rider falls. We can never be justified in what we do to other people when they are wrong. The more we self-justify, the more foolish we look in the presence of the angels.

JUSTICE AND MERCY

There are real thrones in this dimension of Heaven. We sit on them in righteousness and justice, truth and mercy. There is no truth without mercy and no mercy without truth. Justice, righteousness, mercy and truth; Yod, Heh, Vav, Heh. Unless those four pillars are in everything that we deal with in this region, we are going to find ourselves sleeping and in judgment of God.

The things we are trying to show God, God already knows. These issues are just coming out because we are getting closer to God, so now we must deal with it. We have the capacity to know the faults, but the struggle is to function as if we do not know. God has revealed it to us. Unless He tells us to say something, do not say it!

Judging is rooted in self and that is where Dan is. The worst place we can get our self into is the place where we think we are defending God or defending Jesus. We begin to deal with other people as if they are hurting Jesus. The only person we hurt is our self.

"If you sin, what do you accomplish against Him? Or, if your transgressions are multiplied, what do you do to Him?" (Job 35:6)

We cannot hurt God. We make a fundamental error entertaining such a notion. We think God walks by His emotions the same way we do. When we act contrary to our nature, we get hurt. God will still be God. When we are done hurting our self and come back to our true nature, He will take all the pain away. Dan is the constant, active judgment that deceives because what we think we are really judging is not real.

This is the place where God sits in the Heavenlies; the chamber where Satan went into and was defrocked. The priestly garment is called a frock. Defrocking involves taking the garment of a priest from him so he is no longer a priest.

JUDGING GOD

It is the dimension where God allows us to see things we cannot naturally see. It is where God allowed Ham to see the nakedness of his father (Gen 9). It is where God may have allowed Satan to see His weakness in dying for humanity, in the future. When Satan saw that from that dimension, he judged God and fell. In this dimension, an opportunity is created to see if one will side with God or look at His weakness as a weakness.

"This foolish plan of God is wiser than the wisest of human plans and God's weakness is stronger than the greatest of human strength." (1 Cor 1:25 – NLT)

What we perceive to be a weakness on God's part can mislead us into bringing ourselves under judgment. When we perceive God's "weakness" it can become a problem. Everyone must go through this dimension. It tests our capacity for judgment, to see if we can trust God and stand with Him, no matter what. In this dimension, we can perceive God as not doing anything or acting too slow and change sides.

The greatest Satan we will ever encounter is our own personal body. When our flesh is trained to resist the spirit, it brings our spirit and mind into bondage to do only what the body desires.

Judgment is vital, but judgment must be tempered with righteousness.

GAD: THE DIMENSION OF REST AND COVENANT

"A troop shall overcome him but he shall overcome at last." (Gen 49:19 - KJV)

Gad is where the capacity to wage warfare is trained. In this region, there is harmony, disharmony and dissonance. It can be likened to liturgical antiphonal singing where somebody sings and somebody else harmonizes. They blend together and create something magical. Several African tribes have their own traditions of antiphonal singing. It sounds to Western ears as if they are being disharmonious, but they are creating something quite deliberate.

A TROOP IS COMING

When Rachel's servant Zilpah had Gad, the first thing Rachel says is "a troop is coming" (Gen 30:11 NKJV). The name Gad means 'a troop is coming.' (Gad also means "good fortune," as seen in other translations). It is that which is inherent in him that calls forth his own trouble - but also causes him to have victory! The word 'GAD' is 'G-D', Gimel and Dalet, which numerically equals to seven. Seven is the number of rest)(but the rest in this dimension is not the 'seven-day rest' granted by God). Gad is in a mirage. He is resting in his own superiority, his own capacity. So how does a troop overcome another troop? Why does Gad lose in the beginning? Because he is over-confident. He is resting in his confidence. What happens in the process that makes him overcome at last? He changes the place of his rest. It is all the same mirage. It is by disharmony that we learn harmony, by antiphonality that we learn phonality and by dissonance, we learn resonance.

There is a distinction between the rest found on the 7th day of creation and the rest found in the dimension where we go to sleep and enjoy what we think is the real Heaven (but it is not). The rest in the dimension of Gad is a place where our kingship, sonship and our capacity for judgment is being tested.

In the dimension of Gad, the angelic begins to appear in great numbers because he is a warrior. There is also an angelic realm called the Gadiels who are the troop masters. This group of angels never appear alone. First Chronicles mention men who fought with David. These men were human beings with lion faces. They had trained themselves to transmute their body to take on the four faces of God. Human beings already possess this ability.

"From the Gadites they came over to David in the stronghold in the wilderness, mighty men of valor, men trained for war, who could handle shield and spear and whose faces were like the faces of lions and they were as swift as the gazelles on the mountains." (1 Chr 12:8 NASB)

GAD IS A WARRIOR

Gad can be spelled in two ways - "Gimel, Aleph, Dalet" or "Gimel and Dalet." So, the name is 8 and 7. Gad is the dimension of operating in covenant. It is the operation of moving from Sabbath into Covenant.

Gad is the only one that the seven constellations are connected to in Israel. Ursa Major is directly connected to Gad. Gad is not that great from a Biblical perspective because he is not a king, but his father calls him a lion. He is the fourth lion that makes Judah complete.

"Blessed is he who enlarges Gad; He dwells as a lion, and tears the arm and the crown of his head. He provided the first part for himself, because a lawgiver's portion was reserved there. He came with the heads of the people; he administered the justice of the Lord, and His judgments with Israel." (Deut 33:20-21)

Gad is a warrior. The Book of Jasher chronicles that when Joseph introduced his brothers to Pharaoh, he did not introduce Gad. Gad was so strong and powerful that if Gad were introduced to Pharaoh, Pharaoh would have made him a guard and they would have lost Gad to Egypt. Gad was so powerful that his voice could shatter stones (Book of Jasher). One of the tribes of Gad was involved in the gross practice of scalping. This is still practiced anywhere we find a tribe of Gad. They were warriors of fearless power. They could transform themselves and change form.

We don't need to be agitated to be a warrior. We can fight from rest and peace. Gad's perspective is "I am on the 7th and the 8th day. I am resting in God. I have a covenant." There is an apparent contradiction in this dimension because we cannot get anything without a fight, but it is a warfare of rest.

Gad is the tribe Elijah came from. There was no other prophet, except Samuel, who could kill 400 people after a prophecy. God knew what He was doing when He chose somebody from the tribe of Gad. The Scripture says those from the tribe of Gad commanded 100 men and the greatest commanded 1,000 (1 Chr 12:14). This is the dimension of warriorship.

In the book of Revelation, Jesus is sitting on His throne and every time He opens the book, something comes out. The Bible says we are a book (2 Cor 3:2). Jesus is trying to create a body so when the body becomes one, the book becomes one. He is the One to open the seal. Until man is opened, Heaven cannot be opened.

REST AND COVENANT

Gad embodies rest and covenant. A covenant is the alignment of Heaven and Earth upon the human body. The 8th day fuses together the two dimensions. Circumcision was done on the 8th day because it is the unification of the Heavens and the Earth.

Gad's warrior style is to be at rest, in covenant. A man in covenant who establishes a connection between two dimensions can become whatever he desires a human being, at a certain point, can transfigure, not just into light but also into lower creatures!

There is a story in the scriptures about a young prophet who God told to go to the city of Bethel and prophecy against the altar of Baal. Let's enjoy it!

"Now an old prophet dwelt in Bethel, and his sons came and told him all the works that the man of God had done that day in Bethel; they also told their father the words which he had spoken to the king. And their father said to them, "Which way did he go?" For his sons had seen [a]which way the man of God went who came from Judah. Then he said to his sons, "Saddle the donkey for me." So they saddled the donkey for him; and he rode on it, and went after the man of God, and found him sitting under an oak. Then he said to him, "Are you the man of God who came from Judah?" And he said, "I am." Then he said to him, "Come home with me and eat bread." And he said, "I cannot return with you nor go in with you; neither can I eat bread nor drink water with you in this place. For I have been told by the word of the Lord, 'You shall not eat bread nor drink water there, nor return by going the way you came.'" He said to him, "I too am a prophet as you are, and an angel spoke to me by the word of the Lord, saying, 'Bring him back with you to your house, that he may eat bread and drink water.'" (He was lying to him.) So he went back with him, and ate bread in his house, and drank water.

Now it happened, as they sat at the table, that the word of the Lord came to the prophet who had brought him back; and he cried out to the man of God who came from Judah, saying, "Thus says the Lord: 'Because you have disobeyed the word of the Lord, and have not kept the commandment which the Lord your God commanded you, but you came back, ate bread, and drank water in the place of which the Lord said to you, "Eat no bread and drink no water," your corpse shall not come to the tomb of your fathers.'"

So it was, after he had eaten bread and after he had drunk, that he saddled the donkey for him, the prophet whom he had brought back. When he was gone, a lion met him on the road and killed him. And his corpse was thrown on the road, and the donkey stood by it. The lion also stood by the corpse." (1 Kin 13:11-24)

Lions don't tear people to pieces unless they are provoked. A lion only kills a man out of self-defense, never out of aggression. What or who was this lion? We don't understand all that is in us as human beings. Scientists are trying to activate in us the things that God is keeping secret. There is a divine trigger in human beings with the capacity to make one look like a lion. It is in the Gad dimension we see people transforming and looking like lions. In Moses, we see a man transform and look like a bull (Exo 34:29, in Hebrew).

GAD'S STRENGTH AND WEAKNESS

Remember, Gad is also 'good fortune.' Gad received everything he needed. This can lead to restlessness, which is dangerous for warriors. Gad had three cities of refuge. There was manslaughter among the Gadians because those who had not worked on controlling their warrior nature were restless. When we become restless, we destroy other people.

The function of rest is a renewal of strength. The weakness of rest is laziness. The strength of warriorship is the capacity to get supply anywhere and to strike fear in the hearts of people. The weakness of warriors is fear and anxiety. The strength of someone who goes into the Gad dimension is the availability of the arsenal of God. The weakness is wanton destruction where we destroy because we can. Nothing satisfies.

(When God wanted to destroy a particular set of people, He would sometimes create someone who looks like them to fight them. Most of the people David led, except for his family members, were all Nephilim. They were giants whose DNA had been transformed).

It is an apocryphal legend that Gad was a warrior and a lion killer. There is a story that says Gad wanted to wring Joseph's neck! In the apocryphal Testament of the Twelve Patriarchs, Gad complains that the reason he wanted to kill Joseph was because Joseph was not used to being in the field. He came with them to take care of the sheep but he did not know what to do. A lion came around and took one of the sheep and Gad went after the lion, killed the lion, and took the sheep back. The sheep was too wounded to leave, so he killed it and they ate. Joseph went home and told their father his brothers just killed his sheep and ate it. So Gad wanted to wring his neck. After Joseph had been sold, Gad missed him.

(The Bible is an incredible book that will lead to salvation, but it is not the whole story. Some are accurate histories; others are not. There are other people who wrote stories about Jesus. We rightly rejected them as 'inspired' because the authors were trying to justify their own actions by Jesus Christ, their human personality being inserted. They were trying to justify idolatry or certain behavior in trying to tell the story of Jesus. However, others, like The Book of Enoch was rejected because of its capacity to draw people into witchcraft if misused).

STAYING AWAKE

In 1 Kings 22, we read of two kings in Heaven who want to go to war on Earth. They are together and they call all the prophets.

> "Then the king of Israel gathered the prophets together, about four hundred men, and said to them, "Shall I go against Ramoth Gilead to fight, or shall I refrain?" So they said, "Go up, for the Lord will deliver it into the hand of the king." And Jehoshaphat said, "Is there not still a prophet of the Lord here, that we may inquire of Him?" So the king of Israel said to Jehoshaphat, "There is still one man, Micaiah the son of Imlah, by whom we may inquire of the Lord; but I hate him, because he does not prophesy good concerning me, but evil." And Jehoshaphat said, "Let not the king say such things!"

Then the king of Israel called an officer and said, "Bring Micaiah the son of Imlah quickly!" The king of Israel and Jehoshaphat the king of Judah, having put on their robes, sat each on his throne, at a threshing floor at the entrance of the gate of Samaria; and all the prophets prophesied before them.

Now Zedekiah the son of Chenaanah had made horns of iron for himself; and he said, "Thus says the Lord: 'With these you shall gore the Syrians until they are destroyed.'" And all the prophets prophesied so, saying, "Go up to Ramoth Gilead and prosper, for the Lord will deliver it into the king's hand." Then the messenger who had gone to call Micaiah spoke to him, saying, "Now listen, the words of the prophets with one accord encourage the king. Please, let your word be like the word of one of them, and speak encouragement." And Micaiah said, "As the Lord lives, whatever the Lord says to me, that I will speak." Then he came to the king; and the king said to him, "Micaiah, shall we go to war against Ramoth Gilead, or shall we refrain?" And he answered him, "Go and prosper, for the Lord will deliver it into the hand of the king!" So the king said to him, "How many times shall I make you swear that you tell me nothing but the truth in the name of the Lord?" Then he said, "I saw all Israel scattered on the mountains, as sheep that have no shepherd. And the Lord said, 'These have no master. Let each return to his house in peace.'" And the king of Israel said to Jehoshaphat, "Did I not tell you he would not prophesy good concerning me, but evil?"

Then Micaiah said, "Therefore hear the word of the Lord: I saw the Lord sitting on His throne, and all the host of heaven standing by, on His right hand and on His left. And the Lord said, 'Who will persuade Ahab to go up, that he may fall at Ramoth Gilead?' So one spoke in this manner, and another spoke in that manner. Then a spirit came forward and stood before the Lord, and said, 'I will persuade him.' The Lord said to him, 'In what way?' So he said, 'I will go out and be a lying spirit in the mouth of all his prophets.' And the Lord said, 'You shall persuade him, and also prevail. Go out and do so.' Therefore look! The Lord has put a lying spirit in the mouth of all these prophets of yours, and the Lord has declared disaster against you." (1 Kin 22:6-23)

God does not operate at the same level we do! God sent a spirit to go and lie. In this realm, our capacity for judgment is tested. God will deal with the lies we tell about other people, then deal with the lies we tell ourselves. His goal is not our comfort but that we will become like Him. He will not stop processing us because we like to feel good, comfortable and spiritually asleep. God desires for us to be awake, make choices and willfully implement things that look like God. God deals with our self-projection when we project things on to other people and consider ourselves superior. If we think nothing is wrong, we set ourselves up to be overcome by hubris, because we have gone to sleep.

In this realm, we are asleep to the things that are happening in us. However, God is trying to get us to make a distinction between what we project out of our self and what God has created anew in us.

In this place, there are marvelous angels who are ready for warfare. They are warrior angels who are ready to fight. If we are self-projecting, we are going to hurt everybody. If we go to sleep, we will be powerless over what happens and be overcome. God wants us to remain awake. God keeps us awake by cognitive dissonance or 'shock.' He creates deep darkness, so when the light comes, we see better.

"For behold, the darkness shall cover the earth, and deep darkness the people; But the Lord will arise over you, and His glory will be seen upon you." (Isa 60:2)

The Father is the measure of what He wants to do with us. God does not want anyone manipulated into coming into the kingdom. He wants people to come by their free will. God will not give us power while we are trying to be more righteous than Him.

God will not save everybody because He doesn't want to. The true heritage of every child of God is God Himself, without measure. He trains us or we would sit in judgment over Him, thereby condemning ourselves, as Lucifer did. We think God should heal everybody and, if we had His power, we would march down the street and heal everyone. We would justify our action with the scripture that says, "Jesus healed all." In Hebrew, "all" means most or more practically, everyone who came to Jesus. Not all sick came to Jesus to be healed. A proper interpretation of scripture involves making a distinction between the Hebrew exaggerations. God does not want to heal everybody. If He did, there is nothing that could stop Him. The Father can do whatever He chooses to do and He always does it sovereignly.

In the flesh, Jesus could not heal unless people trusted Him. God's ultimate goal is to develop people with freedom and intention who can operate like Him. People who are not moved by emotions; people not sentimental in the way they handle business. Why doesn't God just let us operate in the power that He has already prepared for us? Because we are not mature enough to handle it.

Look at what we do with the ordinary power we have. Our self-righteousness can be detrimental. The eyes of our understanding need to be opened.

When we come to this realm and overcome the temptation will arise to go to sleep. We can become satisfied with ourselves to the point of becoming passive. Consider, for example, the rich man who says, "And I will say to my soul, "Soul, you have many goods laid up for many years; take your ease; eat, drink, and be merry." (Luke 12:19).

THE ANGEL DANIEL

The word "Daniel" means "God is judge." One of the angels (messengers) who operate in the Dimension of Gad is called Daniel. Angels always carry the name of God. In the days of Nebuchadnezzar, Daniel could stand in the gateway of the city, because he knew how to judge righteously. When we understand this principle then that angel is released to us. The judging angels are symbolized in the person of Daniel who stands as a judge over a foreign nation.

Daniel was sitting as a judge over Babylon when Nebuchadnezzar was sent as an animal into the bush (Daniel 4). Daniel was among the people to receive him back into his kingdom and to restore his kingship. Daniel knew how to make a distinction between the mirage and the real thing. Daniel was the one who delivered the verdict against Nebuchadnezzar. He could have taken over the throne of Babylon. He did not because he understood the operation of those angels that he was named after.

Whenever we deliver a judgment there is an angel to carry it out, who stands as a witness against or for us when we stand before God. This is where true kings are tested because they judge nations.

Daniel was a king, though he was a slave. He judged over the major gateway of the world, standing in that gateway for almost 70 years with power to shut the mouth of lions, close the Heavens, command kings, pierce veils and to see beyond. He had the power to step into fire with his brothers and sisters. Whenever the scriptures speak of someone 'like the son of man', it is talking about a human being.

BECOMING A LION

Human beings can train themselves to transmute their body to look like a certain aspect of God. They can take on the four faces of God. The Book of Jasher documents human beings who, with one hand, could lift rocks weighing tons and shatter it with their voices. People in the East still have these legends in their minds where they have a hero who, by the shout of his mouth, shatters a mountain.

Those who have overcome the troop that overcame them take on the nature of the Lion of Judah. So then, how do we deal with the mirage that is rising in the Gad system? There is the temptation to be lulled to sleep so that the lion in us doesn't come out. When we get into judgment, we destroy ourselves. There is a danger if we allow the lion to go to sleep. The key is to have the lion awake but without always being agitated. We hold the key.

MOVING IN THE HEAVENS

There are keys in life to move in the Heavens. One of them

is suffering. One of the best ways for a Christian to access the Heavens is to identify with the suffering of Jesus Christ. Many Catholics begin to see angels and experience the supernatural because they know how to identify with the suffering of Christ.

Key: Trauma

Daniel could move through the Heavens quickly because of trauma. Trauma or conscious spiritual activity forces our soul to shift. Anything that moves us deeply can cause our soul to shift physically. At a certain level of education, our consciousness shifts in the field of study.

Daniel could shift because of trauma. He identified with the suffering of his people. Then there was a shift because of education. He studied astrology and astronomy, amongst many other things. It was not part of his cultural background. Astrology was not even allowed in the open, even for kings. It was only allowed for prophets and priests. It wasn't common for all of Israel because many of them would turn it into something else. These things will cause the whole consciousness to shift.

This is what God wanted to do with the people of Israel - to get them to a place of understanding. They knew what God was doing. God throughout history was trying to shift them. This is probably why God used warriors so much in those days. Warriors are always on the edge of experiencing death. Paul says, "reckon yourselves dead" (Rom 6:11) because that reckoning shifts consciousness.

Key: Teamwork and Separation

Another key is to work in groups. The ancients always worked in a group. They would not walk alone until a certain level. There were very few who walked alone. Men walked with men, women walked with women, until they got to a certain level. Afterward, the schools are put together. To put a woman amid men when she is not mature is to mess with what it is she brings. To put a man amid women when he is not mature weakens the sexual center. Most cultures don't understand why they separate men and women. It is the strengthening of the sexual center that allows for strong spirituality in most cultures. The constant mixture of men and women does not strengthen the sexual center. It weakens it because one is constantly sexually agitated.

The cultures that develop spirituality always separate the men and the women in a spiritual context. There is a direct purpose in developing the woman's spirituality so that it can function at a certain level, while the men function in such a way that they can produce what is needed to produce in the atmosphere. In most cultures, the girls who go to girls' schools do better than the girls who go to co-ed schools because they allow the sexual center to develop. Abstinence is a powerful thing, which causes a transmutation to take place. Sex is a powerful thing when it is used right, not in a moral sense, but what God created it for.

Married couples do not know how to separate and come back, especially in modern Western culture. Separation creates a powerful, spiritual capacity and the transmutation of spiritual power. Paul said: "Do not deprive one another except with consent for a time, that you may give yourselves to fasting and prayer; and come together again so that Satan does not tempt you because of your lack of self-control." (1 Cor 7:5).

Satan gets involved between a husband and wife because of the sexual power and the possibility of what can get produced in marriage through sexuality.

Fornication affects the sexual center, so it cannot be used. One cannot create what needs to be created by having sexual encounters outside of marriage. In fact, the real definition for fornication is to give away our sexual energy. Nothing can be produced outside of a covenant. A single individual who keeps their sexuality will harness the power of that sexuality to manifest what needs to be manifested. When the urge for sex is aroused, that is the time to focus the mind on what we desire to create. God created sex for productivity. It is our power, something God put in us to cause things to come into existence. It is this act that produces a child. Sex has the power to pull a soul from another dimension and put into a body, into an egg and then the soul expands the egg into a body. That power resides in us.

Separating must be intentional. Separate, come back and then separate. There is a time for embracing and a time for separating.

GODS ARSENAL

We need to understand what assets God has in His arsenal. This is so we can understand the power of warfare that comes from rest.

There are Heavenly dimensions where implements of warfare are created and encountered and where warriors are made. God has protocols. In the Book of Revelation, beginning with Chapter 5, a book was brought to the Lamb.

> "And they sang a new song with these words: "You are worthy to take the scroll and break its seals and open it. For you were slaughtered and your blood has ransomed people for God from every tribe and language and people and nation. And you have caused them to become a Kingdom of priests for our God. And they will reign on the Earth." (Rev 5:9-10 – KJV)

The Lamb takes the book and breaks the seals. When He breaks the first seal, there are seven angels. Each angel controls a dimension of a creative arsenal. They are beings that are weapons of themselves. Remember, these beings in the Book of Revelation are not coming from Satan or hell; they are coming from the Lamb's book that He opens. This is a direct creature from God!

"And I beheld and I heard the voice of many angels round about the throne and the beasts and the elders; and the number of them was ten thousand times ten thousand and thousands of thousands." (Rev 5:11)

That is a number close to one hundred trillion. God is not just interested in the Earth; He is interested in the whole universe that He created. That is every creature which is in the Heavens. There are other creatures in the Heavens that cannot be numbered.

"And then I heard every creature in Heaven and on Earth and under the Earth and in the sea. They sang: "Blessing and honor and glory and power belong to the one sitting on the throne and to the Lamb forever and ever." And the four living beings said, "Amen!" (Adonai, Melech, Elohim, Naaman). And the twenty-four elders fell down and worshiped the Lamb. As I watched, the Lamb broke the first of the seven seals on the scroll. Then I heard one of the four living beings say with a voice like thunder, "Come!" I looked up and saw a white horse standing there. Its rider carried a bow and a crown was placed on his head. He rode out to win many battles and gain the victory." (Rev 5:13-14 – 6:1-2 KJV)

In most cultures, white has always been the color of death. It was changed to black by the Europeans.

"And when he had opened the second seal, I heard the second beast say, Come and see." (Rev 6:3 KJV)

Jesus is releasing these beasts. The seals are hidden in the human DNA. Everything in this chapter is in us. The time is coming when these things are going to be released. Revelation speaks about things that are going to be birthed out of our DNA that God inserted there because they are in us; in Heaven. They cannot be manifested except through us!

"And there went out another horse that was red: and power was given to him that sat thereon to take peace from the Earth and that they should kill one another: and there was given unto him a great sword." (Rev 6:4 KJV)

This rider is Jesus.

"And when he had opened the third seal, I heard the third beast say, Come and see. And I beheld and lo a black horse; and he that sat on him had a pair of balances in his hand". (Rev 6:5 KJV)

This rider is a judge.

"And I heard a voice in the midst of the four beasts say, A measure of wheat for a penny and three measures of barley for a penny; and see thou hurt not the oil and the wine." (Rev 6:6 KJV)

The oil and wine referenced here is the anointing and the joy.

"And when he had opened the fourth seal, I heard the voice of the fourth beast say, Come and see. And I looked and behold a pale horse: and his name that sat on him was Death and Hell followed with him. And power was given unto them over the fourth part of the Earth, to kill with sword and with hunger and with death and with the beasts of the Earth." (Rev 6:7-8 KJV)

The language of America is based on the language of the Illuminates. They have categorized us in ways that allow us to be opposed to one another. They tried to put "red" on the Indians and "yellow" on the Asians. Color labels are a symbolism of division among humanity. The goal is to tune our consciousness, so we are constantly opposed to one another in thoughts and vibrations. Thus, we are divided in our consciousness, resulting in wars being fought around the world. It creates a cognitive dissonance in terms of sight. The whole world is being tuned this way to kill each other.

Note, the pale horse is being ridden by death and hell. This is coming from the Lord, not from the Devil.

"And when he had opened the fifth seal, I saw under the altar the souls of them that were slain for the word of God and for the testimony which they held: And they cried with a loud voice, saying, how long, O Lord, holy and true, dost thou not judge and avenge our blood on them that dwell on the Earth? And white robes were given unto every one of them; and it was said unto them, that they should rest yet for a little season, until their fellow servants also and their brethren, that should be killed as they were, should be fulfilled." (Rev 6:9-11 KJV)

In many cultures, when one dies, they put on a white robe. Part of the reason for putting black on death is the fear of death. The ancients never feared death. In our day when an old man is dying at 90 years old, he is afraid and everybody is crying. In the old world, when somebody is that old, people just celebrate the homegoing. We don't celebrate the homegoing anymore. Even if they are 120, we still cry because the color black has blinded us. We don't see any good thing in death.

"And I beheld when he had opened the sixth seal and, lo, there was a great Earthquake; and the Sun became black as sackcloth of hair and the Moon became as blood; And the stars of Heaven fell unto the Earth, even as a fig tree casteth her untimely figs, when she is shaken of a mighty wind. And the Heaven departed as a scroll when it is rolled together; and every mountain and island were moved out of their places." (Rev 6:12-14 KJV)

If the mountains are moved and the islands are gone, is anything left? For the first time since the creation of man, human beings will see nature as it is; without gravity, mountains and beaches. At that moment, everything will just be pure energy. In one moment, we will see how we are all connected to one another and then some of us will be cut off.

"And when he had opened the seventh seal, there was silence in Heaven about the space of half an hour. And I saw the seven angels which stood before God; and to them were given seven trumpets. And another angel came and stood at the altar, having a golden censer; and there was given unto him much incense, that he should offer it with the prayers of all saints upon the golden altar which was before the throne." (Rev 8:1-3 KJV)

God's arsenal comes out of God's throne when the prayers of the saints are offered.

"The first angel sounded and there followed hail and fire mingled with blood and they were cast upon the Earth: and the third part of trees was burnt up and all green grass was burnt up." (Rev 8:7 KJV)

When the prayers of the saints were sent up, this is what came down. Those in the occult know this is going to happen when believers begin to get into their position. That is what they are fighting. They believe Christians are going to be the destroyers of the world.

"And the second angel sounded and as it were a great mountain burning with fire was cast into the sea: and the third part of the sea became blood;

And the third part of the creatures which were in the

sea and had life, died; and the third part of the ships were destroyed.

And the third angel sounded and there fell a great star from Heaven, burning as it were a lamp and it fell upon the third part of the rivers and upon the fountains of waters;

And the name of the star is called Wormwood: and the third part of the waters became wormwood; and many men died of the waters, because they were made bitter." (Rev 8:8-11 KJV)

The prayers and work of the saints are cleansing the Heavenlies from all the things that are there which should not be there.

"And the fourth angel sounded and the third part of the Sun was smitten and the third part of the Moon and the third part of the stars; so as the third part of them was darkened and the day shone not for a third part of it and the night likewise." (Rev 8:12 KJV)

Fallen angels have places where they have nested themselves around the universe. Some are nested by the Sun, the Moon, planets, stars and other places. When these prayers are sent up from the believers, the fallen angels begin to leave their positions and are dropped on the Earth. They are supposed to be cast down on Earth for judgment. Our prayers are not just about us, but it is a way to cleanse the world, the universe and bring it to the place where it can birth sons and daughters of God. The sound of our voice impacts creation. Our prayers and worship cleanse the Heavenlies.

"And I beheld and heard an angel flying through the midst of Heaven, saying with a loud voice, Woe, woe, woe, to the inhabiters of the Earth by reason of the other voices of the trumpet of the three angels, which are yet to sound!" And the fifth angel sounded and I saw a star fall from Heaven unto the Earth: and to him was given the key of the bottomless pit.

And he opened the bottomless pit; and there arose a smoke out of the pit, as the smoke of a great furnace; and the Sun and the air were darkened by reason of the smoke of the pit.

And there came out of the smoke locusts upon the Earth: and unto them was given power, as the scorpions of the Earth have power. And it was commanded them that they should not hurt the grass of the Earth, neither any green thing, neither any tree; but only those men which have not the seal of God in their foreheads." (Rev 8:13 - 9:4 KJV)

In God's arsenal, there is this locust with a scorpion's tail coming out of the bottomless pit, which is being opened by an angel from the Lord and is the result of the prayers of the saints. They are released to fight those who don't know God, who refuse to be sealed by God and who don't have Yeshua Hamashiach upon their life.

"And to them it was given that they should not kill them, but that they should be tormented five months: and their torment was as the torment of a scorpion, when he striketh a man. And in those days shall men seek death, and shall not find it; and shall desire to die, and death shall flee from them. And the shapes of the locusts were like unto horses prepared unto battle; and on their heads were as it were crowns like gold, and their faces were as the faces of men. And they had hair as the hair of women, and their teeth were as the teeth of lions. And they had breastplates, as it were breastplates of iron; and the sound of their wings was as the sound of chariots of many horses running to battle. And they had tails like unto scorpions, and there were stings in their tails: and their power was to hurt men five months." (Rev 9:5-10 KJV)

The locust looks like a horse, prepared for battle. It is wearing armor. Its feet are like crickets' feet. It looks like a horse but it is a cricket. This is a creature we have never seen and it is one of God's weapons. God has creatures in this dimension unknown to man. Some of them have a tail like a serpent but a face like a lion or a leopard and their serpent's tail will bite people and their mouth sends out fire.

We need to understand what God has in his arsenal and what he wants to give us, or through us. We must stay awake and allow Him to deal with ourselves and our character so we judge and rule correctly. Allow God to deal with the Gad warrior nature within you.

NAVIGATING THE DIMENSION OF GAD

AN EXAMPLE OF OPERATING IN THE GAD DIMENSION

When we operate in rest, the arsenals of Heaven and Earth come together. Warfare is taken care of by that which emerges out of the Book of Christ, based on the prayers of the saints!

Prayer becomes a fundamental principle that releases Heaven on Earth. Prayer is our voice and its frequency carries great power and significance.

When we were in a church in a certain city, we were trying to buy a building. The city had a witch coven that decided that no spirit-filled Charismatic churches were ever going to be established. When a Charismatic church wanted to buy a building, the city bought it from under them. Only the Catholic Church, the Reformed Church and the mainline churches were allowed. Spirit-filled churches were not allowed there. So we walked throughout several buildings. Every building we prayed around became a church. These are buildings in commercial areas where there are not supposed to be churches. We went and we prayed around a building and within two months it became a church.

The day came when we wanted to buy a property. I was decreeing, declaring and speaking things into the atmosphere every morning. The property in question was slated as commercial. A federal law was recently passed that a commercial building could become a church. There was a certain woman in power there who said, "You can't make it a church." I went to the mayor and I told him we needed this place for a church. We bought the place, but they wouldn't give us the license. I kept going over and the mayor said, "Okay. We're going to permit you to use it. We're going to give it to you because I have a letter from my lawyer that says we better do this." Now the woman was sitting there and I knew she was a practicing witch. She said, "We're never going to give you that letter."

The mayor wanted to give me the letter but the woman would not. Every time I went to the office, she was out. One Thursday I came in and said, "Okay, if I don't have my letter by tomorrow or by this weekend, this city will be uninhabitable." I walked away, went home and started praying.

In the middle of the night, a tornado landed only in our city. It is a small town between several other towns. The tornado landed and went through the city hall road, pulling out every tree and destroying everything, including the houses of some of the councilmen.

There had never been a tornado in our city before. The people said they heard an angry voice running through the city, uprooting trees. A tree fell and covered the city hall gate. In the morning, when I heard what had happened, I ran over there. When the mayor saw me, he said, "Please come and get your letter on Monday."

WE HAVE ACCESS TO AN AMAZING ARSENAL

This is the kind of power believers have. There are weapons in God's arsenal. Gad is one of those places where we encounter these weapons. Gad is a symbolic manifestation on Earth of the dimension where God puts His arsenal. (They are not just in one part of Heaven. They are in different parts of Heaven). In Gad, we experience the arsenal and meet angels beyond our imagination.

A good way to acquire an understanding of some of the things in Heaven is to look at insects. Truth about Heaven is embedded in the smaller things. Look at the creatures in the sea. There are all kinds of creatures there. God did that on Earth so we can know the things that are available to Him (and us). If God wanted to do certain things to the Earth, one fish could mutate and destroy all the oceans!

Scientists are trying to play on man's genetic structure and initiate mutation to the extent that man will become different from what he is today. They are using food and medicine to manipulate human DNA. They are putting DNA markers and triggers in us, trying to manipulate the frequencies of sight, hearing, smell, feelings, etc.

A WARRIOR WORKS FROM REST

David created many instruments of music and warfare. Why music and warfare? Rest, resulting in warriorship. One must operate from a seat of rest to be a great warrior and not a destructive one. A warrior needs to be creative.

"Then Jesus said, "Come to me, all of you who are weary and carry heavy burdens, and I will give you rest. Take my yoke upon you. Let me teach you because I am humble and gentle at heart, and you will find rest for your souls. For my yoke is easy to bear, and the burden I give you is light." (Matthew 11:28-30). Jesus is known as the Prince of peace. To function at rest as a warrior is not mutually exclusive, it is how they are balanced.

Gimel and Dalet (Gad) is a 'camel with a hump of supply' going through an 'open door'. In this dimension, the arsenals of God are available to us. In this dimension, that which comes to destroy is destroyed, so that which is productive will remain. That is what a good warrior does. True warfare is taking the non-productive things that are not supposed to be there and leaving the productive. Nebuchadnezzar was a great warrior because he took all the wise people and artisans with him.

Nothing is won without a battle, but the battle does not always have to be with complete destruction. In order to function in the Gad dimension, one has to deal with the heart first.

REST AND COMMUNION

Remember "Gad, a troop shall overcome him, but he shall overcome at last." The only way a troop overcomes us is when we step out of the covenant and rest of God.

If we take the first letter of Gad and the second letter and vibrate them with chanting, the Gimel and the Dalet, we have the capacity to vibrate resources, enlargement and treasures. They call it the seven-fold riches. We can create the vibration to open the door by which we go from one dimension to the other. If we put the Aleph in the middle, then we have the pathway of the name of God that allows us to go through. We operate in this dimension in rest and in covenant. The only person that can give us rest is Jesus. He's the only one who has created an atmosphere where humanity can find rest. A covenant is always made by blood. The infusion of the blood of Jesus Christ into our system deals with the serpentine nature. It deals with the demon seed that has infected us all. The blood of Jesus Christ cleanses us from all sins.

"This is the message which we have heard from Him and declare to you, that God is light and in Him is no darkness at all. If we say that we have fellowship with Him, and walk in darkness, we lie and do not practice the truth. But if we walk in the light as He is in the light, we have fellowship with one another, and the blood of Jesus Christ His Son cleanses us from all sin." (1 John 1:5-7)

If we are out of fellowship with believers, we can't live righteous because the blood is activated in fellowship with other believers. This is how we maintain covenant. That is why the world produces more than the churches, because the church doesn't know how to maintain covenant.

Today, we have believers walking away from community and thinking that it is okay. The Bible says if we have fellowship with one another, the blood of Jesus Christ, His Son, cleanses us (1 John 1:7). This is Communion, which has two references - fellowship and the Lord's Supper. If we don't have fellowship with other believers, communion is not activated. Communion means fellowship with one another. It is communion with the blood. That is how we become one as it is activated in the Body. Discerning the Body means being in fellowship with one another.

Section 2: Gad: The Dimension Of Rest and Covenant

ASHER: THE DIMENSION OF JOY

"And Zilpah Leah's maid bare Jacob a second son. And Leah said, Happy am I, for the daughters will call me blessed: and she called his name Asher." (Gen 30:12-13)

JOY PRODUCES LIFE

One way to experience dimensions of Heaven and allow our kingship and priesthood to come forth is to carry an aura of joy. If we open up to joy, it will act as a magnet. People will be drawn to us, and it won't be fake. Some Christians say "Well, why should I be smiling when I am not feeling good inside?" That is precisely why we should be smiling; to transform and transmute what is happening into what we want it to be. For every new project we want to start we will run into mirages, things that want to make us back off and go back to sleep. But the infusion of joy produces life.

That is what the Asher dimension is - to yield that which is fit for a king. There are kings in the kingdom going hungry; kings in the kingdom suffering because they spend so much of their time trying to figure out how unrighteous other people are and how other people are not doing right. Every time joy is infused, the mirage disappears, the soul awakens to a greater consciousness and then that which is fit for royalty gets produced.

We consider Asher to be of Leah, through her servant Zilpah.

What did Leah do that Rachel did not do? Leah focused on bringing the Heavens and the Earth together. She didn't just focus on moving behind creation to manipulate the gods as Rachel did. Leah aligned herself with God and with the purpose of God. She was trying to create an alignment on Earth. As we will see, Naphtali was successful and satisfied, but he was a deer moving freely with the favor of God. Naphtali is from Rachel's handmaid Bilhah, when Rachel thought she was infertile. Leah responds by offering her handmaid Zilpah to Jacob and names and raises the two sons (Gad and Asher). Naphtali, the 6th born, needed Asher, the 8th. Leah answered Naphtali, and God answered Naphtali, by providing Asher.

FULLNESS OF PROVISION

Asher means happy, but the blessing of Asher relates to the happiness that comes from the fullness of provision. There is a reason Leah says the women will call her blessed. A big issue faced by the world is that provisions are not made by society for the woman to be who she wants to be. Women understand the necessity of provision and sufficiency. They recognize it when they see it.

Most women in the world worry about providing for their children and their household. When men make war, women suffer because there are not enough provisions to take care of the family. Women have the capacity to see when provision is coming. A woman will beat a man any day in management and the capacity to manage resources, to cause resource to manifest. She can take what is small and make it into something else. She has the transmutational power of wealth.

In marriage, if done the right way, a wife will be a gateway for wealth. She can see provisions coming where a man cannot see it. The people who provided for Jesus in his ministry were all women. They could see the full provision for humanity in Him.

Asher is the basis of happiness. Leah, in trying to bring forth Asher in using her servant Zilpah, seems to have connected with the divine heart. She was not just trying to create someone who can be great and do miracles and can have access, but creating someone who could tie Heaven and Earth together. Naphtali is the result of God's intervention through Rachel's servant Bilhah. If God did not intervene with Rachel she would have brought forth a demonic force, just like Aaron.

THE TECHNOLOGY OF JOY

"Blessed is the man who walks not in the counsel of the ungodly, nor stands in the path of sinners, nor sits in the seat of the scornful" (Psa 1:1)

The text should read, "happy is the man..." It's the same "Asheri va'ish". The first word in Psa 1 is the word for Asher.

"But his delight is in the law of the Lord, and in His law he meditates day and night." (Psa 1:2)

The word "delight" is also used when Moses talks about Asher. Asher is the last person Moses blesses. The last point God meets us is the point of joy, happiness and delight.

"Asher is most blessed of sons; Let him be favored by his brothers, And let him dip his foot in oil. Your sandals shall be iron and bronze; As your days, so shall your strength be. "There is no one like the God of Jeshurun, Who rides the heavens to help you, And in His excellency on the clouds. The eternal God is your refuge, And underneath are the everlasting arms; He will thrust out the enemy from before you, And will say, 'Destroy!' Then Israel shall dwell in safety, The fountain of Jacob alone, In a land of grain and new wine; His heavens shall also drop dew. Happy are you, O Israel! Who is like you, a people saved by the Lord, The shield of your help and the sword of your majesty! Your enemies shall submit to you, And you shall tread down their high places." (Deut 33:24-29)

Asher is a place of joy; a being of joy. Asher carries with him the technology of joy, happiness and delight. There are things that Naphtali cannot overcome because of where he comes from. But Asher, by being joyful, changes everything because joy waters the ground. Joy will make any hard ground fallow. Joy will protect the head of the person who has it.

Asher, even in natural, was the farmer of Israel. He grew crops. The land of Asher was fruitful. Asher operated in providing delights for the king. The realm of Asher is the realm of the fullness of joy. Asher is not heard of much because what they did was create an atmosphere for other people to rejoice in.

The reason joy is important in this end time is because joy is a technology for rewriting atmospheres. A servant who is joyful will be made a son and a joyful servant is more than sons. The only time a son is more blessed than a servant is when the son causes delight in his mother and father.

THE THREE FOLD CORD OF TRANSFORMATION

Asher causes delight and walks in delight and joy. Asher is the carrier of happiness, joy and delight; the three-fold cords of the transformation of an atmosphere. God told Israel that when those who live far away came to Jerusalem every year they should sell whatever they were going to bring, take the money to the temple and buy whatsoever their soul desires - eat, drink and get drunk in His presence and delight in Him (Deut 14:26).

God gets infused by the joy of His children. Provision is connected to the level of joy. Many struggle because of being too serious. Being righteous does not mean we should not be joyful. Being serious often suggests that we are feeling guilty about or struggling with something. If the struggle has ceased and we have come through Naphtali (first dimension of the fourth triad), the Lord has brought us to an expansive place, free from the snare and we can jump and skip upon the mountain. We will be joyful! The Bible says God rides upon the mountain. If God rides upon the mountain and we operate in the spirit of Asher, we will ride upon the mountain and ride in joy.

BENEFITS OF THE DNA OF JOY

Asher was a very happy guy, filled with joy. He carries with him a certain DNA, an infusion of joy. I remember, when I was going to school, I would study hard. The last two weeks of school, when the exams were going on, I would be playing and rejoicing. I didn't realize the technology of joy was helping my brain. I needed the frequency of joy to swallow the medicine of the studies.

We need joy for certain things to sink into our being. Even the Buddhist monks, occasionally, will throw off all their costumes and go dancing in the streets. These are serious guys who don't talk to anybody.

Go to Israel on Friday nights and look at the serious guys who will not talk to anyone during the week. They are the ones dancing with strangers on the streets because they understand that joy rewrites the atmosphere. It does something to human DNA. It activates what is dormant in us for the good.

A joyful person is not easily rejected. Asher finds favor with his brothers because happiness raises favor with God and with man. It was a law that nobody comes before a king with a frown. That is why Nehemiah was scared. One is not allowed to be sad in front of a king, especially a slave servant.

"Favored by his brothers..." A brother will stand for us when we are in adversity. They may not like us, but when the time of adversity comes most of them will stand with us. They will even travel long distances, after not having spoken to us for years, to visit. Especially if we are a delightful person to be around.

"May you dip your foot in oil..." Oil is usually synonymous with the head, so why is the foot dipping in oil? The place where the Tribe of Asher lived is where oil is being found in Israel today. The 'oil' is a symbol of the feet being able to "see" into the deep recesses of the Earth and the feet being a carrier of victory. The dancers in traditional cultures who don't wear shoes will wash their feet and rub it oil. Oil is always put on the feet so it doesn't crack. The anointing of the feet is to keep the feet healthy so that it can dance before the king or in the community. The feet, when they are in celebration, are the greatest expression of the heart. When the heart is filled with delight, the feet can see treasures!

"Every place that the sole of your foot will tread upon I have given you, as I said to Moses." (Joshua 1:3)

"I will delight myself in Your statutes; I will not forget Your word." (Psa 119:16)

"Your testimonies also are my delight, And my counselors." (Psa 119:24)

David delights in the Word of God. There is a connection where bringing the Word into his heart caused his feet to move. We don't have this finesse in dancing anymore. Today they use music as a motivation for soldiers when they go to war. They don't play sad music for them. Even psychologists have people use drums as a frequency for directing soldiers. They subject their own soldiers to the sound until the sound becomes a positive influence on them and a negative influence on the rest of the people.

JOY AND THE MIND

"The locks of your head are like iron." Why would we need iron locks for our head? Where does our sadness begin? It is our head that tells our heart to be sad. The iron locks will protect our head from all the flying information and the negative processes that grow in it.

The soul in our head can always control how the heart feels. We can speak to our heart, which David did, "Why are you cast down, O my soul? And why are you disquieted within me Hope in God, for I shall yet praise Him for the help of His countenance." (Psa 42:5)

The Hebrew commentary on the soul says the soul in the head can always tell the soul in the heart what to do. It can cause the heart to change its direction. The rational soul must speak to the feeling soul. The head controls the heart, not vice versa. It is only when the heart becomes strong that it is then able to inform the head. If the heart is weak, it will be misled by sentiment. Until the soul in our heart grows up, the soul in our head needs to tell it to, "Stop being depressed and cast down. Occupy yourself with something else until you get healed."

The locks of the head are the protection of the mind. Joy will protect the mind! It will keep us from subjecting our self to the oppression that is around us. A good example of this is the African-American community. If it were not for joy and celebration, African-Americans would have been wiped out by now. They sing and dance for Jesus. It helps them handle what we do to them in US society and in Africa. It is one of the greatest manifestations of the power of joy in the world. Their music helps transform our society. It was birthed from their response to oppression and dealing with an atmosphere. They gave us jazz. Despite how much the blues might make one blue, it makes us feel better.

"As your days, so shall your strength be." According to legend, Asher was able to renew his strength and look young until the day he died. The story is told that Asher died an old young man! If Asher died an old young man, it therefore means there is something in joy that renews the DNA. Why would Jesus tell us not to be anxious? That's why Paul wrote,

"Be anxious for nothing, but in everything by prayer and supplication, with thanksgiving, let your requests be made known to God; and the peace of God, which surpasses all understanding, will guard your hearts and minds through Christ Jesus" (Phi 4:6-7).

CHANGING YOUR CIRCUMSTANCES BY JOY

Can we change our circumstance, with prayer, joy and celebration? The Greek word for 'thanksgiving' is 'Eucharist'; a celebration of a god; a happy or a good christening. "Eu" means good, wonderful, beautiful, celebrative. "Charist" means celebration and thanksgiving. Paul is saying every time we pray, do it in celebration. That will be a hard thing for some of us because we have been brought up to believe the way to pray is to harass God constantly. If we are suffering, we think it is hypocritical to celebrate God. It is not pretending when we do what God tells us to do.

"In everything give thanks." This is the same word, "celebrate." That is Asher's Heaven. The Bible says there is no sorrow there.

If we want to be in Asher's Heaven, we cannot continue to live a life of complaining when relating to a God who celebrates us and who calls us to celebrate for the transformation of our situation.

"A merry heart does good, like medicine, But a broken spirit dries the bones." (Pro 17:22)

When sickness comes, celebrate. Asher is living in a realm where the joy of the Lord is the strength of those who abide in it. Oil on the feet and the head cover you from the influence of all the negativity around. Asher is the principle of joy. Heaven is a place of joy. Stop making Heaven into a place of judgment, make it into a place of joy. When one operates in the realm of Asher, the body responds with greater strength and healing. It releases its own healing.

Leah didn't get Asher by fighting with the dragon. She got Asher by aligning the Heavens and the Earth to create joy upon the face of the Earth. Worship in joy and angels will want to join us to worship because they love what we do. When they are partners with us in worship, they become partners with us in revelation and work.

ASHER SPREADS VICTORY TO OTHER DIMENSIONS

The role of Asher in the Heavens is that it must permeate every other realm. Its fragrance must waft all the way back to Reuben because it is that joy that changes everything. It makes it easier for the one who's struggling at the realm of Reuben (feelings) to rise above their struggle. So to the one who is struggling in the Levi and Simeon dimensions to help overcome their wrath. The one who is struggling with Judah's adultery and tendency towards idolatry will overcome because he is celebrating. Anyone operating in this dimension will discover that victory will come to be easier in many of the things we struggle with and guilt will not be so heavy on us.

JOY IS YOUR FOOD

"Bread from Asher shall be rich, and he shall yield royal dainties." (Gen 49:20) Joy, happiness and delight allow for a majestic provision that is fit for kings. It tailors the DNA of provision towards kingship. If we operate in kingship, we cannot eat the bread of affliction every day. We must learn how to provide 'food' based on the three-fold cord of happiness, joy and delight. This is the basis of the kingdom.

> "For the Kingdom of God is not a matter of what we eat or drink, but of living a life of goodness and peace and joy in the Holy Spirit." (Romans 14:17 NLT)

God is the realm from where manna comes to sustain those in the wilderness. It is only the people in the wilderness who didn't realize that God's provision is angel food that is the result of the angels delighting in God, being celebrated before Him and being joyful in Him. That's how manna is made. Manna comes from the three-fold cord of joy in Heaven. David says, "They ate the food of angels! God gave them all they could hold" (Psa 78:25 NLT).

The food of angels comes from the realm of Asher, where the royal delicacies come. Anyone can get provision, but not every provision is good for a king. If provision is not laced with the drug of joy, happiness and delight, we are not eating food fit for a king.

Everything in the Heavens needs food. Even the offering in the Old Testament is called the food of God. If there is joy, happiness and delight, even the devil will give up what he is holding from us. There is no religion that doesn't have dancing, celebration and joy because it is the food of spirits. As selfish as the devil is, he will give up what he is holding for somebody who celebrates. God set the principle and anybody who walks in it gets blessed. Anyone walking in mourning, sadness and grumpiness is not fit to have the food of a king.

ASHER IS EFFECTIVE IN ALL SEASONS

Naphtali is coming so that Asher can live in sufficiency; a sufficiency of Heaven based on the Asherite domain. Asher is assigned to Libra, then Virgo and then assigned to Cancer (this will be explained in greater detail in future publications on Israel and the Zodiac by Dr. O). Asher is a strange being because some people assign to Asher the sign of water and the sign of air. Asher can rewrite atmospheres. Part of what happens with somebody who operates in Asher is that they know how to adapt to different atmospheres and how to make it work for them.

The key of the nature of Asher is in the constant admonition in scripture to bless the Lord, to praise the Lord, to give God thanks in everything. There is a mystery there for how our circumstance and our situation changes. When we deal with Asher, we are dealing with someone who can draw out plenty in any circumstance. Then we are not controlled by season, circumstance or star sign but can shift from one to another - the capacity to move and access wealth no matter where we are.

By birth, a believer's main position should be operating from Asher. We operate as a king - but who has more power, the king or the one who feeds him? The king depends on the person who understands the season and who can produce when no one else is producing. A believer must not only be a king or priest, but he must be capable of producing wealth. The key of Asher is the three-pronged key of joy, happiness and delight.

Asher's host is 41,500 (Num 2:28). These hosts are angelic beings. They are Israelites, but this is God's way of saying these are the angelic hosts that work in this dimension. They work to create new things and open gates of possibilities when there is no possibility, which is what joy does. Joy and delight are keys for making the impossible happen.

Asher, by his birth, is one person who can deal with curses

because Asher understands how to function in the delight of the Lord amid trouble. A joyful person who looks like he is acting silly can overcome witchcraft quicker than a person who is always somber and sad. It's power to the powerless!

ASHER AND THE CONSTELLATIONS

In describing tribes based on the Heavenly signs, Asher is controlled by Virgo. Virgo carries a grain of wheat, which is a symbol of harvest. Asher is supposed to provide royal harvest. Harvest is always in scripture done with joy. Joy is necessary for harvest. By joy, we draw water out of the well. When we think of the goodness of God and what He has done for us, our soul should rejoice. It always provides an abundant harvest in all circumstances. A person who operates in joy holds the key for opening any door during any season.

The Hebrew word for Virgo is the word 'Bethulah' (הַבְּתוּלָה), meaning 'virgin'. A virgin is always a sign of abundance. When the bible says that the virgins of Israel should weep, it is talking about famine coming upon the land.

Asher is also connected to Libra. Libra carries the scales. In ancient times, the king's diets and foods were measured on scales. Libra is also used to measure food in the time of famine according to the book of Revelation. There is a horse with the rider carrying scales. Anyone operating in Asher can distribute wealth, even in famine. He has sown, distributed and still has more left. There is a famine in the book of Revelation but the scales are for measuring food for everybody. Asher carries the scales because he is the one who distributes wealth and food. The person with the food controls the nation. Whoever he does not give food to will die. If Asher must distribute food without measure, it means something has gone wrong. However, the key is that Asher is supposed to distribute food for kings, not for people who are dying.

The third sign of Asher is Cancer, represented by the crab. It is argued that the reason why Cancer is attributed to Asher is because he lived in red alluvial soil that produced more than any other place in Israel. When everybody else was suffering, Asher was producing. The stone of Asher in the ephod was the onyx. Onyx means 'bleach' in the Hebrew, which is the capacity to change the color of objects. Anybody who operates at this level can shift and not be held captive by context, situations or even geography.

JOY AND THE WORD OF GOD

"And of Asher he said: "Asher is most blessed of sons; Let him be favored by his brothers, And let him dip his foot in oil." (Deut 33:24)

In Jewish tradition, oil represents the Torah. The dipping of the oil (apart from the natural resources that are in the land of Israel where Asher was) means that Asher's feet are grounded in the Torah. Asher delighting in the Torah increased the oil of gladness in the land. The word "shemen" used for oil is the word for an anointing that opens realms and allows for the flow of abundance into the life of a person. Abundance is part of the gospel. Prosperity is not the focus of the gospel, but we cannot preach the gospel and tell people they need to remain poor unless they choose to do so. If somebody is poor in the gospel, somebody else must make money for the person who is pouring out the gospel to survive. Those who teach the gospel should not be poor.

Asher is not just the principle of being happy. Asher is the principle of prosperity. There is a level of prosperity tied to the fact that one has dipped himself in the Word of God. Asher walks in multiple systems and can produce from those systems. The oil that he dips his feet in is the wisdom of the Word of God. He dances in the Word of God, activating the spirits that are in the Word. When Asher steps upon the delight of the Word it produces angels that work with him!

WATER AND THE WORD OF GOD

The month of Asher is Shavuot, the month of the outpouring of water. Asher is the one who carries the symbol of Israel, which is the symbol of a bucket of water. The Torah is a deep well. The great heroes of Scripture met their wives at a well or somewhere at the water. A well or water is a sign of a place to converse about the Torah. When Laban heard that his daughter met a man who drew water for her, he picked up his head. He knew that was a man of mystery.

Women understood that Jacob knew the depth of the mystery of the heart of God, which is the wisdom of the water of the heart of God. Jacob met Rachel at a well. The wrestling of Jacob with the angel was by the water. It was a wrestling to get the depth of the mystery of the record of the life of Jacob.

David picked up five stones from the brook. Five is the number of the Torah. David was operating from the depth of the heart and the law of God.

> "David answered the P'lishti, "You're coming at me with a sword, a spear and a javelin. But I'm coming at you in the name of ADONAI-Tzva'ot, the God of the armies of Isra'el, whom you have challenged." (1 Sam 17:45 – CJB)

David draws from the water. Wisdom and mercy are regarded as water. If that is the case, Asher is drawing from wisdom and mercy (Naphtali, as we will see, draws from beauty and harmony and mercy).

Happiness makes one wise because it releases our capacity to remember what has been forgotten. The water in our body operates at the level of Asher. It is an emotional principle. If we plant joy in the water of our body, it will give fruits of harvest. Instead of sowing sadness and complaint, sow joy, happiness and delight so that the body will bring forth fruit and the gates of the body will be open.

JOY CAN BRING SALVATION AND HARVEST

The month of Shavuot is considered the month of abundant blessing. There is a passage of the Mishnah Taledot that says Asher is the one who stands at the gate of hell. His job is to send back anyone who has delighted in the Word of the Lord from getting to hell. He does so by an expression of joy that leads the joyful back to the heart of God. The Joy of the Lord can save somebody from a life of hell!

Asher has the capacity to look beyond circumstances and see the abundance that is hidden behind what one would consider to be suffering. Paul says, "If we suffer with him, we shall also reign with him" (2 Tim 2:12 KJV). James says we should rejoice when we suffer. We need to bring joy into suffering to harvest what is hidden within it. There is a harvest in every pain, a seed. If we complain and fight, the seed will be destroyed before it comes out.

AIR, WATER AND EARTH

Asher can operate in the fullness of air, water and Earth. If he operates in the principle of the air it means that, by joy, happiness and delight, he infuses the body, soul and spirit with life because air is the food of the body, the soul and the spirit. God is saying the person who operates in Asher can fill the body, soul and the spirit because that is what air does. One who operates in the watery principle has the capacity to cause anything to grow in any season, any place. If water was spread in a desert, something would grow. We are not only carrying the water of the body, but also the water of the Word of God.

Human beings carry water. Wherever human beings plant their feet, the very DNA in the water changes the environment. If it is tuned right, the environment will change. Our incapacity to move and to do what needs to be done is because the water in our body has become stagnant or poisoned by our thoughts. We carry an unlimited reservoir in our physical body. If it is tuned correctly it will attract what is needed. If we spend time judging others and not ourselves, the water in our body begins to stink because it doesn't have an outlet except to punish other people. Pride can stand in the way of breakthrough.

God made our body to carry water for the environment. We carry our own destiny in our body. Nobody is born with poverty written on their forehead. Remove the limitations. The Lord has come to live in us, so move into the realm of Asher, the realm of abundance, overflow, favor and production of the delights of kings. In this realm, if the color doesn't look good, we can change it. We are the carrier of the onyx stone. The spiritual principle is that we can change our environment by language and thoughts.

We are a carrier of the transformative principle of our destiny. When we speak to our body, the rivers of water in the body are agitated. It is stirred to bring forth the records of Heaven that are in the body.

> "For there are three that bear witness in heaven: the Father, the Word, and the Holy Spirit; and these three are one. And there are three that bear witness on earth: the Spirit, the water, and the blood; and these three agree as one." (1 John 5:7-8)

The water, blood and the wind that we carry in our body bear witness to the record that is written about us in the Heavens. If we misuse our breath, we misuse our capacity to activate the record of Heaven about us. If our emotions are wrongly tuned, the witness of Heaven about us changes.

The Spirit, the Word and the blood are also for our redemption. We are not saved by just thinking. We must speak it. When we spoke, God's will and our will aligned and God came into us. Now we carry in our physical body the power and the grace of God. Our body has the capacity to manifest something our minds have never understood.

Asher is God's release of technology into Israel that keeps Israel afloat when everybody else is fallen. We possess the same thing!

JOY OVER SORROW

Joy is one of the fruits of the Holy Spirit (Gal 5:22-23). Jesus said to ask and receive, that our joy may be full (John 16:24). Asher is the realm of celebrative joy. The way to God's heart is not through mourning, fasting, praying, crying, screaming or shouting. One can be engaged in mourning and fasting and the problem persists.

There is something in our being that responds to the rhythm of joy and celebration. It is something human beings carry and God gave it to us deliberately to change atmospheres. God loved David because He was a king who would dance until his clothes fell off. I believe Leah must have been a happy woman. The Messiah could not come from somebody who was stuck in sadness.

God may have picked Mary when she was a little girl because she was filled with joyful exuberance. She said, "Be it unto me" (Luke 1:38). She didn't know what she was getting herself into. God knows what He is doing. We are carriers of this DNA of joy.

Most people don't know how to relate to their Heavenly Father from this perspective. Even in the natural, we think having respect means not being joyful. There is no one so serious that there is no joy in them. In fact, God makes it a point to change our mourning into dancing, change our sorrow into joy (Psa 30:11). It is easier to change our destiny by joy than to do it by sorrow!

Sometimes the happiness that produces life destroys the enemy. In the dimension of Asher, the Lord God will thrust out our enemies. The reality of having anointing on the feet, which flows from the heart, is the reason we are Christians. In fact, our job is to bring the spirit of Asher into the world. The gospel is good, happy news. It is a message of joy or as the King James says, "glad tidings of great joy" (Luke 2:10)

Christians should be dancing down the street talking about the redemption of the Lord. Our gospel has become a gospel of sadness, destruction and fear. Our joy and message must be consistent with the realm of Heaven where we are living.

"Your word is a lamp to guide my feet and a light for my path." (Psa 119:105 NLT)

There is always light and abundance. Naphtali and Asher have the same role as Gad. They are all supposed to correct the serpent principle of Dan. There are always two that correct the one that has a problem.

The true initiation of the believer into the mind of God is not done by suffering and crying. The true initiation is done by delight in God. When God instituted the law and sacrifices, the fat of the animal was always sacrificed to God. Israel was not supposed to eat the fat. The fat around the heart was supposed to be put on the altar and burned. Fat always maintains its purity. It refuses to let other things into it. God says, "Burn the fat and when I smell it, I will restore to you the abundance and I will remember you."

The fat produces oil. There are some anointing oils that come out of fat.

Asher is the director of the affairs of the king. He can sustain destiny and, if necessary, change the environment, even the personal life of a person, to provide them with the resources that they need to fulfill what God has called them to do. Sustenance is needed to move and weave the joy of God as a force into the fabric of the record of the soul and the spirit of the individual. Whenever we walk in joy, the fragrance of our life transmutes a cantankerous life. The joy from the Lord does something to irritability, it does something to a chaotic world. It realigns and redirects it for manifestation and for creation.

If we can overcome and focus on joy and celebrate a person making a mess in our life, we will discover that they get transformed. I was not a very joyful person. I was initiated into mysteries from childhood. My wife taught me joy. I needed somebody to correct me.

JOY CHANGES DESTINY, ATMOSPHERES AND OUTCOMES

If our story can change, so can our destiny. We need to tell ourselves a different story deliberately until our body, soul and spirit believe it. Asher has the capacity to modify what might seem to be constant forces at any time he decides. He can rewrite the wilderness and change it into a land of plenty. He can come into a place where nothing is growing, sit there on the stone and the stone starts sprouting beans. It is such a powerful thing that the whole universe responds to Asher because he is a melodious song, singing in harmony with the galaxies as they expand the creativity of God in time and space. Believers are Asherites who can impact the universe and change the world by the redemption joy that flows from the heart of God through His Son by the Holy Spirit. We can tune the environment around us so that it produces what we want based on the record of who we are in the mind of God.

Remember, Asher is a triangulated technology that joins water, air and the Earth. He moves the Earth to produce what it was meant to produce. That is why traditional people dance before the harvest. They are dancing to create an atmosphere for the Earth to respond to their bodies. Asher must have been a dancer. He was a joyful person, the kind of person who went into the presence of God. He is not necessarily the creator of the universe, but he is one who can redefine, realign, redirect and rewrite the very essence of what has been created. The influence of Asher extends from the inner depth of God to all of creation because the person who operates in joy, delight and happiness has access into the depths of God's heart.

A Court Jester is paid more than soldiers because he makes the king happy and keeps the king from cutting off people's heads. He makes the king laugh so the king forgets. Joy, happiness and delight is a powerful intercessory tool. Whenever we think God is upset with the nation, believers should get together and dance before God for time and space to bend to our will. The triangular principle of joy, happiness and delight form a vector whereby light pierces through the darkness. This is evident in the life of David.

David invented fourteen musical instruments because that is what joyful people do. The greatest witness to a man's life is not the level of wealth he has amassed but the level of joy he has spread around the world. The joyful person, or the Asherite, incorporates all the positive arrangements of creation and turns them into a chariot that carries the fullness of God to wherever their mind wills it to go. This is a temple of joy and delight. God comes into the garden of delight. These garments of God also serve as the garment of the righteous. They are the fundamental principle of creatural coherence. They have the capacity to create coherence, thereby removing fragmentations.

Fractals carry the light of their original forms. Joy, delight and happiness are fractalizing elements. When glass is shattered it still has the wholeness of where it came from. The more joy we spread, the more happiness and delight we have. The more it increases in the world and the more we have. We always have more than we give. We are coming to the place of joy and delight that will rewrite the atmosphere and the very nature of human beings. The more human beings get into the realm of the triadic celebration of the delight, happiness and joy of God, the more we begin to live longer. It is the key to longevity.

The Bible tells us that when we get to Heaven, we will rejoice always. There is no sorrow, tears or crying there. These are the three counterparts to what God provides for us that keeps us alive forever in Heaven. If there was sorrow in Heaven, we would die because sorrow is the result of loss. Asher lives in a dimension where nothing is lost!

JOY CREATES WORLDS

The supernatural waters above align with the water of the Word connecting them to the water of the human body who has come to believe in the Lord. The triadic principle of joy, happiness and delight is not mainly a physical movement. It is both physical, psychological and spiritual. It touches the very depth of who we are pneumatically because from the place of joy we touch the essence of what it means to be spirit.

Through the Asherite, worlds that are still in the mind of God come into existence because of the delight the righteous have in God and the delight that God has in them.

"Then I was beside Him as a master craftsman; And I was daily His delight, rejoicing always before Him, rejoicing in His inhabited world, and my delight was with the sons of men." (Pro 8:30-31)

In Proverbs 8 we see that every creation and manifestation of new worlds is a combination of delight, joy and happiness. Jesus said when a new soul is created in the Heaven, all the angels get up and start dancing and rejoicing (Luke 15:7). All Heaven joins in a chorus of praise, adoration and magnification to God. When we accepted Christ or when we were born, for us to be able to descend, we needed the triangular process of joy, happiness and delight. We were not born out of suffering. Jesus died for us to be saved but our new birth comes through the circle of the joys of angels. Our 'yes' to the new life activated Heaven's joy, forming the pathway for us to manifest on Earth. The Asherite nature is the secret of the poles that holds up the tabernacle. All of Israel praised the Lord and rejoiced when the tabernacle was set up.

It is easier to rectify certain aspects of the world by the triadic principle of joy. It is not done through repentance. It is the triadic principle of joy that rectifies the upper level. Repentance rectifies the lower levels. Repentance is a way to open us to move beyond our present mindset, but to sustain our presence in the Heavenly realms, we need the triadic principle of the Asherite; joy, happiness and delight.

In Proverbs, joy and delight are the divine primal modulation. Joy causes a modulation in the Heavens. The best way to modulate the reaction of God on the Earth is repentance - but we are not in repentance all the time. We sustain and modulate the reaction of God to creation by delighting in His Word and personality, expressing happiness about who He is and what He has done and intends to do. Believers are yet to grasp the intercessory power of joy, happiness and delight.

The body of Christ is coming to a place of understanding these three principles as intercessory principles for changing atmospheres and delivering people out of the hands of destruction.

When the angels came to the birth of Jesus they did not talk about the sins of human beings. All their songs were about joy, goodwill and delight. The shepherds were joyful because creation needed the joy to rewrite its history. The four rivers of the Garden of Eden that we carry, the rivers of abundance, flow into more abundance out of love and joy and delight.

The mental orientation of the Asherite is that which keys the whole being of the person into the heart of God and into what makes creation alive. It allows all the visible forms of creation to be brought into an integration with the will of God by releasing the Shekinah into creation. The Shekinah travels on the wings of joy.

It is possible by love to transmute ordinary realities so that God can be seen even in the worst situation. While there are other means of having victory over the elemental principles of creation and demonic forces of the world, what the demons hate most is delight, joy and happiness. In other words, the enemy delights in our sorrowful approach to God. One of the best ways to cast out demons is to begin to delight in God and praise Him. The demon will just leave.

The joyful person is a spiritual and eternal carrier of spiritual and eternal possibilities. He gains victory over elemental forces and dominion over creaturely vicissitudes. If we operate in joy and happiness, we will sail through circumstances and pain. The joy of the Lord is our strength (Neh 8:10).

God has given a formula to make situations look small. Every substance, season, thought and vision can be rewritten by the triadic principle of the Asherite realm of Heaven! Even stones, by joy, can be squeezed to give water. Why do native people dance in the wilderness where there is rock? They believe that joy in the atmosphere can make the rock give forth water.

Moses did not hit the rock with celebration. God was about to offer His people water. He should have been joyful. He complained over the rock before he acted. Asher understands this power. One of the errors of our generation is that we live a life with a narrative of sadness and complaint, expecting the result of joyful living. We spend hours complaining about everything and expect our situation to change. We use the technology of death and hope to produce life! Everything in the universe is controlled and directed by that which is fitting to it. The fitting principle for life is joy, happiness and delight.

If we want to operate beyond the mechanistic reality of the world in which we live, we must operate in the dynamism of unbridled, unhindered, unhinged joy, happiness and delight. Our mechanical response based on our fallen nature is to respond even to good things with complaint. We must work against this nature to create a dynamic fluidity that allows us to operate non-mechanically, so we are not responding the same way we have been responding since birth.

The sixties were not changed by protest, but by song and dance. It was the sons of the black church who changed American consciousness. There was a tuning of the nation with the songs of delight despite suffering. It wasn't just America that was changed. Other groups who have tried to be free since that time have sung these songs.

It was a song of delight that changed England. John and Charles Wesley, amongst others, wrote hymns that rewrote the atmosphere and the hearts of men and women. The landscape of England changed, so it became a land of life rather than a land of death.

In France, Christians were not allowed to sing. France still suffers from that occultic bloodbath.

Every revival is followed by joy. It begins in sadness but is followed by joy and delight and songs come out of it. The reason God gives songs in revival is so that believers don't turn the revival into a mourning fest.

JOY IS FROM BEFORE CREATION

When we repent and God forgives, it is not a time to mourn but to rejoice! The establishment of divine rulership in its fullness and dominion does not just come from giving our life to Christ, it comes from accessing the delight that Christ had with the Father before the creation of the world. The delight of the pre-creation wisdom is Christ celebrating with the Father as He displayed His fireworks in non-time and non-space. A true initiate knows when to get completely unhinged, get drunk (in the Lord) and literally get naked by their drunkenness before the Lord.

Noah did not get drunk because he was depressed. He got drunk because God had done something for him. It is God's desire for us to become unhinged in response to His goodness!

God says to Israel, "Get unhinged, get drunk, dance before Me for seven days. Celebrate My blessing in your life." There is time for mourning but we have mourned enough. Every prophet keeps telling us to cry but it is time to try the triadic principle of joy, happiness and delight and see how the situation changes. It is time for believers to dance crazy on the street, to come to church, get unhinged and dance until their soul leaves their body and they get catatonic. It is time to stop being so cool and mature and be like children, regardless of who is watching.

We know nothing of awe and the movement of God's ecstatic presence in the Heavens. Heaven is such a joyful place. The atmosphere of Heaven is saturated with the possibility of God's heart and how much God loves humanity. God cares for humanity and He delights in the sons of men. He does not willingly abuse and punish the sons of men. He has a joyful heart towards us!

A person cannot operate truly in the delight, happiness and the joy of the Lord unless they have an inner rest. To be initiated into the higher worlds of spiritual consciousness, we need the thread of joy and ecstasy. We need an actual flow of the wine of Heaven. It is when we operate in this that we can flow in the sweet incarnational incense of God manifesting Himself in creation. Developing higher stages of self-mastery is possible when we operate in this principle.

There is time for being quiet but joy activates what we work for and brings it to the fore. If we bring joy, delight and happiness into our labor, wrestling and pain, the seed will germinate. We will develop a higher level of self-mastery and mastery of our rulership, kingship, dominion and power. We have the capacity to control life's forces. Some life forces need to be controlled otherwise they will destroy other people. There is a place for control, a place for telling the force of nature to stop.

Everything in the universe can be sanctified by the prayer of joyfulness, happiness and delight, which is why we give thanks over our food. If we complain over our food, we would be poisoning our self. We can rewrite the DNA of what we eat by heartfelt thanks. It is the elixir of immortality, the wine of divine nature and activation. It is a way of planting our feet above and our heads downward, of living in a right side up world with our head looking down on Earth and feet planted in Heaven. It is a way of balancing the scales, realigning the 28 dimensional stars of time and space. It is a way of creating a covenant rainbow that delights the eyes of God that keeps judgment away.

Our whole body within and without is purified by the principle of joy, happiness and delight. We overcome the flux and contingencies of other people's emotional baggage by healing our self. When we are elevated to the level of joy and happiness, others will follow.

When witches gather, they sing and dance around in a coven. The key to dealing with witches is not to hide in church, but to dance in the neighborhood at night, celebrating God. Celebrate God under the Moon. Tune the Moon by celebration towards life and not death. Tune the Sun by celebration so the Sun does not smite by day or the Moon by night. It is a powerful thing to participate in the joy of the Lord. The Father delights in us. Draw from the well of delight, the world of happiness, the world of Asher because this is the key to living the full abundance of the record Father has about our life. God's record about our life is not for destruction!

Asher is the one who provides the food for the delight of the king's heart. It is a celebration of joy and happiness that rectifies the universe and realigns the Earth with the heart of the Father. Joy, delight, happiness is a greater medicine than mourning. God will make haste to turn our mourning into joy.

God is interested in us operating in delight, joy and happiness because it is the way of the heart of God. God has mercy on us because He wants to produce a manifestation from the realm of God's heart to the realm of our heart and all creation.

Section 2: Asher: The Dimension of Joy

NAVIGATING THE THIRD TRIAD

We are moving through the 12 Lower Kingdom Intersection Dimension: the Tribes of Israel. Each of the 12 dimensions deal with our soul, based on the character of a son of Jacob as revealed in Genesis 49. Each triad (grouping of 3 dimensions by birth order) deals with a certain facet of our new nature. We have just investigated the third triad of Dan, Gad and Asher; the Warrior Triad.

WARRIORS AND EMOTION

In Genesis 49:19, Jacob says, as for "Gad, a troop shall overcome him, but he shall overcome at last." In other words, Gad's nemesis is in himself and not outside of himself. Gad shall be "gadded." A 'gad' is a huge object that is used to hold things together in buildings. To be gadded means to be held in place so it doesn't move.

Dan judges as a destructive serpent. God put a lion in his way. Gad is that lion. Gad stayed at the boundary of Israel and the other nations. He needed to be strong and able to become whatever he chose to make sure nobody crossed the borders.

If people know that they are called to be warriors, they must learn how to be grounded in themselves. This means that warriors cannot be moved by their emotions because they can become destructive. All the weapons that we throw outside are coming from within us. One needs to be grounded in rest and covenant to know who they are. If we operate from fear, anxiety, likes and dislikes, we are operating from our self. If we operate from our self, based on the negative, we will always get the things we fear.

Fear and anxiety must be removed because, when it is inside, it will attract what we are afraid of. Overcoming fear allows one to draw what is needed.

CREATING AND EMOTIONS

The life of Job teaches a fundamental principle. Everything that happened to Job is what Job called forth. He said "what I feared has come upon me" (Job 3:25). In other words, Job created all that happened in Heaven. God was responding to Job, based on his fear. Let's rephrase: "What I feared, I have created." Job's mind was constantly focused on not losing his children, not losing an opportunity, not losing a house, not making it, so he ended up creating it. Fear is a creator, as much as faith is a creator. The difference is what it creates. Fear always creates what we don't want, and faith creates what we desire.

Operating in rest means operating based on what we desire - not based on what we have, but on what we can create out of nothing. It is the Sabbath; the day of doing nothing. God commands that no work be done on the Sabbath because of our tendency to insert our self into the process, thereby hindering our capacity to create what we want to create. Every time we get anxious and get involved, we narrow our capacity for creation. We end up creating what the body is comfortable with because the body is in control of the mind. When the inspiration comes to do something great, the mind influenced by the fear of death begins to speak, "Look, I have been in control all these years and now you are trying to release your mind to create something that I am not comfortable with. Hold on just a second." The Sabbath is about doing absolutely zilch and just calling things that are unrealistic into reality!

In the quantum world, nothing exists the way it's supposed to. Everything is malleable and in potential form. Everything is particles and waves. We need to release our conceptualization of reality because the particles and waves will become what we put into the atmosphere. They will form around it and become what we want them to be. That is how faith functions. We should develop a big picture but release our self from the responsibility of making it happen and from knowing how it is going to happen.

Envision something big and continue to envision, speak, think and feel it until it comes to pass. Release the details to God. Leave God, Jesus and His universe alone to figure out the details and the outcome. If we knew how it would happen, we would create a narrow image and it would not be as big as God wants it to be. It is unrealistic of us to want to change and transform the world by our own efforts. Think big and be unrealistic. Everybody who has ever changed the world has done this.

How can the people from Gad literally change their form to look like a lion? The people of Gad, like Elijah, understood that nothing is impossible. In the real world, whatever does not exist, can be created.

COVENANT

A covenant is a fundamental connection between that which is inseparable. It is the giving, the intentional connection of the fundamental nature of one thing with another to create something completely different. It is a connection where there is no separation. Jesus says, "I and the Father are one" (John 10:30). He says that we are one with Him, we are His body. The physical body has nothing to do with this. There is a connection that happens beyond what we can see with our eyes.

GRATITUDE: POSSESSION PROCEEDS MANIFESTATION

Gad's name also means good fortune. What happens to a person who has good fortune? They share it. A person with good fortune is always joyful because they are not worried. It is not good fortune that results in joy, but the heart of gratitude that results in good fortune. It is that gratitude that allows one to live as if they are already in the reality being spoken about. If the focus is always on what is lost, there is no gratitude. To operate in rest and in covenant, there must be a central principle: the tone of the scale is a spirit of gratitude. Jesus says, "Whatever you ask, believe that you have it" (Mark 11:24). The possession precedes the manifestation. We can't get it if we don't believe we already have it. Believing we have it creates a spirit of gratitude and joy. Therefore Dan, as judgment, who was supposed to judge in righteousness, could not because he was taking on the serpent nature and he disappeared from the line of Israel. Gad, who is a lion, lives in rest and in the covenant. He is in rest and undergirded by Asher, who is joy.

The problem with Dan is ingratitude. Dan wasn't happy that God saved them and with the land God gave them. He wasn't happy with anything God was doing. He put God under judgment and then ended up selling himself to the serpent. Dan is the problem of the world today. That whole house of the Danites from Europe and the Danites from Asia are the ones who caused the world many problems. The problems have their root in ingratitude. The ingratitude in Dan resulted from the incapacity to conquer the giants who were in the land. Rather, they entered a serpent covenant with those that removed the giants. The difference between Dan and Gad is that Gad took the covenant seriously and stayed close to Asher.

PROTECTION IN COVENANT

In every one of the triads, there is a person that amends for the weakness and the strength of the others. There's someone who helps with the weakness and the strength of the other two, allowing them to fulfill their destiny.

A person who has entered the dimension of Gad always has a troop around him. There are people with 2-3 angels around them; others with 12-14. The Bible talks about the angelic host encampment, and there are those warriors in the kingdom that are surrounded by a host of angels. Elisha was one of those. Elisha said to one of his servants: "Do not fear, for those who are with us are more than those who are with them" (2 Kin 6:16). The servant saw the angelic host of God around the mountains. That is the dimension in which Elisha was walking because Elisha was one who was a warrior and a prophet.

The covenant of seven, which is the Sabbath, allows us to walk in the spirit of prophecy because a prophet operates in rest. That is why a prophet will have music playing around him. The covenant means that we are connected with God in such a way that we are protected. Nothing can change that, no matter where we go, no matter who speaks, we are still in that covenant.

Gad is the only one with the numbers seven and eight joined together and he represents the Messiah. Gad is the 4th lion (Judah is the first 3 lions). He is the only one that looks like a lion. Judah is called a lion but Judah never changes into a lion. The Gadites are the only guys that transform into a lion.

A LION AT REST

"Blessed is he who enlarges Gad; He dwells as a lion, and tears the arm and the crown of his head. He provided the first part for himself, because a lawgiver's portion was reserved there. He came with the heads of the people; he administered the justice of the Lord, and His judgments with Israel." (Deut 33:20-21)

Gad took the place of Dan because he could judge righteously. Notice that Dan is mentioned after Gad in Deuteronomy 33. Dan had already started joining himself to idolatry. Dan leaped away from Israel when he jumped away from Bashan. From that point on, he became an idol-worshiper. Dan is a different kind of lion. He is a young lion but he is also a serpent. A serpent which is a lion is destructive. Dan is already being tied to the one called "like a roaring lion".

Gad dwells as a lion, but he does not move as a lion. He's at rest as a lion. When we walk in covenant rest, there is an inherent principle which is the principle of enlargement. It is not enlargement by force, but enlargement by presence. A lion doesn't need to enlarge by force. Territory belongs to a lion, not by him running and chasing after everything, but by lying down and groaning or roaring upon the Earth. The Earth carries the vibration and his presence gets translated through the vibration of the surrounds. Every animal can hear it. This comes from a place of rest. When a lion is chasing its prey, it doesn't roar. It only roars when it is at rest or when it catches its prey. It doesn't roar when it chases the prey because it is conserving its energy. It is anxiety that makes one roar (some call this prayer).

THOUGHTS BRING REST AND MANIFESTATION

We see in Deuteronomy 33:20-21 that Gad enlarges and he "tears the arm with the crown of his head." There's something in his head that allows him to cut off every adversary. He was seated and he "provided the first part for himself". This is the fortune of Gad that he enlarges. He overcomes by his thoughts. The way he overcomes the hand of the enemy is not through warfare all the time, but by controlling his thoughts. He focuses his thoughts on what it is he wants. While the enemy is agitating, he is focused. That is how he breaks the arm with the crown of his head and he provides the first part for himself. That is the first portion. Only the firstborn has this. Gad is also a firstborn. He is the 7th son of Jacob, but the firstborn of Zilpah. He receives the portion of the firstborn by virtue of where he is at rest.

Gad is also a portion of the lawgiver. Gad never truly ruled Israel. "He executed the justice of the Lord and His judgment with Israel" (Deut 33:21). The only person we see this with is Elijah, but the Gadites were always called when there was a dispute between two tribes of Israel. The Benjamites were defeating Israel until the sons of Gad showed up.

Gad is a lawgiver, an executioner of the justice of the Lord, but this can only come from someone who knows how to use the arsenal that God provides - someone who is not agitated, who is not moved very easily, who doesn't go to war over things that don't matter. That energy wasted being angry could have been used to manifest something. That energy used to complain about everything going on could be used to manifest what is truly needed. When one complains, energy, strength and power is wasted. A lion doesn't waste power. It conserves its power. That's why it looks like a lion is lazy, because a lion will sit there for hours. When it releases energy outside of the place of rest, it affects many things but creates nothing. It just causes more confusion.

ACCESS THROUGH CHRIST VERSUS AN IMITATION PROCESS

The seals of the Messiah are different from the seals of Solomon, which come directly out of the Danites and their worship of the serpent. It is the seal that produces the great harlot that gives birth to the antichrist that causes the manifestation of the dragon, the destroyer.

The seals of the Messiah release things that defend God. The seals of Satan release things that demonize, darken and destroy people's capacity for serving God. It leads to the great harlot. That is the reason for the increase of prostitution.

Slavery is a part of it. Witches speak of the virgin, the wench, the widow and the harlot. They are bringing back these Danite lines that are coming from Europe, bringing back the worship of Beelzebub, the worship of Lilith and the worship of the serpent to Israel and calling it Judaism. That is what the rise of a false 'Kabbalah', which is not the genuine Kabbalah. This false Kabbalah opens the demonic and lays out all demonic processes and mixes God with it. It doesn't work. It putrefies and causes rottenness in our soul. People don't understand what they do when they give themselves to these things. The deception is that they can get power from demons when they are using the God-given power to operate in the realms. Demons don't have power to give.

Human beings don't need demons to have power. That is why unbelievers sometimes prosper more than religious people. They are not tied to the kind of spiritual substance where they must depend on a process or entity that is inferior to get what belongs to them already. Worshipers of the Lord Jesus Christ can fall into the place where we make angels do things for us when we can go directly to the Father. The Bible says "Let us therefore come boldly to the throne of grace, that we may obtain mercy and find grace to help in time of need" (Heb 4:16). Jesus Christ has given us the capacity to come to the Father. We can send angels as God's servants to do other things, but the things we need from God, we don't need to ask angels for. We go to the Father and the Father gives it to us through Jesus Christ. What the son can get from the father, a servant cannot.

Angels should not be worshiped. They would never allow us to worship them. Use angels in their right place and in right proportion. When we come to this triad, we have an arsenal in our hand. This arsenal can only be used by sons and daughters, not by people who want to show off their power.

Jesus is the logical evolution of humanity. The "Christians" who attack Jesus and kill Christians are from Europe. The reason they don't like Christianity or Jesus is because the very foundation that many of them have committed themselves to is contrary to who God is. They try to destroy Christianity by inflicting pain on people and making Christianity lose its credibility. Persecution and oppression came from the Europeans in Christianity. It's the Danite principle. Most of the people burned in Europe were Christians who believed something other than what the official government said.

Everything God establishes, the Devil has a counterfeit to open an arsenal that destroys people. It's not in relation to God's judgment. The Devil's plan is in relation to possessing the Earth and controlling the resources, rather than bringing salvation to humanity. This process thrives on punishing the innocent rather than on bringing justice.

THE FOURTH TRIAD: MANIFESTATION AND WEALTH

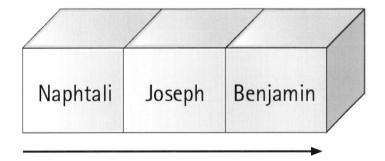

Section 2: The Fourth Triad: Manifestation and Wealth

NAPHTALI : THE DIMENSION OF VICTORY

"So Rachel said, "With mighty wrestlings I have wrestled with my sister, and I have indeed prevailed." And she named him Naphtali."(Gen 30:8 NASB)

PRODUCING ON EARTH FROM THE DIMENSIONS

The word "Elohim" is not in the English translation. There is no place in that verse where it says "God." The word is translated as "mighty" (or "great" in other translations). When the revelation of the Naphtali dimension is discovered it will be the moment when God's people come into their fullness, moving towards the perfection of the capacity to produce. It will be the time when the righteous, those who are in God, begin to move in the dimension of their perfection. The potential that is in them will begin to manifest and move beyond the material into the actual spiritual. We will move from the magical to the magisterial.

Naphtali is the sixth son by birth order, from Rachel's servant Bilhah. He is the one created before the day of the Sabbath. He is the one created when God breathed, when the divine technology came into play upon the face of the Earth. Naphtali is the result of Rachel's wrestling.

WRESTLING WITH GOD AND ANGELS

Jacob, who wrestled with an angel, lived many years before Naphtali was born. He overcame the angel and the angel released the blessings of the life of Jacob. It is not just an issue of wrestling, but an issue of engaging God to the point where we release potentiality into actuality.

Jacob was enslaved for over twenty years before his encounter with the angel. In the middle of the night his destiny shifts. Both his idea of God and his idea of himself gets transformed. Jacob can now live out of the fullness of the future of what God had already promised him (he couldn't get to it previously because he could not key into it). Jacob's wrestling is not the same as Rachel's. In Jacob's life, the angel comes down to find out who this guy is because Jacob gave his angel over to Esau! (He did this by wearing and smelling like Esau and saying to his father, Jacob, that he was Esau). Jacob's life over the next twenty-one years is the life that Esau was supposed to live. Esau was the one benefitting from Jacob's angel because Jacob had said to his father, "I am Esau your firstborn; I have done just as you told me; please arise, sit and eat of my game, that your soul may bless me." (Gen 27:19). The father says to him, the smell is like the smell of Esau, but the voice is like the voice of Jacob.

Angels attach themselves to the fragrance of an individual. Even though Jacob had thought he had tricked Esau, what he did in terms of tricking his father was to exchange what already was his. Now the angel of Esau has attached himself to Jacob. Instead of Esau wandering around aimlessly, which is what he was supposed to do because he was a wild man, Jacob became the wild man. He became the vagabond. He went all over the place and he subjected himself to twenty-one years of being a slave. He still had the magic, he still had the miracles, he still had the capacity to mess with material processes, but not the access to his real destiny.

The angel wrestled with Jacob because it was trying to figure out who he was. He did not know who Jacob was and Jacob wanted his own angel back. The angel came to kill him because the angel is defending Esau. Jacob now has the fragrance of Esau and Esau has the fragrance of Jacob. The angel is defending the Esau that is now in the created reality of Jacobs's makeup. Esau is the one receiving the blessing, who has the keys, conquering mountains, overcoming and prospering. When the angel begins to fight with Jacob and can't defeat him, he says, "Let Me go, for the day breaks." Jacob replies, "I will not let You go unless You bless me!" (Gen 32:26). In other words, Jacob was saying, "I need you to do what you were supposed to do in the first place." Jacob's identity was all mixed up and the angel did not know who he was. Jacob told the angel his name. Jacob's name was then changed to Israel.

Jacob was supposed to be able to see God - to see into the Heavens, not trying to manipulate nature. Jacob was operating in magic.

The Angel blesses him and puts a mark on him. He dislocates his hip, not to torture him, but to have the scent of the angel and to carry this mark wherever he went. His limping was a mark from Heaven to demarcate him from others.

It is in the Father's nature to wrestle, but this is not the wrestling we are talking about with Rachel. Rachel dealt with idols and gained victory over her sister, Leah. Which gods are these women twisting? We can tell from the blessing given to Naphtali that he is not an ordinary being. Rachel did this by controlling the Heavens. She shifted what was the right of Leah to her own handmaiden, Bilhah.

From an astrological aspect, Naphtali could hold the tail of the dragon and the hand of the virgin. Naphtali can control Hydra. He is the only one in Israel who can control the snake. That is why he was put directly next to Dan in the camp. He is also the one who can relate to the virgin. Virgo is the capacity to bring forth something new into existence.

LEAH AND RACHEL

Leah paid Rachel so she could sleep with Jacob for one night. Leah conceived and brought forth Issachar. It was not her time, she was not qualified, so how did she do it? She also wrestled with Elohim and with the idols. She is the one who brought idolatry into Israel. Everybody left Laban's house without an idol and she linguistically connected an idol to her menstruation, which is connected to her capacity to give birth. Unwittingly she messed up her own fertility by connecting it to that god.

Rachel wasn't someone to play with. She could move in the spirit, just like her father. She was a Chaldean. God preferred Leah rather than Rachel for the messianic line. However, Rachel was so inline and imbedded with the process of witchcraft and idolatry that God could not use her. The sons of her first born, Joseph, and his Egyptian wife (Ephraim and Manasseh) ended up in idolatry and they were the first ones to leave Israel and be carried away into exile. (Hos 4:17).

> "For we do not wrestle against flesh and blood, but against principalities, against powers, against the rulers of the darkness of this age, against spiritual hosts of wickedness in the heavenly places." (Eph 6:12)

Rachel wrestled with flesh and blood. She wrestled with things above and caused the constellations of Heaven to manifest. Naphtali was a child born from another dimension brought in by controlling the serpent principle and opening the womb of the virgin.

Rachel wants Naphtali to carry what is in the Heavenly realm. We can enter the supply of Heaven, which means we create an atmosphere that can be manifested on Earth. Naphtali is one of the tribes that is hidden in scripture because it has a secret of secrets. Scriptures have a way of hiding mysteries, like Naphtali, to be hidden until the last day.

FREEDOM AND WEALTH TRANSFER

"Naphtali is a deer let loose; He uses beautiful words." (Gen 40:21)

Naphtali, Asher and Zebulon are a key to eschatological freedom and wealth transfer. Naphtali carries the possibility of Jubilee, the capacity to free one from shackles. It cannot be bound. Naphtali is a deer set loose. He has an inherent capacity for renewal and reinvigoration, reverting back to the point of creation where everything is liquid form and we can create anything. We have not yet seen the manifestations of Naphtali.

When Naphtali emerges to take their position, Israel and all those engrafted with them will develop technology beyond what we have seen because Naphtali holds certain keys in the spiritual dimension.

Rachel understood that, in order to wrestle with her sister, she had to leave this Earth and go into another dimension and take the tail of Hydra and make the virgin step on it. Even though Rachel was not a virgin at the time of the birth of Naphtali, she didn't have a child.

Jacob's blessing is "Naphtali is a deer let loose; He uses beautiful words." Deer can get out of traps as if they float on air. In the Book of Jasher, Naphtali ran onto a row of cornflowers and he didn't bend them. He was known for his capacity for long distance running, floating in the air and moving at the speed of wind. In another account, to settle a dispute, Joseph turns to Naphtali and says "Go get a record from Egypt" and within hours Naphtali brought the record back to the battlefield. This is a man whose mother wrestled with Heaven to have him born by a handmaiden.

JESUS AND NAPHTALI

There is a connection here between Jesus and Naphtali. Naphtali caries the frequency of the manifestation of sonship. For it is written "Israel is my son, my first born son" (Exo 4:24). Naphtali's name begins with the Hebrew letter Nun. If we use the 'final Nun', which is 500, we get '9-5-8'. 9 + 5 + 8 becomes 22, which ends up in 4 (2 + 2), – the full name of God "YHVH." Everything in this passage is pointing to the dimension of creation, the name of God, finite and infinite, connection of upper and lower level Heaven. The righteous are the people that know God and are able to shift creation. Naphtali points us to this secret. Again, that is why this tribe is hidden in scripture.

The word "ayyalah" is for a female deer ("hind" in KJV). Naphtali is a female principle which carries the full supply of who God is. There is a dimension in Heaven that is feminine - always pregnant with possibility. The Jewish dealing with Shabbat is feminine. The Bridal paradigm only works with Shabbat. It is the Shabbat that is the bride - not us. It is the Shabbat that brings in the Shekinah and always comes pregnant with wealth and possibility from the supernatural realm.

NAPHTALIS HIDDEN TRUTHS

When getting ready to conceive Naphtali we read Leah spoke to herself. Speech is a connection to this realm and others that carries the potential of bringing the non-existent into existence (Heb 11:3).

In Genesis 1, the 6th sentence is a manifestation of light

and revelation. Naphtali is the 6th son who gives "goodly" or "beautiful" words. Jacob may be going back to the story of creation when light came into darkness. Naphtali is a carrying and manifesting being. He cannot get to manifestation until he wrestles with Hydra and tames the virgin. This is about relationship between female and male. Naphtali can bring forth words of beauty to unlock the coded realities of Heaven for other fragrances to be manifested on Earth.

When Jacob wrestled, his true fragrance was released when the angel blessed him. This is the seminal principle of Naphtali in the life of Jacob that allowed angels to ascend and descend through him. When Jacob was lying down and angels were going up and down the ladder of his DNA, they were going down through the 3-fold cord of the life of Naphtali in Jacob's DNA before Naphtali came into existence in this world. This was a result of Rachel's struggle to make sure the ladder came down so that she was connected and able to go up and down, to bring down Naphtali to this dimension. Naphtali is the ladder, wrestling with the supernatural, with angels.

Naphtali brings a hidden code of divine cypher. He is the 6th word spoken. God commanded and there was light in the 6th sentence of Genesis. God commanded light to shine out of darkness and into our hearts in the face of Jesus Christ. Naphtali is that part of Heaven that when we get there we no longer go through struggles. We stand in fullness of supply, taking captive the serpent and waiting for the birth of our destiny.

Rachel knew how to operate in the Heavens. Until we find Naphtali and begin to connect with him (hidden in the North East of Europe) there are things we cannot have. They are not in Russia. God has hidden them because, when they come out, the time for divination and false prophecy will be over.

RESTED WARFARE

About Naphtali, he said: "Naphtali is abounding with the favor of the LORD and is full of his blessing; he will inherit Southward to the lake." (Deut 33:23)

Naphtali was in charge of making sure the curse was turned around when it starts. In the blessing of Moses above, there is something important to look at in this dimension of Naphtali. Naphtali is satisfied with the favor of the Lord. When God is saying "Come and enjoy," this is us being born from Heaven.

When Jesus is talking to Nicodemus, He says, "those who are born of the spirit are like the wind" (John 3:8). This is a reference to Naphtali. He is a master at rested warfare, operating from victory. A victory that is already won by his mother. He is not afraid of his enemy; he has no fear of losing- he has already won!

Naphtali draws on the fullness of the Name of God. There is palace where we enter where we have no other identity but the name of the Lord. It carries the hosts of Heaven and is available to us, making us fearless. It is a real tower. Naphtali understood this. Every blessing in Israel is unique. Every dimension is unique. We can explore these places of mercy, favor and God, overflowing with compassion.

REST AND ABUNDANT SUPPLY

Naphtali was in the North of Israel. Jesus began His ministry there. The Jewish mystics started in this open realm. Naphtali was a nation open to the world. He knew how to draw people from different dimensions, looking toward the full supply that comes from the South. (We can find them today in North-East of Europe and in the South toward Argentina). They know how to operate in the Heavens because they understand it. They go by the wind. When we look from Israel to the South-West, we see creation displaying power and light (forming and reforming). The wind from the South brings rain, which means that it brings a level of abundance. In the South of Israel, there is no need to water anything for it to grow.

Naphtali is the 6th division lot in the land of Israel. There is a connection to kingdom manifestations appearing in the life of Naphtali. This tribe contained one of Israel's cities of refuge (and there were only three). Naphtali is a free place where burdens are no longer counted against us. It is a place of abiding in fullness where the past is not counted against us. The Tribe of Naphtali was the place for refuge.

If Naphtali is not operating in the full abundance of God in rest, he can operate in occultic nature. For example, Hiram, the descendant of the King of Tyre and the son of widow from Naphtali, gave Solomon 666 talents of gold for the temple, to allow him access into the realms. Hiram knew he had access to other realms illegally. The donation was to give him a 'legitimate' access through Israel. He needed Solomon as a key for this access. The design of Solomon's temple was attributed to Hiram, from the other side of the serpent's tail - which is what will happen to Naphtali if he is not operating in rest, the fullness in abundance of God (see 1 Kin 9:11 and 2 Chr 2:14)

THE ESCHATON, MYSTERIES AND SECRETS

The Eschaton (the final act of God, in this age) is where there will be no night and the darkness will be removed. The mystery of God will be finished according to the book of Revelation. The hiddenness of God will be completely removed and with an unveiled face, we shall behold Him! (2 Cor 3:18) It will be an exploration of the infinite radiance of divinity. This is what God has planned because, when we get to the 24-dimensional city, it is a gateway to infinity. Jesus Christ is in the center of the city because He is the light of the city. He becomes the beam of light that steps in the center of the city. The 24 dimensions, the gateways and elders serve as a prism, a refracting process whereby that light manifests infinitely. God is light and in Him there is no darkness. There is darkness around Him because of the necessity of the mystery and keeping hidden the things of God from the profane, unsanctified and unredeemed eyes. He surrounds Himself with darkness as a way of keeping the Holy away from the eyes of the profane. This is the same way the temple was built to keep the Holy away from the eyes of the unbeliever, pagan and the immature.

Mysteries are not for everybody. Not every mystery is meant to be shared publicly. Jesus knew far more than He spoke. He concealed a lot of knowledge and revelation in the parables He told, but He did not say everything He knew. Our interpretation of scripture can be skewed by the evangelical paradigm (that I believe is a false paradigm). For example, the eschatology of the West has been formed by Western occultism. Most evangelicals will not agree that they are involved in Western occultism but much of their theory is based on Western occult practices and a rejection of Jewish understanding. (An example is the misunderstanding of the Jewish idea of the 'seven' leading to the return to the 'eight').

The Hebrew language still holds the key to hyper physics. The Jews are under attack because, if we destroy their culture, then we destroy the capacity for other people to know the secrets of what God has embedded in nature. Also, if they destroy native / first nation culture, then the destroyers are the only ones who hold the secrets.

We need to really criticize ourselves. There is a reason why God put the secrets in different cultures. There is a group of people in the world who think it is their job to gather the secrets and wipe out everyone who held them before so that they can use this knowledge to control everybody else. This is history. Wars in Europe and around the world have been fought by secret societies using us, the people, as pawns. The wars were all about different secret societies trying to get ascendency over everybody else.

Embedded in Israel, God has put secrets of physics, finance and more for the purpose of the manifestation of the Sons of God and the rulership of creation! Many of the tribes are being kept away from what is going in the world today. They that hold the secrets are scattered all over the world, waiting for the manifestation of the Sons of God!

Naphtali carries the binary principle, where the world comes through struggle to a place of rest for new creation. It is surrounded by a creative possibility of new light by the manifestation of the dimensional principle that brings Heaven / the Kingdom into the creation realm. Naphtali has this capacity, when we have gone through many struggles, to arrive at a place of rest.

DEALING WITH THE SERPENT AND ITS LINEAGE

Naphtali's nature was birthed from the conquest of Hydra and the raising of Virgo. It is the virgin stepping on the tail of Hydra and literally forcing it to regurgitate what it has swallowed. Naphtali also has the capacity to turn the head of Hydra against its enemy, the world or even friends. Embedded in Naphtali is the serpent nature, but not all serpents are evil. Serpents can be a symbol of renewal, salvation and even redemption.

"And as Moses lifted up the serpent in the wilderness, even so must the Son of Man be lifted up" (John 3:14)

Dan didn't need to worship the serpent, but he chose to. If Naphtali is operating at the level he is supposed to, then he becomes the tamer and the destroyer of the serpent's power and finds rest. He does so by the words of his mouth and he "escapes the traps." Naphtali is able, by speech, to change atmospheres and context. Naphtali delivers "goodly word" and can decipher the codes of God. Solomon knew this, so when he was building the temple, he invited Hiram. David was a good friend of Hiram, but he never invited him to contribute to the temple. Solomon did. Remember, Hiram was a son of a Naphtali widow and a descendant of the King of Tyre, which means he has insight into the realms of the Heavens.

Hiram is regarded as the builder of the temple and he is the hero of the Masonic. He is a worshipper of Satan because he is from Tyre. Hiram came out of that lineage - the same lineage Jezebel came from to trouble Israel. Solomon understood the power of somebody with the blood of this lineage to be able to access that realm of Heaven where the treasures of Heaven are released upon the Earth. Solomon also knew the connection between the virgin and the serpent. Solomon knew Hiram represented how Naphtali was born into the world. What Solomon didn't count on was the serpentine position, the serpent nature and what it was going to do to the temple.

Solomon was wise above all men of the Earth but, in the case of Hiram, he made a big mistake. This is the reason why Israel was removed from the land. Solomon not only asked Hiram to come in and help build the temple, but he took gold from him - six hundred and sixty-six talent of gold. This is the number of man. Not the number of man who reaches into God, but the number of man who stands in opposition to God and wants to take position of the Almighty. The temple is built with that gold and Hiram's hand is all over the temple that Solomon built. God honors this temple because it was built for Him, but the seed that is in the temple did not take more than 1000 years before it germinated to its fullness. By the time of Ezekiel, reptiles were being worshipped in the temple! The negative side of Naphtali had gained ascendancy and gained superiority over Israel. It wasn't Naphtali as a tribe, but an individual who was a descendant of Naphtali. Hiram had the right to access the stars, but didn't have the right to access Heaven because he was a son of the King of Tyre, who was a High Priest of Satan.

NAVIGATING THE DIMENSION OF NAPHTALI

Holiness and righteousness are tested in Heaven. If our heart is not dealt with, we will block what needs to be done. We possess the capacity to shift our selves and stay kind and loving, despite what people are doing, and lead them to their destiny (even though we can wrestle with their destiny and make them fall). Naphtali is a man whose life is based on the capacity to wrestle; to bring out beautiful words and light into darkness. We must train ourselves to show mercy and make our language "goodly."

Naphtali was blessed by Jacob. David says, "You make my arm to break a bow of steel" (Psa 18:34). A deer is an animal that is supposed to be weak, yet there is an inner strength to change. When we move in the Heavens to change the lower Heavens controlled or led by Naphtali, we are going to discover a place of full supply, freedom, Jubilee and new revelations! We will also discover a place of hiddenness because Naphtali is not talked about a lot in scriptures. We will be clothed under the tallit of the wrestling of God.

THE RESPONSIBILITY OF NAPHTALI

"On the twelfth day Ahira son of Enan, the leader of the people of Naphtali, brought his offering. His offering was one silver plate weighing a hundred and thirty shekels and one silver sprinkling bowl weighing seventy shekels, both according to the sanctuary shekel, each filled with the finest flour mixed with olive oil as a grain offering; one gold dish weighing ten shekels, filled with incense; one young bull, one ram and one male lamb a year old for a burnt offering; one male goat for a sin offering; and two oxen, five rams, five male goats and five male lambs a year old to be sacrificed as a fellowship offering. This was the offering of Ahira son of Enan." (Num 7:78-83)

When Naphtali shows up, it is because something needs to be finished. When we operate in this dimension, it means we have gone through the battle and come into place of seeing things clearly. Revelation has come, the code has been broken and joy has come in the morning. What is the significance that Naphtali is last to offer up offerings? Naphtali brings closure to pain. Rachel wrestled for Naphtali to enter rest. Rachel struggled so Naphtali can be born. Naphtali carries the result of Rachel's suffering.

On the 12th day of offering, Naphtali brought 53,400 angels. Positive angelic powers surrounded him. Rachel was trying to make Naphtali controller of constellations to get what he wanted. Having goodly word can allow him to get what he wants, to receive wealth inherent in them.

Naphtali was part of the group that pronounced curses on Mount Abal (Deut 28:13). The pronouncers of the curse are the ones that defended against the curse, trying to turn it around. They have the tonality of Heaven to change what is happening in Israel.

When we get to this dimension, the first thing that happens is we live in a state of satisfaction with favor. We will walk the dimension of favor. Stop hanging around courts of judgment. Move beyond that and be satisfied with favor. Stop fighting. Warfare always costs blood.

It is important that we understand spiritual principles because we are the one making things happen. We need to stop allowing people to use the tail of the dragon to direct us by false prophecy that raises hope without due process and divine protocol.

THE COUNTERFEIT

Naphtali comes out as a seed from God and builds a tent with God. Then this other Naphtalite, Hiram, uses the serpent to access the things of God. He carried the capacity to see into the spirit realm, but from a wrong gateway. This is important because every time God's people are supposed to come to a place of manifestation, overcome and operate in their victory, the enemy raises a counterfeit.

So, Israel is at rest. God has given David rest all around and has granted a son for him to reign. What is the enemy going to do? He is going to raise somebody who seems to be an insider. Hiram looks like an insider. His mother is a Naphtalite. The moment the temple is finished, Solomon begins to draw all the idol worshipers into Israel. He brings Pharaoh's daughter and created alliances that are based on the pattern of the King of Tyre, who created alliances with all the people of the world so that all the gods of the nations now had a place in Israel. Hiram was not raised up by the enemy.

David was too smart to bring Hiram into Israel. He made alliances but never brought Hiram into Israel. His son, Solomon, was too wise for his own good and brought him in. Hiram is dealing with Virgo and Hydra. Instead of dealing with the the tail of Hydra, he is dealing with the head of Hydra. Hydra is a serpent with many heads. Hiram comes in and Solomon begins to now duplicate the principle by bringing all the women in to continue to create. The Bible says Solomon's heart was turned from the LORD because of all the foreign women (1 Kin 11). Israel was told not to marry from the outside because they would be led away from the LORD. It is always about idolatry.

SUPERNATURAL ESCAPE AND TECHNOLOGY

"Nevertheless the gloom will not be upon her who is distressed, as when at first He lightly esteemed the land of Zebulun and the land of Naphtali, and afterward more heavily oppressed her, by the way of the sea, beyond the Jordan, in Galilee of the Gentiles." (Isa 9:1)

The whole idea of the coming of the Messiah is tied to the breaking of light in the land of Naphtali. His word brings light. The entrance of our word brings light. Naphtali is a revelationary being that operates in a place of satisfaction, escape, Jubilee and freedom. These come from the battle that has already been fought by someone before we get there. Naphtali is not the wrestler. The scripture does not say that Naphtali wrestles, it says that his mother named him Naphtali because she wrestled. Naphtali is the result of somebody else's wrestling. Somebody else paid the price.

The book of Jasher says Naphtali can run over cornfields. For Naphtali to do that he needs to be able to levitate. That is a problem for a lot of people because levitation is of the devil to them, even though Jesus did it. Philip couldn't do what he did unless he could levitate (Acts 8).

Naphtali, in his very nature, is a trans-dimensional traveler. If he is a hind it means he has the capacity to jump space. David says, "You sprung my foot out of the trap that they have laid for me" (Psa 140:5). Israel will always have a way of escape.

"The temptations in your life are no different from what others experience. And God is faithful. He will not allow the temptation to be more than you can stand. When you are tempted, he will show you a way out so that you can endure." (1 Cor 10:13 NLT)

This portion of the Heavens is a place of Jubilee, a place of celebration. Jubilee is the end of the struggle for every slave, every sufferer, for every person who sold himself either by choice or by force. Jubilee is a time when people stop their labor and their bondage and move into their freedom.

The next phase of revelation of the people of Israel will be the revelation of Naphtali. There is technology coming that will allow people to jump space, to be able to move from one dimension to another and that technology will come out of Israel. The breath technology was embedded in the DNA of Naphtali. This is freedom from materiality, the capacity to move to another dimension. That is what the book of Jasher is hinting that Naphtali could do; to bend time, freeze time and jump to places before an era is over. This is a person that, after they have gone through what they are supposed to, cannot be held captive. They become free in their expression of their destiny in God. Nothing can hold them back.

The development of the modern Jewish mysticism happened in the territory of Naphtali and in the whole Galilean area because there is a gateway there. The birth of the Messiah and the Heavenly battle attending His coming from Heaven and Earth will be carried out by the Heavenly dimensions of Naphtali. The Bible says the gate of Naphtali in the Book of Ezekiel shall be East of Asher (Eze 48).

An individual can possess three dimensions while living in the fourth dimension. Naphtali is one of the hidden aspects of God. Once the tribe of Naphtali appears, all of Israel will begin to come together.

There were two wars in Israel led by two Naphtalians. Deborah is believed by the Rabbis to be the wife of Barak. That is why she could tell him to come and do what she wanted. The Bible says Deborah lived under a palm tree. The righteous are like palm trees. A palm tree in Israel means always living under righteousness or the Mitzvoth. Her whole life was spent doing the Mitzvoth while her husband was out there fighting because the country was under bondage. Deborah was, by righteousness, balancing the forces of Israel. Deborah was a Naphtalite and so was her husband Barak. This was the only war fought in Israel where the ancient seas and the stars themselves came down and fought the battle because of who was leading the war. Not even in David's wars did the stars come down from Heaven. Deborah says the stars came down and fought, the ancient river rose to fight against them.

"They fought from the heavens; The stars from their courses fought against Sisera. The torrent of Kishon swept them away,

That ancient torrent, the torrent of Kishon. O my soul, march on in strength!" (Judg 5:20-21)

The river turns like a snake, and the virgin holds the stars in her hands, so Barak and Deborah could turn the serpent's head against its enemies and raise up the stars of Heaven (the angels of God to participate in warfare). There are things we consider to be evil that are God's weapons. God has a right to use any weapon and to use anyone.

For example:

"Micaiah continued, "Therefore hear the word of the Lord: I saw the Lord sitting on his throne with all the multitudes of Heaven standing around him on his right and on his left. And the Lord said, 'Who will entice Ahab into attacking Ramoth Gilead and going to his death there?' "One suggested this and another that. Finally, a spirit came forward, stood before the Lord and said, 'I will entice him.' "'By what means?' the Lord asked." 'I will go out and be a deceiving spirit in the mouths of all his prophets,' he said." 'You will succeed in enticing him,' said the Lord. 'Go and do it.' "So now the Lord has put a deceiving spirit in the mouths of all these prophets of yours. The Lord has decreed disaster for you." (1 Kin 22:19-23 – NIV)

Another example:

"Then they journeyed from Mount Hor by the Way of the Red Sea, to go around the land of Edom; and the soul of the people became very discouraged on the way. And the people spoke against God and against Moses: "Why have you brought us up out of Egypt to die in the wilderness? For there is no food and no water, and our soul loathes this worthless bread." So the Lord sent fiery serpents among the people, and they bit the people; and many of the people of Israel died. Therefore the people came to Moses, and said, "We have sinned, for we have spoken against the Lord and against you; pray to the Lord that He take away the serpents from us." So Moses prayed for the people.

Then the Lord said to Moses, "Make a fiery serpent, and set it on a pole; and it shall be that everyone who is bitten, when he looks at it, shall live." So Moses made a bronze serpent, and put it on a pole; and so it was, if a serpent had bitten anyone, when he looked at the bronze serpent, he lived." (Num 21:4-9)

There were serpents fighting for God. Most of the beings in Revelation - angels, demons or creatures - are fighting for the name of God. Most of them, except for the ones attacking Christ, are fighting for God. When they appear as a human being, they do that for our own safety. There are some angels only God can like! God's sense of beauty is not our sense of beauty. Human beings tend to judge things from the external perspective and we define beauty by our standard.

There is a fragrance that we all carry. God put a fragrance on us so we do not smell in front of the presence of angels. We stink because of the residue of sin, yet we are made into the fragrance of Christ.

NAPHTALI IS VITAL

In Heaven there is no distance, space or time. We can move at the speed of light while appearing to go nowhere. Time and distance disappear when we come into the realm of victory! There is going to be a mastery of time coming out of the hills of Israel. This is part of the manifestation of Naphtali, but it will not come to its fruition unless the present people in Israel allow certain tribes to return. A lot of these technologies embedded in Hebrew DNA, which God put in different tribes, will remain scattered until the Sons of God take their place. It is like a war machine. God's goal is to create a world where the whole system is complete. A world where humanity can defend itself while living a life of peace, with access to other dimensions - all without having to exert too much energy. Naphtali is the capacity to bridge distances and time, gaining access to time and dimensions.

The Book of Jasher speaks of Naphtali having access to the records of the ancients because of the way he moved. He could access records in any time of history and any dimension of creation. Joseph could in dreams and visions, but Naphtali could go there. Naphtali is very important because if he doesn't come, Asher cannot come.

HARMONY AND MERCY

Naphtali is the number six. When we engage the principle of ascension, in a lightning process from the Earth, Naphtali is either Chesed or Rahamim ("Mercy or Compassion"). Naphtali is operating in mercy going up. (That is why it seems like Naphtali does not commit any sin, but he does). He operates in mercy in fullness and overflowing. The mercy is the water that washes the sinner.

When Naphtali comes from above, he brings beauty or harmony. He operates in the convergence and harmony in the laws of nature. Wherever Naphtali operates, the elements are not fighting against each other; there is no continuous struggling. In this realm, when we are ascending, we need mercy, when we are descending, we need harmonization.

The Arc Angelic Prince Michael sits in the centre of the Naphtali dimension according to the Jewish mystics. Michael is a warrior angel, but the real nature of Michael is to balance the forces of the universe. Michael is a harmonizing angel. The reason he fought the serpent was to create harmony in the universe. He wants to balance out the forces of Heaven and creation.

Naphtali is this being that perpendicularly balances harmony and mercy. This is what mercy does. Mercy brings harmony and restores the balance of things because it removes that which separates people. If we have mercy we can float above the air. One of the reasons we don't ascend is because we carry too many grudges, bitterness and regret. There is too much payload that cannot be lifted without carrying the right fuel. The right fuel is mercy. To move, go through walls, jump over walls, go from one dimension into another, there must be a certain fluidity or liquidity to the individual.

THE CATALYST OF FREEDOM AND HUMAN POTENTIAL

The Tribe of Naphtali is an example of what it means to be born from above. Everything about them is about liquid form. They move easily. They are not easily caught in their own trap or in the mess of other people. They can always escape, so their pasts do not determine their position. When we deal with them, we are dealing with people who, because of their past, can face their future.

The true rise of Naphtali will be the elevation of Israel and the true Tzadik (the righteous person who can perform miracles or act as a "pipeline" between man and God) coming from the nations of the world. The revelation of the Naphtali dimension will bring an accessing of the force of creation, a move towards purification and an activation of the DNA in the human body, soul and spirit. Further, it will bring the capacity to take on various forms of the Godhead, accessing the life and the creative power of the Godhead in creation itself!

Jesus stayed in the area of Naphtali in order to begin His ministry because of the capacity to access certain things that were present in the atmosphere. Naphtali is a revelation of mystical power bearing fruit. He is able then to call forth the life potential of all that he touches. When we are able to operate in this realm, we are able to reach deep to the hidden potentials of other people and draw it out. A true Naphtalite does not touch people and submerge their destiny; he brings it out.

The rise in Christianity, in our faith of the Naphtalite, will be a group of people who have the capacity to touch others. The potential in them will be stirred to do what God is calling them to do without destroying the family.

Naphtali never said, "I'm more gifted than you guys and I am going to do my own thing." Every time he was needed, Naphtali did what he was supposed to do. Every time there was warfare, he was present. When Israel was fighting in the book of Jasher, Naphtali shows up. Israel was busy struggling at the bottom of the hill and Naphtali was somewhere playing with time and space. The Israelites were still sitting at the bottom of the third wall. Naphtali arrives, jumps up the third wall and opens the place up so Israel can come in.

Whenever Naphtali comes around, somebody gets access, a victory, a possibility. Somebody's potential gets activated. When the Naphtalite shows up we will not be commanding light to come. Instead, we will see light in its fullness. We will see the revelation of the deep potential of what it means to be human and what God has made us to become. Naphtali will call out the potential of humanity towards the fullness of who God is. This is the entrance of the mystic light into the chaos of creation that turns darkness into light, mourning into joy, a slave into a king and raises the poor and places them with kings and princes. The downtrodden will look up and those who are about to lose the war will gain new strength and victory.

In this dimension, victories and the record of victories, are kept and are accessible to those who are willing to walk in the struggle that has already been won through Christ. In this, the aspiration of the soul of the human being reaches to the very heart and the core of Heaven. This is the place where we celebrate what has been won for us.

Naphtali is the result of wrestling. Jacob wrestled. Rachel wrestled. Naphtali lived out the fruit of their wrestling. The Father wrestled. Jesus wrestled. Now we live out the result of the wrestling. It is finished!

It is possible to live a life of harmony, mercy and grace, filled with the compassion of God - a satisfied and content life. It is possible to live a life of the flow of light, where our words are the revelation of the fullness of who God is. It is possible to live at the gate of the serpent's mouth and still be free from its bite.

Naphtalites are determined to reach inward and upward towards a greater manifestation of the Godhead. This is the ladder by which angels ascend and descend. It is the first movement out of the grasp of the magical into the technology of the divine spirit. An infusion of the breath of God animating a new form of movement upon the face of the Earth, unhindered by materiality and by egoism! We are in the time for the search of Naphtali because Naphtali's army is the army of the 13th principle. This is the 13th angel of Israel that opens the womb of Heaven for the manifestation of the fullness so that we can participate in the full supply of God's provision!

There is a legend that Naphtali, because of his capacity to bend space and time, was born to control the length of time. In fact, there is a legend that Naphtali was born on the longest day of the year (the longest day is the Solstice, June 20th). It is believed that the day Joshua commanded the Sun to stand still was on the birthday of Naphtali. The Equinox is the longest day, the day of Naphtali. The day is stretched so that the day can be extended, made longer and more can be accomplished. God created everything on the days of creation in less than 12 hours. God-time can be shorter and accomplish more. A spiritual person can do more in the context of worship that bends time.

THE EAST GATE

In a vision recorded in the Book of Enoch, chapter 94, Enoch tells us about the 6th gate of the city where he goes. The 6th gate is considered the gate of Naphtali. Enoch tells us that the 6th gate of Heaven is in the East. Naphtali's gate is East of Asher in the book of Ezekiel. The Sun rises in the East, but the Sun doesn't move. The Earth moves. The East Gate is the gate of the Messiah. The Messiah does not go out of the West Gate because it is the gate of death. The East Gate is the gate of the rising from the dead. It is a gate of Messiah that never dies. Enoch says it shall be open and shall never be closed. It speaks of the rising of the Sun, of the resurrection, of coming to life and chasing away of darkness.

In the new age coming, which is the coming of the Kingdom

of God, that gate is always open. It shall never be shut by day or by night. Nobody else goes through it except the Messiah and His entourage. It is said that on the day that the Messiah goes through the East Gate, the period of the day is twice as long as the night. The night becomes shorter. In the New Jerusalem there is no night, so it's a perpetual day. Once the Messiah comes through the gate, there is no more night and everything changes.

BRINGING MERCY TO THE EARTH

What is it that was so inherent in Naphtali that made Jesus begin His ministry in his realm and physical area? There must have been something because a lot of the stories about Jesus happened in Capernaum. A lot of the mercies Jesus showed to people happened in the Naphtali area.

When we operate in Naphtali, we are operating in the fullness of the victory that has been won for us. We are not laboring. This victory has been won. Naphtali is the one who runs in the air, shows up, enters dimensions, gets records from different dimensions and brings them into this dimension. We can move into another dimension and get the records of the past, bring them into this dimension and read it. That is what we do when we go to Heaven to try to get the 'scroll', but we can go beyond that and get other scrolls from other dimensions and realms.

Someone who has access to this realm, knows who they are and has permission from the Lord, can correct the scrolls! In Proverbs 10:25 the Bible says the righteous are the everlasting foundations of the world ("Yesod Olam"). Only the righteous can annul the decree that God makes because the Tzadik is like Elohim upon the Earth. Jesus even said "whatsoever you bind on Earth is bound in Heaven" and "You shall have whatsoever you say".

The revelation of the tribe of Naphtali is vital for Israel and the Earth. As you navigate this dimension, enjoying the victory already won for you the struggle of Christ, you will begin to walk in its benefits and release them upon the Earth. You will have victory from rest!

JOSEPH: THE DIMENSION OF MANIFESTATION OF PROVISION

"Joseph is a fruitful bough, even a fruitful bough by a well; whose branches run over the wall. The archers have sorely grieved him and shot at him and hated him. But his bow abode in strength and the arms of his hands were made strong by the hands of the mighty God of Jacob; (from thence is the shepherd, the stone of Israel;) Even by the God of thy father, who shall help thee; and by the Almighty, who shall bless thee with blessings of Heaven above, blessings of the deep that lieth under, blessings of the breasts and of the womb. The blessings of thy father have prevailed above the blessings of my progenitors unto the utmost bound of the everlasting hills; they shall be on the head of Joseph and on the crown of the head of him that was separate from his brethren." (Gen 49:22-26)

MATURITY

Joseph is a fruitful bough, a parah. The word "parah" refers to a female cow, a heifer, that has not carried any burden or yoke. It can be used as a deriding statement, which God does in Hosea 4:16 where He calls the narcissistic women of Israel "heifers." So parah can refer to narcissism and Joseph is a parah. That might explain why he went through the sufferings he went through. Joseph was narcissistic.

There is nothing as bullish as a cow or a bull that has not had a burden laid on it. Jacob begins his blessing by saying that Joseph is a fruitful bough. That translates, "he is a fruitful cow," but a cow that has not been trained.

Joseph has a dream in which he sees all his brethren symbolically as the 11 stars and his parents as the Sun and the Moon bowing to him. He tells his brothers and they get angry at him. Then his father, Jacob, doesn't help matters. He clothes Joseph with the coat of many colors. This means within Joseph is embedded all the colors of Israel. He is the fundamental embodiment of Jacob, not as a twin, but separated from Jacob. Jacob is a twin with Esau, a parallel universe that can never break itself away. Jacob could not conquer Esau because he was his twin brother. So, Joseph becomes the one who is separated, to deal with Esau. The Bible says there were wars between Ephraim (Joseph's son) and Esau. Joseph is the one who doesn't have the attachment.

In Joseph's life we see his prideful nature. God deliberately sets him up so he gets broken. There are experiences in Joseph's life that are parallel to what God does in somebody's life who He wants to use or who is gifted. All gifted people must go through a brokenness in which they transmute their weakness into strength. This is the greatest process. It is not that God wants to punish us. We might not come to an understanding of who we are until we have gone through certain things. We may never submit our life to purpose until something is broken. The brokenness is not intended for death. It is not outsiders that break us, but the people we know. It's a hard thing.

FRUITFULNESS

The next thing Jacob says is "even a fruitful bough by a well." A well is the word "Ayin." There are many feminine words referring to Joseph. The first one is "fruitful." The second one is a "cow by a well." The word "Enayin," which comes from the word "Ayin," is a feminine noun meaning an 'eye, a spring, a fountain or a womb from which something bubbles up'.

A womb is not just a place of life; it is a place of death. More things die in the womb than are made alive. The womb is selective as to what it allows to live within it or how many it allows. But Ayin also represents an eye, and the eye is the door to the unconscious, to the soul.

Joseph is a fruitful bough, whose branch is by a well, whose "branches run over the wall." The word "ba'at" from which the word "fruitful branch" is used, is also a feminine word meaning 'daughter'. It designates a female child. But here, when defined properly, it literally means a daughter-in-law, who comes into the family to propagate the seed of the family. We now have three feminine words. In the first blessing, the father speaks of Joseph three times in feminine terminology.

"The archers have sorely grieved him and shot at him and hated him."

Archer is the word "ba'al" which means "lord or husband, owner, possessor" or even "a god." It is masculine. It denotes one who rules. The archers are not his brothers. They are spiritual beings. The archer in the Zodiac is Sagittarius. The archer shoots at the cow. The archers shoot at this female pluralification principle to cause it to multiply. When translated into English the verse says the archers shot at him, suggesting that he was wounded. In Hebrew it means the archers have caused him to increase.

The archer is male. The triple principles are female. This is talking about impregnation. It is metaphoric. In the life of somebody like Joseph, when the enemy shoots at him, the enemy thinks he is decreasing him, when in fact the hatred helps to increase him. Without the hatred of his brethren, what would have happened to Joseph? He would have stayed in Canaan, worn nice clothes, lived and died. He would have never been broken or achieved what he was supposed to achieve. He would think he was too good for everybody.

"But his bow abode in strength."

His bow is his "qesheth". This is also a feminine term, which is connected to "rainbow," - "his rainbow remained firm." Rainbow refers to the colors of the garment that was given to him through prophetic annunciation by his father. It also refers to a weapon; a bow and arrow. It is a play on words harking back to the clothing that his father gave him. It is also a play on his strength, however Joseph never went to war.

In the Ebo language, the language of my youth in Africa, a steady stream coming from a spring is called "atani" - a stream that is constant. There is a rainbow stream that continues its flow, unstopped in spite of hardship. Rainbows will come out during, before or after a storm. It is a reflection / refraction of water.

"his hands were made strong by the hands of the Mighty God of Jacob."

The word "God" is not in the original. The word "God" is in italics. It should be that his hands were made strong by the "mighty one" of Jacob.

"From thence is the shepherd, the stone of Israel."

This is where confusion sets in about who the Messiah is. The stone of Israel is not about Jesus.

"Even by the God of thy father, who shall help thee; and by the Almighty, who shall bless thee with blessings of Heaven above, blessings of the deep that lieth under, blessings of the breasts and of the womb."

There are four blessings mentioned here six times.

"The blessings of thy father have prevailed above the blessings of my progenitors unto the utmost bound of the everlasting hills: they shall be on the head of Joseph and on the crown of the head of him that was separate from his brethren."

TRANSMUTATION

Joseph is that dimension of transmutation (The name "Joseph" has Yod + Vav, which is 16. 16 plus 60 = 76. 76 + 80 = 156. 1 + 5 + 6 = 12). That is, the capacity to transmute something from one dimension into another is embodied in Joseph. He has the capacity to transmute one form of character into another - to transmute arrogance into humility, hatred into mercy. Joseph must have been bitter for years, yet at the end he was able, in all honesty, to forgive his brothers and to take care of them. The way he dealt with this was through a certain kind of drama when his brothers came to visit. He had the power to do them evil and throw them into jail. Joseph shows them that he could have done anything he wanted, but instead he showed them mercy. The reason the male and the female is used constantly is because it is a combination of the male and female that transmutes human energy into a person.

In Joseph we find something that is not in a lot of the brethren. There is a capacity for nurture, and that is what he does. That is what a cow does. A heifer nurtures, not just its young but it becomes the common food for most human beings. It is the meat that most people in the world eat, apart from chicken.

In this dimension, one can transmute arrogance into humility. We have power, but we bring it under control. In the physical realm, Joseph transmutes arrogance into meekness, victimization into victory, bitterness into forgiveness and hatred and revenge into mercy.

When Joseph left his father's house to go look for his brethren, he met a man in the field who directed him to his brothers (Gen 37:15). This was an angel who deliberately led him into the trial he was about to go through. His father says it this way: "he is a fruitful bough by a well; whose branches run over the wall." That means he stands by a source of water with the possibility of constant watering. Joseph cannot be circumscribed because he embodies within himself the capacity to transmute into a new kind of person at every level of movement. Joseph's father is also making a reference to the fact that Joseph was the one who could interpret the dream of Pharaoh. The dream of Pharaoh was about transmuting famine into plenty and providing amid lack. Everything about his life is about transforming the circumstance.

ACCESSING DIMENSIONS, DREAMS AND ANGELS

Why did Joseph's father clothe him in rainbow-colored clothes? When did the rainbow first appear? After the flood. And the rainbow is in the form of a coat. It is a priestly garment, which meant that Joseph could see from the time he was a child. He could walk in the dimensions. He could move from one dimension to another. Why did his father put the garment on him when he sent him into the bush? Why did his brothers take away his garment? What were they trying to stop? They were trying to stop him from moving and from escaping them. When they saw him coming they referred to him as the dreamer. A dreamer goes into other worlds. That's why old men dream dreams, because old men are now traveling to other worlds. They don't belong here anymore. They took off his garment and they deliberately soaked it in blood. It was not just about lying to the father, it was about making sure Joseph had no access to come back. It was also a symbolic slaying of Joseph by magic. The brothers themselves were involved in wickedness. They wanted to wipe out his memory. They closed the door to his being able to connect with them.

Joseph goes into Egypt and God takes him directly to Potiphar. Even as a slave Joseph is still an untried heifer. Everything he does God blesses, so God starts training him how to deal with loss. One cannot be trained any other way.

In the dimension of Joseph, we are dealing with angelic activity. When Jacob decides to bless Joseph and his sons Ephraim and Manasseh, he says "may the angels that kept me throughout all my journey keep the children." In other words, there is a specific function of angels within this dimension where Joseph has rulership.

Joseph transmutes his context first, by suffering. Second, by being able to operate at the level of his soul, where he understands what is happening in the supernatural realm. When other people are dreaming, he participates in their dreams. People who operate in the Joseph realm can enter that realm of unconsciousness, or that realm of super-consciousness, where people's dreams happen. That's what Daniel did. Daniel literally entered that realm.

STRENGTHENED BY SUFFERING

Now we are looking at the principles of Joseph as a transmuter, as one who can go into the spiritual realm, come out and change what is actual (in the spiritual realm) into what is possible. To do this, we must be strengthened by suffering so we are not transmuting based on our victimization. We can stand apart from it and see victimization as if it is happening to somebody else. This is not schizophrenia. This is a deliberate schizoid state in which we literally separate our self from our suffering so that we can look at it. It is not the suffering that is splitting us, but we are standing apart from it and saying "okay, I see myself in this condition and this is where I want to take myself to".

A person who is moving in the spirit realm is not operating based on likes and dislikes. The question that we are always asking is "How do we move stuff from the Heavenly dimension to the Earth dimension? How do we transmute this feeling into a finer understanding of the cosmic reality that is in God?"

Joseph became the shepherd of Israel. He became the stone. He is the only person who was buried in two places. His body was buried in one place and his bones were buried in another place. In other words, Joseph is the only person who is going to have two resurrections. He is going to resurrect because he is an ark. He is both a shepherd and a stone. Joseph carries all his father Jacob said. In his body he carries the three-fold feminine principle: the principle of impregnation, the principle of inner nurture and the principle of birthing. It happens within the context of his enemies.

"You prepare a table before me in the presence of my enemies; You anoint my head with oil; My cup runs over." (Psa 23:5). This is a direct reference to Joseph.

A KING, A PRINCIPALITY AND A GATEWAY

Suffering produces the capacity to move into a new dimension. Nothing that we go through can circumscribe us. In the case of Joseph, from the time he was a child his father knew he was a king. His father knew that he had the capacity to see and enhanced it by putting on Joseph the rainbow garment. A person who lives under the rainbow sign is a person who lives in a place of covenant. This person is never overwhelmed by judgment, even though they may be arrogant. God stays with him until his life is transmuted from immaturity to maturity. Joseph operates in that realm of transmutation.

For us to operate in this realm, the arsenals of God must be available to us, especially in the angelic form. Many people will say that in the realm of Joseph are the archangels because he is a king and a shepherd. In other words, Joseph is a principality. There are people on Earth who God has raised to be principalities. That means, no matter where they are, they go through a process and they get to a point where they themselves become the gateway.

Joseph became the gateway in Egypt. He became the gateway for Egyptian survival and for understanding what God was going to do. We must go through Joseph to get to Pharaoh. Joseph became a principality, which means he had the lives of people in his hands. Someone who is going to be a principality or a king cannot walk by emotion (Simeon and Reuben) and cannot operate from the place of their pain.

Joseph did not operate from a place of pain when he confronted his brothers in Egypt. If he did, the outcome would have been remarkably different! It wasn't about emotions anymore. His ultimate response was not based on what his brothers did to him. Something happened to Joseph's mind and heart. Joseph said to his brothers, "It is not you that did what you did to me. God sent me ahead." He understood something about the nature of God. This life is not about what we like and what we don't like. Emotions are good but they are only to be experienced and then move on. When we deal with other people we must check our emotions. If our emotions become the basis of our dealing with people we can never be a king. It becomes difficult for us to transmute and transform things because we are so embedded in emotion that our weight keeps them from moving from one dimension to another.

THE FEMININE

The context of "his hand was made mighty/strong" is in the feminine expression. We have not come to understand the feminine principle within the spiritual development of Christianity. We always try to short-circuit it, to keep it on the side, because we don't want to deal with the feminine. We don't even want to look at the Holy Spirit symbolically as a woman. We are not saying he is a woman, just like we are not saying God is a male. The principle is about impregnation, nurture and birth. It is about moving from one dimension to another, doing the things that produce newness.

In the dimension of Joseph, the dimension of the feminine and the masculine come together, but it is a dominance of the feminine. A dominance of impregnation, inner nurture and birth. It is a place of kingship and it is also a place of production. (This explains the number 12, which is $1 + 2 = 3$. Three is not a binary principle, but a complete principle. It is a triangle, which is a gateway). Joseph is a gateway for the survival of the people. He is also a gateway to the future of Israel because he is the one who predicted that Israel is going to possess the land. He did that because he was anticipating the resurrection. This is the dimension of the hand that possesses and the productive hand.

THE ANGEL OF GODS PRESENCE AND MELCHIZEDEK

Genesis 49:24 (KJV) says Joseph's hands were made strong by the hands of the "mighty (one) of Jacob." The mighty one of Jacob is not a reference to God. Later on when Jacob blesses the children, he says "may the angels that led me through my journey keep the children." God is with Jacob, but Jacob doesn't use the word "God" there. He doesn't say "Almighty." He says the "mighty one." So literally, Jacob transferred his personal angel to his son, Joseph.

Jacob then says to Joseph, "The blessings of thy father have prevailed above the blessings of my progenitors unto the utmost bound of the everlasting hills; they shall be on the head of Joseph and on the crown of the head of him that was separate from his brethren." The blessings of Jacob surpassed the blessings of his ancestors. Then he says to let these blessings be on the head of Joseph.

Joseph is the only one who receives the blessing of Abraham and Isaac directly. The blessing of Abraham is the blessing of the angel of God's presence, which God then transfers to Moses. "And I will send My Angel before you, and I will drive out the Canaanite and the Amorite and the Hittite and the Perizzite and the Hivite and the Jebusite. Go up to a land flowing with milk and honey; for I will not go up in your midst, lest I consume you on the way, for you are a stiff-necked people... And He said, "My Presence will go with you, and I will give you rest." Then he said to Him, "If Your Presence does not go with us, do not bring us up from here." (Exo 33:2-3, 14-15). Moses is the first one to say "I don't want Jacob's angel, I want you."

Look at the blessings that God gives in this dimension. This is a dimension of the capacity to transmute lack into plenty and of transmuting natural elements into useful elements. It says "his hands were made strong by the hands of the mighty of Jacob; (from thence is the shepherd, the stone of Israel). Even by the God of thy father, who shall help thee; and by the Almighty" (Gen 49:24 KJV). Joseph and God, arms locked together, are hand in hand. The hands of Joseph became the extension of God's hands. Joseph saved more people than Moses. Moses saved Israel, but Joseph saved a whole nation and the future generations of Israel.

The scripture also mentions "the stone of Israel" and it is not an upper case 'S'. This is not Jesus. We know where Jesus comes from. Jesus comes from Judah. This is Joseph. What is the stone of Israel? "Eben" is a feminine noun meaning "a stone". It's not a rock. The word is used often and has both figurative and literal meanings, depending upon its context. Eben refers to a small pillar that is set and defines parameters.

Jesus is referred to as an eben - the stone which the builders rejected that became the head cornerstone. A cornerstone is something that can be carved into a particular form. It is malleable. This stone in Genesis 49 is not Jesus, it is not a person.

"Out of Joseph comes the stone." What is the stone? It is a boundary mechanism, an arch, which is really what a cornerstone is. It is a capstone.

"But his bow remained in strength, and the arms of his hands were made strong by the hands of the Mighty God of Jacob

(From there is the Shepherd, the Stone of Israel), by the God of your father who will help you, and by the Almighty who will bless you with blessings of heaven above, blessings of the deep that lies beneath, blessings of the breasts and of the womb." (Gen 49:24-25)

Even though it says "el" in that passage, it might be referring to the angel of Jacob. The angel that kept Joseph was the same angel that met him on the road when he was on his way to Dothan. Joseph was strengthened by the angel of his father and by the Almighty. That is where the distinction is made. If we say "by the mighty one of Jacob" and "by the Almighty," we are making two gods. The first one represents an archangel, which represents Israel, given to Jacob. Almighty refers to El Shaddai!

"He that dwells in the secret place of the Most High shall abide under the shadow of the Almighty" (Psa 91:1). It says he "shall abide under the shadow of the Almighty." The Almighty casts his shadow upon the boundary stone as a form of protection. Accordingly, Joseph is the one who abides in the secret place. Jacob says Joseph's hands were made strong by the God of his father. By the 'El' and by the 'strong one' of Jacob, which is the gift of Abraham to Isaac, that Isaac bequeaths to Jacob, and that Jacob bequeaths to Joseph by the Almighty. If Joseph is under the Almighty and the angel is the strong one of Jacob, he is

Joseph's strengthener. He is that angel of God's presence, who is Melchizedek because he is the only one we know of in the Old Testament who is a transmuter of things! By giving communion, Melchizedek transmutes the DNA of Abraham, who was from Ur of the Chaldeans with all that mixture, into one who is under God. For it was through Abraham that the name El Shaddai was first mentioned. "I AM Elohim El Shaddai. Walk before Me, (walk in My shadow) and be thou perfect." (Gen 17:1 KJV)

The gift to Joseph, symbolized by the coat of many colors, is directly from the throne of God. The garment that was put on Joseph was a direct gift that was given to Abraham, that was given to Isaac, that was given to Jacob, that was given to Joseph.

There were two garments created. One was the garment of Nimrod (Book of Jasher). The other was the garment given to Abraham by Melchizedek. One is the garment of the hairy one. One is the garment of the smooth one. Jacob did not throw away the coat of many colors because it was bloody (by Joseph's brothers). He cleansed and kept it because it was the clothing of the Heavenly one. "Melchizedek blessed Abram with this blessing: "Blessed be Abram by God Most High, Creator of Heaven and Earth." (Gen 14:19 – NLT)

Jacob gave Joseph the four-fold blessings, which meant full participation in the name of God, "YHVH". The angel of God's presence was given to Abraham when he met Melchizedek. Notice what happened after Abraham met Melchizedek. Think about the people he began to meet. Until then, God was only talking to him. After he met Melchizedek, Abraham started seeing God and angels kept coming to him. A spiritual garment that represented Heavenly patterns and covenantal patterns was given to Abraham and the garment was tested by suffering. It was the angel of God's presence.

Jacob blesses Joseph and then Joseph transfers those angels to Ephraim and Manasseh. The angel was not given to Judah, it was given to Ephraim and Manasseh.

"The blessings of your father have excelled the blessings of my ancestors, up to the utmost bound of the everlasting hills.

They shall be on the head of Joseph, and on the crown of the head of him who was separate from his brothers." (Gen 49:26)

They are the ancient, everlasting hills. Some people have used this passage to prospect for oil and gold in Israel, trying to go into the Northern hills of Israel, but this verse is referring to the mountain of God. When it says "the blessings of your father have abounded to the everlasting hills," what is it that comes out of his father? The Messiah and the people that then occupy the other side, the other wing of God. The blessings have prevailed above.

What is it that makes Jacob say "The blessings of your father have excelled the blessings of my ancestors"? Abraham, Isaac and Jacob are a three-fold cord. The fourth dimensional principle was coming into existence through Joseph, and it contains within it the capacity to overcome adversity at a higher level.

"Who shall bless thee with the blessings of Heaven."

This refers to all the planetary systems and the sound from all the planets. All the sound from everything God created is directed towards Israel and towards Joseph. He then becomes the recipient of the fundamental divine intention for good from all creation!

People have all kinds of theories about what people group is from Joseph, or who is from Esau, etc. We know who Dan is because the Bible tells us who they are. But we don't know where Ephraim is in the world today. In other words, the real blessing of the firstborn is no longer within the borders of Israel. It is somewhere hidden all around the world. (The British people say that they are the descendants of Ephraim because they are the firstborn. They rule the greatest part of the world. The claim of power knows no end).

The scriptures say "who shall bless them with the blessings of Heaven." 'Blessings' is plural. This is hope made real and actual. That is what Joseph can do. He can endure the vicissitudes of life until the longing becomes a reality. In Joseph, we can focus on what is said and do whatever is needed to avoid derailing the process (and thereby derailing our destiny). We can only do that with the help of the mighty one of God and by the hands of the Almighty. Without Him, we cannot be strengthened but distracted, dissipated and misdirected.

If 'Heaven' is plural (Hashamayim) that means there are things in the universe that are in the material realm and in the spiritual realm or the pneumatic realm, where God is, that flow into the life of Joseph. Joseph could know dreams because the Heavens opened the dimensions of dreams and he could walk in them. It is not prophecy. It is an experience in the soul realm that allows one to experience other people's experiences, thought systems and visions that are embedded within them. We enter with people into the reality of the other realm and we help bring the meaning back to their lives.

All things come from Heaven. Paul says we are blessed with all spiritual blessings in the Heavenly places (Eph 1:3). The first blessing is having access to the throne of God. There, the Father is saying we are going to have access to the very place from which the Heavens were founded. We are going to have access to all the systems that are in the Heavens, the rotations of the Heavens, the movement of the Heavens and the ascendancy and descendancy of planetary systems. We are always going to be able to access them. In other words, Joseph is the one who is steady and has the capacity to transmute reality into something new. He is not moved and never derailed by the vicissitudes of life or by the movement or the motions of the stars or the planets.

THE BLESSINGS OF THE DEEP

There are two ways to look at the deep here. We look at the deep as the Earth. In other words, a time is coming for Jews, Israelites or anybody with the blood of Israel, that as we are going into space and planets, things will begin to happen. People who have Jewish blood are going to find themselves attracted to new minerals that are coming from space. Jewish scientists will go into space and start mining from planets and outer space once this process of travel is accomplished.

There is a scientific revolution coming that is beyond what anyone ever thought. The people who claim to be Israel, whether accepted by the Ashkenazi Jews or not, are going to be at the helm of these discoveries. They are the ones with the DNA and the capacity to create. They will be able to bring back some technologies from the Heavens and the planets. We are going to mine planets. We are going to need new kinds of technology to produce the next wave of science that will allow us to quantum leap and travel beyond the present limits. Humanity has the capacity to build from materials (that are available in planets in certain star systems) that allow people to bend time. There are young men who have been so gifted by God who are going to begin to develop some planetary shifting technology.

The Earth has a depth. There are things on Earth that have not yet been mined or moved. It will be the same group of people. There are all kinds of people with the Jewish blood of Israel that the current nation of political Israel does not recognize. They carry something in their DNA to allow Israel to access things on the Earth that have never been accessed before. They will develop the technology, the capacity to use certain things that are still underneath the Earth.

There are more things in water than just elements. There are certain characteristics that it can carry. When water is tuned, it becomes healing for the human body. We are going to develop technology to tune water, to change the water in the human body, to give the human body a new kind of water to make it live longer.

There are things coming that God has situated and created in the depths, in the veins of God, that are yet unformed that are going to be formed. They were not there before. God is going to cause them to be discovered. People are going to think they have been there for years but in fact they are being created for Israel and humanity. There are technologies of metals, far better than platinum and chrome, that have no name yet that are going to be discovered.

Joseph becomes the embodiment of the capacity to harness the powers in the Heavens and what God has specifically deposited on the Earth for the maturation of humanity.

THE BLESSINGS OF THE BREASTS AND THE WOMB

The word breasts is a masculine noun. The original word is "shad." It is used for a woman's breasts, but it is the principle of "macho." The concept of macho is tied to a masculine word. Why is breasts a masculine word and not a feminine word? It is a place of provision. This is a euphemism, an allegorical word.

The blessings of the breasts and the womb mean provision and maturation. It is a place where human beings are formed and protected until they mature. Feeding happens at the breast.

"The blessings of your father have excelled the blessings of my ancestors" (Gen 49:26)

This is Jacob talking about himself. While the breasts feed people, there is a reference to the male organ impregnating the woman with child, bringing forth life and nurture. The womb is still the zero. It is a woman, but it is a combination of male and female that brings forth life upon the face of the earth.

Two words are used for the father; the 'father' of Joseph and the 'ancestors' ('progenitor' in the KJV). An progenitor is one who carried someone in their bosom. A progenitor does not have anything to do with fathers. Some translations use "my fathers" but the word progenitor is a better word because it is the word for those people who came before, who carried us in their bosom.

Men have a spiritual womb where they nurture seed in their body. That's why it says Levi paid tithe in the bosom of Abraham. We should engage our imagination to work differently to be open to some of the new things that God wants to reveal. If our imagination and structure of thought keep operating the same way we cannot be used to bring the new.

When God is showing Zechariah the menorah (Zech 4) he shows him a forty-nine-candlestick menorah. There is no such thing. He was trying to change Zechariah's grid for understanding because God was going to talk about Jubilee. When Zechariah saw the candlestick, he did not know what it was. Later, it is revealed that the angel was talking about the Jubilee that God is going to celebrate for Israel with years 49 and 50. It is necessary we study to shift our paradigm of the perspective we see from.

Genesis 49:26 is a reference to mother and father. However, there is more to it. When God says female, He is talking about things much more deeply than just physical appearance. When he says "thy father," he is talking about our existence in another person.

There is a reference to the blessings of 'bringing forth' and of 'pre-existence' in the father. In other words, when Joseph was born, something new was created inside of Jacob. Joseph was specifically created within the bosom of the seed. It was a unique seed, not like the other brethren. It was a seed that could overcome Jacob's weakness. "The blessings of thy father have prevailed" and have become stronger and stronger, moving from one level of glory to the other, above the blessings of his progenitors.

The word for progenitor is "harah" which means to be pregnant. He is talking about progenitors, but he is also talking about pregnancy. Some translations say greater than the blessings of "my fathers." But the word 'progenitor' means whoever's seed we are. That which was carried in the bosom of our father and mother is who we are. There exists the capacity to transcend what was carried in our father and mother. If Joseph did not transcend Jacob, he would have fallen when Potiphar's wife pursued him. He would not have told the truth about the money. He would have acted to make everything Potiphar had become his own. Joseph transcended his birth place. (Joseph's mother lived a life of jealousy and anger, which is probably why it was difficult for her to have a baby.)

"unto the utmost bounds of the everlasting hills."

The word "hills" is not the word "har." It is the Hebrew word "gibah" denoting a small hill. The word "har" is for "mountain." That is why mountain is usually a male noun. Gibah is a female. The use of gibah is referring to a woman in full term, whose stomach is a hill. When the Bible talks about Israel putting its images around hills, most were female deities from the pagan world, not just the masculine Asheroth. God had a problem with it because they were not only impregnating themselves, but they were impregnating beings that were going to affect them and make them unable to remember God. Worship is spiritual intercourse.

We need to be careful what we worship because we can get impregnated by it and impregnate it, so we mutually produce. The word "har" denotes an everlasting mountain or everlasting hills. The word "olam" is an eternal hill. A mountain or a hill is a place that things can flow from. Springs flow from out of the hills. The blessings of his progenitors, the blessings of his harah, of those that carried him, have come to fruition. They have come to fruition in olam, in eternity, not just in the natural. There are people who, by virtue of who they are, operating in a dimension where their desire is put in eternity and allowed multiplication. It is unbounded by time and circumstance. It is not kept by genetic or environmental determinism. It operates at a different level.

JOSEPH IS FREE FROM TIME, STARS AND SORCERY

Joseph is different because everything in Joseph's life indicated that he should have been a failure. If he is operating "unto the hills of the eternal," it means he has access to this aspect in eternity. Remember, his father has released his angel and has given Joseph access into the shadow of God, the place of the Almighty, the place of El Shaddai. He is the one who is able to carry what was in the bosom of Abraham, Isaac and Jacob, into eternity. He is not bound by his birth sign. Joseph has the capacity to transmute into something new because of that access into eternity, the availability of the mighty one of Jacob and because he is dwelling under the shadow of the Almighty.

Then Jacob says these five blessings will be on the head ("rosh") of him that was separated. Rosh is the place of imagination and the place of continuous analysis of thought. The brain is not the source of thoughts. It is just a storehouse and a place for analyzing and mixing thoughts in order to create action. The blessings fall upon Joseph's head, so his mindset is different from the mindset of his brethren. A big problem we have is that we allow ourselves to be bound by our circumstances and by experiences. The Zodiac world and the so-called astrologers and other people don't help us. They shift us into a way of looking at ourselves that doesn't allow for us to change. In fact, if we are reading astrology, we are setting our day and making it impossible for change.

The day is not set by planetary systems for those who are connected to God (even though they do have some influence). The capacity to move from one dimension to another is always present because our God rules the planetary system. We have the nature of our Father in us. We live in Christ, who is both a Lion and a Lamb, which is a mixture of the most unlikely signs in the universe. He is the one who says we must be baptized with fire and with water. We can move in the elements, we are not stuck.

As a child of God, when we operate in the dimension of Joseph, we don't worry about star signs. In fact, the people who understood this in ancient times would change their names about three times in their lives. They realized if their name was giving them a 'bad rap' and it was not allowing movement, they could create a new name that allows them to get into a new dimension. That is what happens when we are baptized. That is why Christians started giving people new names - to allow them to function differently.

The Zodiac has a definite effect, but it shouldn't be our Christian view since we have come to understand the things of God. It shouldn't be the basis of our movement because we can move from one principle to another. We can be an ox, a lion, a lamb or an eagle. We can be whatever it is we choose to be because our nature is now the nature of God, not just an ordinary nature. For example, anyone born under Aries likes to sacrifice themselves. We don't have to always remain in the form of a sacrifice because the same lamb that came into the world became a lion. If a lamb can be transmuted into a lion, that means we are not stuck. We must understand what our true nature is. We must step into the systems to be the one in charge, not the one controlled by fate. Jesus came to create a people who understand how to take their place in the universe at every given time. That is why the Bible says that there is no divination and no sorcery against Israel. Sorcery cannot touch someone who can transmute from an Aries ram to a Leo lion!

Just because we are born poor doesn't mean we should remain poor. The capacity to move from one dimension to another has been given to us the moment we came to Jesus Christ. When we came to know Him, something about us changed. We became a son or daughter of God, a manifestation of God. We don't have to be stuck where we are.

Joseph is the one with two inheritances; Ephraim and Manasseh. He has the capacity to move on Earth and the capacity to move in the Heavens. The capacity to operate as one who serves on Earth and as one who rules as a king from Heaven. He is a warrior and a caretaker.

We were created in this dimension by the voice of the Lord - the logos - the Word of God. A Christian who knows Jesus Christ shall never be under the power of any sorcery. We should never be afraid of it because we are in God. We move in God. We don't have to worry about demons. They can't go where we go because we go into the throne of God! This is where Jesus, who came as the Lamb, was seen in Heaven as the Lion. We crucify the Lamb and He comes back as the Lion. We kill the dove and He comes up as an eagle. The nature of a born-again child of God operates in this kind of dimension, the four-fold blessings and in a constant pregnancy with possibility from the eternal realm.

JOSEPH'S ACCESS TO BLESSING

Joseph is the 11th son. In the Book of Deuteronomy 33, Moses does not change the blessings of Jacob for Joseph, he just adds a little bit. "And of Joseph he said: 'Blessed of the Lord be his land, for the precious things of Heaven, for the dew, for the deep that croucheth beneath." (Deut 33:13 KJV). There are blessings on the (1) land, for the (2) precious things of Heaven, for the (3) dew and for the (4) deep. Those are four blessings. Joseph is the embodiment of Jacob. He is Jacob without the attachment to Esau. He is the one able to deal with Esau. He is the one in whom the name of God, YHVH, dwells completely and fully.

"And for the precious things brought forth by the Sun and for the precious things brought forth by the Moon." (Deut 33:14 KJV)

These are the two things that Moses adds. The ancient people believed the Sun and Moon affect the lives of human beings either in a positive or in a negative way. The Moon affects human beings. Even scientists acknowledge that. It's why we call craziness 'lunacy', from lunar. Our body and how we function can be affected by these elements. The Sun affects us as well. We can actually eat from the Sun and feed our body and mind!

The Bible then says that Joseph gets a four-dimensional gift: the land, the Heavens, the dew and the deep. The deep refers to "tehon," which is found in Genesis 1, when God creates the world out of nothing. It says "and darkness covered the face of the deep" (Gen 1:2). Access to the things that come out of darkness means having the capacity to acquire from hidden places and to get mysteries. Joseph had the capacity to draw from mysteries, even the mysteries and the hidden darkness of people's hearts and dreams.

Moses added the Sun and the Moon, which are the major principles that affect life on Earth. The stars also affect the Earth, but the immediate effect on Earth is from the Sun and the Moon. If we move in the dimension of Joseph we can control certain things. From that dimension we are able to affect the Sun. There are people working on bending the power of the Sun and the

Moon to create. This is Joseph's power and movement in the Heavenly dimension.

In this dimension we find the capacity to cause things to grow, to cause things to reach up. That is what the Sun does. We also find the capacity to change chemical structure itself, which is what the Moon does. Joseph is being given power to control what gives life.

The "dew" is the same word that is used in Genesis 2, "and the mist went out and watered the Earth" (Gen 2:6). Dew is an element from Heaven that covers an unproductive area to preserve seed until the moment of production. Look at the life of Joseph. Look at how his seed remains intact until the time when God literally speaks to him and it comes to pass.

"With the best things of the ancient mountains, With the precious things of the everlasting hills." (Deut 33:15 KJV)

There are chief things embedded in the mountains of God, in every mountain that is covered by an individual, an angel or a particular being. God now tells Joseph that he has access. He has access to the things that come out of the dark and the depths. Joseph can cause things to come into manifestation that have been hidden and he can access things that are covered in mountains.

Mountains are where the dragons or other beings rule and where gifting's and treasures are kept, covered and protected. Joseph, in moving in the Heavenlies, has access to this. If we move in the dimension of Joseph, we begin to get access to this as well. However, the dimension of Joseph does not come without some sort of tribulation and humiliation - the movement from pride to humility, where God knocks down arrogance so that the bull is brought under control. The Bible says that Joseph is a bull that has not been ridden. This deals with taming that aspect of our life that moves us into doing things that are not under control.

There's a reason why the distinction is made between the hills and the mountains. A hill is a mound created by human beings. It can be natural and it is not as high as a mountain. A mountain is a God thing. A hill can be created by creatures. The mountains are set by God. A hill can be devastated and brought low but God's mountains abide forever. The treasures of the hills can be exhausted. The treasures of the mountains are not exhausted because they are God's mountains. Joseph has access to both; the perishable and the imperishable, the mortal and the immortal.

"With the precious things of the earth and its fullness, and the favor of Him who dwelt in the bush. Let the blessing come 'on the head of Joseph, and on the crown of the head of him who was separate from his brothers." (Deut 33:16)

It is God who dwelt in the bush. God told David that He preferred to dwell outside, living in nature. He did not ask David to build a house for Him (2 Sam 7:5). When Solomon finished the temple, he said "You said you wanted to dwell outside in the open, but I built you a house". God's response is "What house are you going to build for me that I can dwell in?".

Moses repeats their father's blessing over Joseph. Then he says:

"His glory is like a firstborn bull, and his horns like the horns of the wild ox; Together with them he shall push the peoples to the ends of the earth; They are the ten thousands of Ephraim, and they are the thousands of Manasseh." (Deut 33:17)

This is referring to Joseph's expansion as a people. Most of the other tribes of Israel can be pinpointed, but Joseph's expansion from Israel, even after going into exile, is very strong. Joseph's people are all over the world. Israel doesn't want to admit the fact that many people who are in Africa and in the East are descendants of Abraham. Descendants of Abraham's children make up at least one-third of people on Earth today! We are not as different as we think we are. In India and Northern Pakistan we can find descendants of Abraham who went East. Many of them are from Africa, except for the older races. There are ancient ones like the Egyptians and Ethiopians. The younger races are all people who descended from Abraham, Esau, Isaac and Jacob.

God said to Abraham, "Out of thee shall all the nations of the Earth be blessed." We look at it from the perspective of Jesus, but in seed form most people on Earth, most nations on Earth, have some form of Israelite and Jewish people dwelling there. Otherwise they would have no blessing.

NAVIGATING THE DIMENSION OF JOSEPH

When we navigate the Heavens and we move through the dimensions of Joseph, treasures are made available to us from different places. They are the treasures of Joseph - treasures of the dew, the Heavens, the Earth, all that secret treasures that are there. There are about 8 treasures in Joseph that we have access to when we navigate this dimension.

When we enter the Joseph dimension we enter a place both of political power and the ability to do. We enter a dimension of restoration and of preservation. We enter this dimension of being able to access what the Sun and the Moon provides. In this dimension, we have access to these blessings, at least eight of them.

The blessings of:

- Seership

- Interpretation of Dreams

- Thriving in Foreign Lands

- Access to Rulership

- Provision for Nations

- Reunion and Reconciliation

- Prophetic Future

- Assurance of Inheritance

The Joseph realm is something every believer needs to come in touch with. The dimensions of Joseph's blessings are dimensions of Heavenly movement, of transmutation and bringing Heaven to Earth.

Section 2: Joseph: The Dimension of Manifestation of Provision

BENJAMIN : THE DIMENSION OF POWER

"Benjamin is a ravenous wolf; In the morning he shall devour the prey, And at night he shall divide the spoil." (Gen 49:27)

THE TWO NATURES

In Hebrew, when the spelling of a name is changed, it affects the force of the word. Benjamin is one of those words that are spelled differently. He is one of the few people in the Bible who has a double 'Yod' in his name. A Yod is a masculine principle and force. The deep mystery of the masculine force is the stirring up of the masculine divine force. Benjamin is considered by the Father to be "a son of his right hand." In other words, when the Father names Benjamin, he names him specifically after the Messiah - the righteous one who shall stand at the right hand of the Father.

Benjamin had two natures. One was a warrior. The other was illegitimate lust. There is lust that is legitimate, which is desire. Benjamin had a form of illegitimate lust. The lust didn't show so much in his personal life. However, it showed up in the tribal life.

"As they were enjoying themselves, suddenly certain men of the city, perverted men, surrounded the house and beat on the door. They spoke to the master of the house, the old man, saying, "Bring out the man who came to your house, that we may know him carnally!" But the man, the master of the house, went out to them and said to them, "No, my brethren! I beg you, do not act so wickedly! Seeing this man has come into my house, do not commit this outrage. Look, here is my virgin daughter and the man's concubine; let me bring them out now. Humble them and do with them as you please; but to this man do not do such a vile thing!" But the men would not heed him. So the man took his concubine and brought her out to them. And they knew her and abused her all night until morning; and when the day began to break, they let her go. Then the woman came as the day was dawning and fell down at the door of the man's house where her master was, till it was light. When her master arose in the morning and opened the doors of the house and went out to go his way, there was his concubine, fallen at the door of the house with her hands on the threshold. And he said to her, "Get up and let us be going." But there was no answer. So the man lifted her onto the donkey; and the man got up and went to his place. When he entered his house he took a knife, laid hold of his concubine and divided her into twelve pieces, limb by limb and sent her throughout all the territory of Israel." (Judg 19:22-29)

Israel was incensed. This event was God's way of stirring them up. They cried and wept, decided to fight Benjamin and drew lots to see who would go first. The tribes went to the Benjamites to ask for the criminals, to deal with them. The Benjamites refused because they were their brothers and would not allow them to be punished. So they went to war and the Benjamites desolated the tribes. Then Israel attacked them from the back of the city and wiped out the entire village, including the women.

Benjamin decided to go capture wives for themselves in another village during a festival where the virgins of the land came and celebrated.

"I will build you up again and you, Virgin Israel, will be rebuilt. Again you will take up your timbrels and go out to dance with the joyful." (Jeremiah 31:4 – NIV)

They captured wives to rebuild the tribe of Benjamin. There was now a mother from every tribe in the tribe of Benjamin. Benjamin is the only tribe that has the seed of the woman from every tribe and is a summary of all the tribes.

TRUE PROPHECY

A few years later there arose a king, Saul, from the Benjamites. He was impulsive. He became the first tribe to rule Israel. Saul, the son of Kish, is a great story of the prophetic power of the Benjamites. Saul prophesied, was ecstatic and left his body. They wondered if he "was among the prophets" (1 Sam 10).

Just before this moment, when Saul goes looking for Samuel, his servant says "We can't go see a prophet empty handed" (1 Sam 9:7). Samuel feeds him and says "Then the Spirit of the LORD will come upon you mightily, and you shall prophesy with them and be changed into another man" (1 Sam 10:6 NASB). He gives Saul two loaves of bread and a calf. He doesn't give him three loaves, which means Saul's kingdom was not supposed to last. The one loaf he doesn't give him is the loaf of forgiveness.

Prophesy is when the Spirit of God comes upon someone, they have no control and begin to speak by the power of the Holy Spirit. We don't do that anymore and that is why, sometimes, there is no real transformation. In Hebrew tradition, when the spirit of God comes upon someone the person loses control. That is why Paul was telling them the spirit of the prophet is subject to the prophet. We can now control it, but only to a certain point.

I was in a US city to have a conference. During worship, I stood up and I saw the Lord standing by the back of the sanctuary. I hid my face because I knew what was going to happen. Suddenly I felt this weight come upon me and my knees buckled and I started speaking in tongues in such a vibrant and powerful way that I couldn't control myself. Saul, the first king of Israel, was filled with that kind of power.

The Spirit of God can come upon us and we can prophesy. Speaking in tongues and interpretation is a great way to prophesy because we are not speaking ourselves. We can discern issues and speak to edify, but that is not prophesy. Mysticism is an ecstatic movement that gets us into real ecstasy with the Holy Spirit. Saul was the first person recorded to openly prophesy.

Benjamin will possess Gilead (Obadiah 1:19). Gilead is a very important place in the prophetic movement. Elijah was from Gilead and Elisha had dealings there.

BENJAMIN AND KINGSHIP

Benjamin's father blessed him as a "ravenous wolf." He said that a ravenous wolf has the meat and shares it. Wolves share as they eat in packs. They never eat alone. They are a community and they operate in community. Benjamin is a communal person and is important for the fulfillment of somebody else's destiny.

Saul becomes the first king and Benjamin is loyal until the end, until David calls them and receives them back into the kingdom. Saul's daughter, Michal, became David's wife. Benjamin is the owner of Jerusalem. It was Benjamin's territorial land and Judah received it through David. He was the one who gave the seat of power and a lamb for the Messiah's throne. The Benjamites gave the land willingly. King David is from Bethlehem. The lineage of Benjamin is in the King of Kings. In the book of Psalms, it says, "There goes the little Benjamin, their ruler" (Psa 68:27).

By virtue, Benjamin is a wolf and he can sniff things out. If we train a wolf, he will be loyal until the end. When Jesus talked about the stone the builders rejected, the cornerstone of Judah, He was making a veiled reference to Benjamin because he was the only one in the tribes whose name contains the word 'son' (ben). Not only does Benjamin contain the word son (ben) but also 'Eben', the stone that serves as a marker. The scripture about the stone that the builders rejected is a play on 'the son' and 'stone'. A chief cornerstone of a family is a son.

The person who preached the Messiah to the Gentiles was a Benjamite. Paul was a Benjamite (Philippians 3:5). Even though he was not the first apostle, he was a chief among the apostles. Benjamin runs through scripture much more than a lot of other tribes.

The king and the warrior are combined in Benjamin. Let's spell his name: Beth, Nun, Yod, Mem, Yod and Final Nun "בנימין." If we spell it without the final Yod it equals 152, which is 1+5+2, which equals 8. If we add the final Yod, it equals 9. His name is spelled with two Yods when the male power of the Godhead is activated. Benjamin is one of the people who bypass the 'seven times' and moves directly into the now. He goes from margin to the "Sod" (the depth of God). Benjamin can move into the heart of God faster than any other as his life was joined to his father's life.

Benjamin was always connected to Judah. His part in the kingdom is a part of kingship. He participates in the King of Kings. In Genesis, when the brothers leave Egypt to return to their father Jacob, Joseph puts his silver cup in the bag of Benjamin. A silver cup is a sign of authority and a test of one's emotional stability. When the brothers discovered that Benjamin had the cup, they came back. Joseph said he would keep Benjamin. Judah was his target though, not Benjamin. He knew Judah would be king. Joseph wanted to know if Judah was willing to protect someone other than himself. When Joseph reveals his true identity to his brothers, he gives Benjamin a double portion. A double portion belongs to the first born. Joseph knew something. He was a seer and knew that Benjamin's tribe would become the head of Israel through Saul. He kept them in their birth order and gave the last one double. He brings Benjamin back and binds him. Everything that happens to Benjamin happens to the Messiah.

Joseph had given them the cup he used for divination. Communion is a powerful way of seeing into the future. It is a powerful way to move tri-dimensionally. Joseph could see Benjamin through the cross. Jacob weeps for Joseph as he is weeping for Benjamin. Benjamin is the ravenous wolf, who does not eat alone. Benjamin is the one with the silver cup, which is a cup of prophetic perception. Joseph does this to bring him back but gives him the cup as a king because a king must see. A king should be able to divine what is going on in his kingdom.

All the seeds of Israel are co-inherited in Benjamin. We find elicit sexuality in Judges, which is destructive to kingship. Benjamin was also involved in witchcraft.

The reason for sexuality in Hollywood is to access supernatural power, not just sex of itself. The reason we encourage marriage before sex is because we can access certain things to deal with what is coming from the other dimensions. We must learn how to use our sexuality positively to access something from the other side.

King Saul is the first king whose first seed remains today in the Messiah and a part of our capacity to know God through the person of Paul. The greatest Apostle was named after Saul. His name was Saul, not Paul. He was from the tribe of Benjamin and boasted of coming from the family of the King (Philippians 3:5). Benjamin was the one person in whose family a foreigner, Ruth, a Moabite, was inserted and became part of the Messianic line.

BALANCE

Benjamin operates in a redemptive principle of sacrificing his life for the person who does something for him. He is even willing to lose his identity so the person he is supporting can be lifted up (like Judah, in David's kingship, replacing Saul). Benjamin is a kingdom principle connected to understanding. Benjamin doesn't just understand theoretical processes, he understands actual warfare. Benjamin is a son of the right hand who operates by the left hand. Many of the Benjamite military were skilled, left and right handed (Judg 20:16). He was the only balanced person in Israel. He understood how to balance mercy and severity, wisdom and understanding and victory and glory because he uses both hands.

The balance is important for Benjamin. That is how Saul lost the Kingdom. When it came time for him to use the left hand, the hand of severity, he wouldn't use it. When it came time to use the right hand with the people, he used his left hand. If a Benjamite doesn't work on this issue, they will do the wrong thing to the right people and the right thing to wrong people. Look at the life of Saul, how he treated his friends, including his own son. We find in Jonathon and Saul the capacity to go after an enemy and also to be loyal unto death. This is a tribe that must remain balanced.

At the end of the ages, Benjamin remains steady. He does not change his position. He remains steady all the way to the book of Revelation. He remains constant, but needs to stay in the mode of balance.

ABOVE AND BELOW

"Blow the ram's horn in Gibeah, the trumpet in Ramah! Behind you, O Benjamin!' (Hos 5:8)

Benjamin carries a cup and a shofar. He is an activator of that which is hidden in the Heavens. He can smell what is going on in the Heavens. He is loyal and stands as king in his own right even when he is no longer a king. He has the king's DNA. A Benjamite is someone who will deal with severity but is quick to balance it out with the right hand of mercy. If he doesn't, he will also be destroyed, like Saul.

In the Heavenly dimension, there is the portion for a king who willingly gives his kingship over to a greater king. When Benjamin comes, prophets are reconciled and stars are put in their right places. They will be like a Barnabas who operates on a level to support us, to get to our destiny, even though it costs them personally. They enjoy all the gifts of Kingship but not the responsibility. The crown of kingship is not what makes a king - it is the nature of what is inside the person.

Benjamin starts with the 'Bet'. He is a house of plenty. Benjamin is a 10 with the capacity within his name to create. The Yod on both sides is not connected because it is separated by water.

In Genesis 1, God divides the waters above from the waters below. In Benjamin's case, God uses the water as a separation so that Benjamin can create in the Heavenly dimension and in the lower dimensions. He doesn't need to go to Heaven to change anything on Earth because His 'Yod' is at the top and on the bottom. When he vibrates the Yod at the bottom, the Yod on the top vibrates also. He's the only one in the tribe of Israel who can do that.

"Your kingdom come, your will be done, on Earth as it is in Heaven." (Matt 6:10 – ESV)

When the Kingdom is manifest on the Earth, everything we do in the Kingdom is done in Heaven. Until then, to change something on Earth we need to go to Heaven. There is something in Benjamin that connects the Yod above and below. The Yod equals 10, so it is the binary principal for creating things (1 and 0 are the male and female principle). God looks upon someone operating in the Benjamin principle as someone who deserves to shake the Heavens from wherever they are. The Yod is also a sperm. It allows the seeding of God's nature into circumstances.

Issachar knew the times and looked into the Heavens but he needed to shift his position to do so. Benjamin didn't need to change his position because He carried the Yod and the DNA of God, so when he engages, Heaven responds.

SEXUAL PURITY

"About Benjamin he said: "Let the beloved of the LORD rest secure in him, for he shields him all day long and the one the LORD loves rests between his shoulders." (Deut 33:12 NIV)

The Yod is in between the waters, which is where things occur between the Heavens. The Yod is in between the legs, not between the shoulders as interpreted above. The Yod in Hebrew is the circumcision point. The test of covenant is in the man's circumcision. The enemy wanted to mess up Benjamin because the Yod was in the center and that was his power. He wanted the Yod to be defiled so he couldn't stir the Heavens.

Our sexuality is something the Lord put within us so, when it is stirred, we can manifest from Heaven. If we draw the energy from ourselves during that stirring, we can birth something new that God desires.

A lot of stories about Benjamin relate to women and marriage. The Yod is the mark of the circumcision, which is why children are called unclean in Israel when they are not circumcised. The Yod is also a fist for breaking something. There are three things the Yod represents: circumcision, a fist and seed. A folded fist gathers power in it, which becomes a seed gathering the power of the universe. The power of creation is unfolded in the seed. If we could harness the power in the seed we could destroy the world. The power it takes for a seed to grow is larger than thousands of tons of a nuclear weapon. What makes a seed to go from death to life is stronger than any destructive force in the universe. We are at a place where God's good intention flows into the world.

SUPPORTING THE CALL OF ANOTHER

If we get to the point where we are content to be second in command, to support another who is responsible for an area of the kingdom (and God has called us to do it) we will benefit from it. If God doesn't call us to be the one ahead, we should not push our self. Benjamin had more influence on the gospel by being under Judah than what he would have if he was independent.

God has not called us to be the head. There is nothing we benefit from that we don't suffer terribly for. Benjamin wasn't supposed to be the king, he was supposed to provide the DNA for the next king. This is why he messed up a lot when he was king. Saul got angry, going around and killing because it was a Benjamite principle. For someone who isn't satisfied helping another get to their destiny, that person has a problem with themselves for their future and the future for everyone around them. The Benjamites hubris is stronger among 'spiritual' Christians than any other group.

THE NEW JERUSALEM

Benjamin has a prophetic spirit. He releases himself to the Holy Spirit and stays on the ground screaming and shouting for hours. They are passionate and were respected for their spirituality, not just the warfare. What is the goal of entering the dimension of Benjamite in the Heavens? The reason we have been drawn by the Lord is to bring Heaven down. When Heaven is manifested here on Earth then we don't need to go anywhere else.

We build the New Jerusalem in our being. Jerusalem belongs to Benjamin, not to Judah. It is Jerusalem below that stirs up the Jerusalem above. There was also a Bethlehem in Benjamin. The goal of going to Heaven is to get to the place where the structure of the holographic Jerusalem dances around us. That is the goal; to sit with Christ in a holographic New Jerusalem above so it can respond on the ground. Benjamin is the one where we transition to the upper Heavens.

In the New Jerusalem there are twelve dimensions above (apostles) and twelve dimensions below (tribes). Benjamin can transition and connect the two. He opens the way to speak to each other. It happens by commitment. Every structure of the Heavens underneath in the lower Heaven demands that we deal with certain things in our life. In the case of Benjamin, it demands that we deal with the sorrow that is embedded in our DNA. We narrate or find a new name - either we get it or someone gives it to us.

There are several ways a Jew changes their destiny. They either change their name or change location. We can do it because we are above principalities and powers. Our system and direction is not controlled by the systems of the world or creation. Creation doesn't have control of us. If it does, it is because we have not figured out how to bring the Yod from Heaven to Earth. When this section is complete, there will be no divination or sorcery against Israel. That is why the sorcery with Saul (1 Sam 28) was such a big deal. He was a person with two Yods stirring the underworld which affected Heaven. He was never forgiven because he did that. At the end of the age Benjamin is listed but some other tribes were not because they did not have both Yod's to justify and correct their lives. They did what Benjamin did, but He had a holographic possibility of the transformation of Heaven that he walked in every day. He could tune Heaven from the Earth and operate in that perspective. He knew how to do it by the transference of his DNA into the next King.

KNOWING BOTH SIDES

We cannot be a Christian without beholding the Benjamite, because our life is in the Messiah. The Benjamites were known for the capacity to look into something and being curious about spirituality. They understood what it meant to seek out the spirit. What made Benjamin so powerful in Israel and Judah was that Benjamin understood both the righteous and unrighteous parts of spirituality. We are a Benjamite when it comes to connecting the Heavens and the Earth and knowing the left and right side. This knowledge is not for everyone because there are many people who have gone into mysticism and have denied Jesus.

Solomon brought all the women from all the nations with their idolatry. His son, King Rehoboam, didn't know how to deal with this issue. Jeroboam lived in Egypt and learned all their ways. He came back and took the kingdom from David's family (1 Kin 12). He did that because he was unbalanced. That is the danger of being in the dimension of Benjamin. There must be balance. Daniel knew both ways. Daniel was said to be among the astrologers. Daniel could control the king. He put a dream in the king's mind and interpreted it for the king. He gave that dream to Nebuchadnezzar. He was the fourth man in the fire. It wasn't Jesus. The reason we keep saying it is Jesus is because we don't think we can do it. The phrase "son of man" is the phrase the angels used to refer to Daniel. He was like "a son of man." It didn't say he was "the son of man."

The power that someone who operates in Benjamite principle is being seated in Heaven and having a seat on Earth, learning and knowing both sides and balancing them. Not everybody is a Benjamite. Not everybody is ambidextrous. This is the one place where believers need to be careful. This dimension of Heaven, even if we have it, must be kept quiet.

David had two advisors; Ahithophel and Hushai. David could not defeat Ahithophel because he knew both sides. He could bring this side and use it against David. David had been told, "Ahithophel is among the conspirators with Absalom." So David prayed, "LORD, turn Ahithophel's counsel into foolishness." (2 Sam 15:31 – NIV). David used cunning to deal with him because he couldn't go to God. God doesn't attack people who operate in this level. We must learn how to operate in wisdom to deal with those who operate here. There are certain things in the spiritual realm that cannot be dealt with by spirit alone, so we need wisdom and the capacity to change the atmosphere by practical knowledge.

The temptation for someone who knows both sides is always to be drawn by one side, with out balance. Aaron could call forth a bull from hell. He didn't do it in the name of the Lord. He used what he knew from Egypt to call forth the fallen face of the cherub. The cherub is named after the bull (of the four faces). Aaron stepped into hell and pulled out a fallen angel's face because he knew both sides. The reason God made him priest, even after he did that, was because he knew both sides.

Moses knew both sides. He was trained in all the ways of the Egyptians. When we operate in the Benjamite principle, we need to pray for the capacity to balance. We need to pray for the capacity to lean on the right hand of the Lord so we are not constantly trying to hurt people. Benjamin is an incredible person when he is balanced. He is a dangerous and terrible person when he is not.

There are certain principalities that only God can deal with. We don't have a right, especially when the principality is assigned to people God has given a blessing to. Before we take out a principality we must know where we are standing in Christ and how to use our position in Christ to deal with it. It doesn't mean we are not powerful. We can stop them from working, but we can't invade their authority or territory. We want to be one who knows how to agitate the Yod below and the Yod above - to cause the waters above to stir so the waters below can bring forth. If we cannot, we need somebody else who will. Believers have come to the house of Benjamin. We have come to the house of the "right hand", to the place of the star system that carries the goblet, the cup of relationship, the cup that drinks the wine of the king. We are in a place where we can control the Earth from the Heavens. Not all of us are called to go deal with such issues. We must be careful or we could become a casualty of spiritual warfare.

I remember flying into an Asian country while they were having a ghost festival. All the spirits came to look at me. I simply looked at them. It was not my right to ask them to leave the land where they were born. Christians do that. They go to somebody else's country and want to change a person's country without permission. There are sons in the land that can do it. Ignorance causes believers to fail because they approach situations on presumption.

"Benjamin shall raven as the wolf. In the morning he shall devour the prey and in the night he shall divide the spoil." (Gen 49:27)

If we spell his name Ben-yamin, we have to add 1. So, he is 2-2-2 (6), but he's also 2-1-2 (5). The 2-2-2 is important because Benjamin becomes the first gateway to kingship, not according to God but according to man (6).

2-1-2 equals 5 and 5 is the number of the principle in man for man to be a full divine being. How many blessings did God give to Adam when He created him? Five blessings. "And God blessed them saying (1) have dominion, (2) be fruitful, (3) multiply, (4) subdue and (5) replenish" (Gen 1:28). Always remember that about mankind. They either will multiply based on the divine principle of man (5) or they are going to act as man independent of God (6).

Benjamin's story begins in sorrow and death. His mother names him Ben-oni, which is "son of my sorrow". His father names him Ben-yamin, which is "son of my right hand". So here is a fundamental schizophrenic idea. Benjamin had a split personality because his parents caused it.

How does this relate to the Heavenly dimensions? We need to develop a clear and clean desire because we have two sides in us. We have the fallen desire to be completely human - which is trying to be God without God. But we also have the potential of being divine - which is being human the way God wants us to be. A human being tied to God is made divine, not an independent being, so we are not an idol.

NAVIGATING THE DIMENSION OF BENJAMIN

After going through the process of going through the different dimensions in the Lower 12 Heavens, we come to the dimension of Benjamin. This is where we begin to benefit and inherit as Joseph inherits. We have come to that dimension where treasures are available. God opens the treasure house of Heaven to us. God opens the treasure house of wisdom and knowledge. Wisdom has come to us. We have overcome our capacity to judge as a serpent and now we are judging as a righteous judge. We are now standing in our kingship, ruler-ship and priesthood.

Our waters have already come under control because Reuben's agitation is gone. God has done all of that work in us. To get to Benjamin we have come through the place of Joseph. We have suffered and God is now going to open the dimensions of the treasures of Heaven where Melchizedek and Enoch rule. This area of Joseph is where Enoch and Melchizedek are! This is the place where the treasures of the garden are, where the waters of Eden still flow.

After God has brought us through to Benjamin our capacity to have a split personality comes up. We must be careful when God brings us to that place; where we enter this dimension.

Jesus shares a story about the servant whose master leaves him in charge of the other servants. He says, "Who then is a faithful and wise servant, whom his lord hath made ruler over his household, to give them meat in due season? Blessed is that servant. But and if that evil servant shall say in his heart, my lord delayeth his coming; and shall begin to smite his fellow servants and to eat and drink with the drunken;" (Matt 24:45-49 KJV). Who is that servant whom his master will leave over his brethren that will begin to beat and tear them up? Jacob says Benjamin is a ravenous wolf. His major issue is trying to prove himself, even after God has already done everything. This can happen to us when we start going to Heaven and start experiencing the dimensions. Then we come down and try to prove to people we are who we say we are.

Jacob says Benjamin's tendency is towards tearing, destroying and messing people up. He sits on the side waiting for someone to pounce on. He expects the worst to happen. When Benjamin was born his mother named him Ben-oni (son of my sorrow) and then she died. Everybody reminded Benjamin of that. Benjamin had an inferiority complex. They would go to war against their brethren because they wanted to prove that they were powerful enough. They were the only ones who stayed attached to Judah.

Although Benjamin is also the 'son of the right hand', as a 'son of sorrow', he is someone who traffics in self-victimization and self-death. He is constantly reminding himself "nothing good happens to me" and expecting something bad to happen around every corner. In this manifestation of Benjamin, when things are going well, we begin to think it will never last. Something else bad is going to happen. When somebody comes around us, we think they want something. If they become our real friend we are looking for the day when they drop us and walk away. Some think it is because they are "spiritual" or "prophetic." People walk away because we are the ones drawing and creating the atmosphere where people do that to us.

On the other side of Benjamin (a son of the right hand) is a man created in the image of God, not thinking from the perspective of loss, but thinking from the perspective of strength. Once God gives us what we are looking for, He will create opportunity to see if we are going to use it as man without God or use it in the strength of God. The tests do not stop. In every dimension of Heaven we enter we must work through certain things in our self. In this Benjamin dimension what we are going to work through in our self is our experience of loss. If we are not careful, we chase the things we have lost rather than building what we can become.

This concept is clearly embedded in movies, where a character gets to a place and there is potential to become victorious, but he sees all the things he has lost. He sees someone close to him who has died and starts moving towards that. Rather than gaining strength, he loses strength. In fact he moves towards the ghost world rather than moving towards his target.

When we gain victory we always get this temptation. If we travel to Heaven this test is put before us. Things are given to us and we may see them based on our suffering, experience or our personal pain. We must make a choice - whether that is going to define what we do as a man (the '6') or whether we are going to move towards the potential of what God really wants us to be (the '5').

A big problem in the church is many operate from the dimension of our loss and of our pain. We are reacting. Our experience of loss and disappointments can be the greatest hindrance to where we are going. God has already brought us into dimensions where we can inherit things of the kingdom. Are we going to be a son of sorrow or a son of God's strong right hand?

This is the crossroad, where every pain we have experienced is pulling us to stay in the same circle we have been going through. There is a way through here but it's not pulling us as much. It is just there. We must make a choice of our will to go that way, rather than to keep repeating. The whole world is in a conspiracy to make sure we keep repeating the failures we have experienced. The world empowers it to keep us under delusion, illusion and to keep us weak.

When we are at Benjamin and begin to emphasize failure or loss we fall back to Reuben and become unstable as water. Or we fall back to Simeon and become ruled by fire, which is anger, destruction and vengeance. We think we are controlled by reality and not vengeance. What we experience in that moment of falling back towards Reuben, Simeon or Levi is Benjamin's victimization syndrome. We fall back with no transition towards kingship. We stop being a king and become a victim. It happens to us at least once a month and we are not conscious of it happening. The enemy is sucking the life from all the processes we have been through where God has purified us, where we have worked and made choices in our kingship, priesthood and dealing with the serpent nature. All the things we have lost come rushing towards us. In mysticism, this is what is called "Rachel's grave." Rachel cursed her son, Benjamin. She was a bitter woman, who died bitter, which is why she couldn't have a baby. She was bitter from the beginning against her sister and her husband.

LACK OR ABUNDANCE MINDSET

This is also the area where we choose whether we operate from a perception of lack or a perception of abundance. The whole issue about a wolf is that a wolf is never satisfied.

"Benjamin is a ravenous wolf. In the morning, he shall devour the prey and at night he shall divide the spoil." (Gen 49:27)

Benjamin never rests, he is not satisfied with just getting. He is not satisfied with destroying and maiming and taking for himself. That is what living with a sense of loss causes - ultra-possessiveness. What we pursue to possess we always lose, especially if the idea of possession is coming from a sense of loss. We are trying to make sure we don't lose anything else.

God will test us when He begins to take us into the Heavenlies by putting things in front of us that look like they are real. In every dimension there is something to see that is not real before we see something that is real. We must figure it out. Most of what is unreal is coming from our experience in our body and our perception. We need to clear up our natural perception so we can see what God is trying to do. The Bible says we walk by faith, not by sight. Sight is illusory. It's ephemeral. The things we see are not what we think they are. God wants us to see with a pure, inner eye, not just with a physical eye.

In the sphere of Benjamin, loss becomes a strength because our loss should teach us that nothing material is permanent. It is funny how it works the other way with human beings. The more we lose something the more we think we can hang on to something. In fact, the lesson in loss is that nothing is permanent on this planet. So, we begin to look for what is permanent. Hebrews 11 says that the people were looking for a permanent city whose builder is God. To them, this world did not matter because it was passing away. They had seen what is permanent. We need to focus our mind on what is permanent.

When Benjamin understands the power of loss as an implement of learning, as a cleansing phenomenon, as a clarifying or clarification of the inner eye, he becomes more powerful. When he hangs on to what he has lost and tries to get it back, he becomes weaker. He falls back to the dimension of Reuben, Simeon and Levi, not as a priest but as a victim. He becomes somebody who feels victimized and who attaches himself to what he thinks is going to help him and what he has lost.

THE 12TH HOUR TRANSMUTATION

Benjamin is the 12th hour. The 12th hour in the day is a time of judgment. The midday also has transmutation qualities because it is when Jews pray for forgiveness. When we are in a desert at midday we see all kinds of mirages. The capacity to see mirages is what we have got to deal with to see clearly. It is where our loss begins to become real - but what we have lost is no longer here. We need to let it go and focus on our strength.

Benjamin is the level of transmutation - in terms of forgiveness and also in terms of name. His mother names him Ben-oni. His father names him Ben-yamin. His father transmutes his loss, which had already happened in his life. Rachel had died giving birth to Benjamin. Jacob doesn't need to go about fighting, so he names him as a way of transmuting his experience of loss into a possible gain.

As a believer, we are already here by the fact that Christ has given us a new name. That is a transmutative process. By renaming our self we can change our destiny. This is why kings take a new name. In the early days, when Christians were baptized, their name was changed. Those born a Christian or a Jew are given two names. In some cultures they are given three names. The name we choose will depend on what we want to happen at a particular time.

When Jacob changed Benjamin's name, a transmutative process was initiated towards possibility, but the experience of loss is still there. Benjamin can always go and wake it up if he wants to. He needs to focus on being the son of the right hand.

A right hand is the place of power, the place of protection, the place of provision. The Bible says that Jesus is seated at the right hand of power. But scripture also says that if we serve Him and we are in Him, Jesus will make us sit with Him at the right hand of the Father. Is this in the future or is this what happens now? The Bible says we are seated with Him in the Heavenly places now. (Eph 2:6). This is the place for a believer.

When we get to this dimension and move toward the place of this power, our past will continuously come up. We must decide whether we live our life by reaction to what has happened to us or by will and creation. When people who have not experienced Heaven before - experience Heaven, they come back down and they want to change their name. They want to change everything about themselves.

In the natural, when Ben-yamin overcomes his sense of loss, he dwells with Judah. When we get taken up to Heaven and experience the right-hand side of God we really don't want to come back. We don't want to go around and do life because we can now see what is in God, as opposed to what we think we are losing on Earth. Most people don't want to come back when they have that experience.

THE FATHERS SECRET PLACE

When we experience this dimension we experience the Father's secret place. This is also revealed in Benjamin's relationship with his father. We should always use the natural things in Scripture to understand what is happening in the Heavenly realms. When the brothers go to Egypt, Jacob keeps Benjamin under his shadow and he refuses to let him go. In fact, the brother Reuben said to Joseph, "for the lad's life is bound in a bundle with his father's" (Gen 44:30 KJV). Imagine our lives bound with the life of God because we are always at His right-hand side! He is not going anywhere. But when Jacob releases him from His right hand, He sends gifts with him that will make sure he doesn't get taken prisoner.

When we have this experience, and we have dealt with loss, we get to experience what Job was talking about. "If there is a messenger for him, a mediator, one among a thousand, to show man His uprightness, then He is gracious to him, and says, 'Deliver him from going down to the Pit; I have found a ransom'" (Job 33:23-24)

Judah became that ransom for Benjamin. This is what Psalm 91 is about; "He that dwells in the secret place of the Most High shall abide under the shadow of the Almighty...I shall say of the Lord He is my refuge and my strength...I shall not be afraid of the terror by night nor the arrow that that flyeth by noon. A thousand shall fall at your side and ten thousand at your right hand; but it shall not come near you. Only with your eyes shall you behold and see the reward of the wicked." (KJV). This dimension is based on somebody who has come to the right hand side of God and has accepted the transmutation of his name from victim or loser, to the "son of the right hand".

"He shall give His angels charge concerning you." (Psa 91:11)

An angel is one who stands for us. Judah became an angel of protection. It was the same Judah who sold Joseph. Now Judah has become a strategy for Benjamin. The only reason Judah does this is because Benjamin has started to take his name seriously. He stayed with the father. He was at the father's right hand. It was when Benjamin was at his father's right hand, obtaining favor from the father, that Judah had to deal with Benjamin in that way. It was because Benjamin stayed with Judah that Judah continued to obtain favor. We cannot separate the choosing of Judah from Benjamin's presence. Benjamin and Judah became bound together forever. When they went into exile, they went into exile together.

FIGHTING FROM LACK OF IDENTITY

There is a tendency to constantly fight for fighting's sake because we have something to prove at every moment. We need to watch that human aspect. The tribe of Benjamin caused Israel the most trouble. They fought their brethren. They were great warriors. There is a situation with a concubine in Judges 19. Benjamin was one of the first tribes in Israel to practice homosexuality because of that motherless syndrome. The Bible says God wanted to punish Israel because of what Israel was doing. They came to war against the Benjamites but the Benjamites defeated them. Israel went and cried before the Lord. When Israel came back they killed almost all the Benjamite women and men. They killed and burned down cities so that there were no women left in Benjamin.

When the war was over, all the men of Benjamin went to hide in the bush because the tribe of Benjamin was completely decimated. The Israelites treated them like Canaanites. All the men of Israel vowed they would never allow a Benjamite to marry their children. Israel had a dance every year that the young girls went to. They decided if a Benjamite came and took one of the girls that they were not going to ask for a dowry. The Benjamites would take the girls and the Israelites would act like nothing happened. There was an agreement to re-people Benjamin. It was out of that tribe that Saul came. Saul fought against losing the kingdom. He fought against losing his reputation, losing something that was given to him freely. That Benjamite sense of loss was still in him. There was a sense of fear that God was going to abandon him. That is why he made the sacrifice and didn't wait for Samuel (1 Sam 13: 8-13). If we act in order to prove something, we will end up messing our self up.

Benjamin's name begins with "Beit." This is the letter that begins the Torah - in Genesis the first letter is Beit. There is a creative principle in Benjamin. The "Nun" represents Jubilee. There's a Jubilee, a principle for setting free all that is in him. The

"Yod" of course is the vibrating letter of the name of God which appears in Benjamin's life twice. The "Mem" is the water which can draw us back. The final Nun is '100' - one on, two offs. It is a binary code. When Benjamin starts going down the wrong path it is much more difficult to bring him back. God puts two Yods in Benjamin, knowing his tendency to slide down, so that he always has a capacity to return.

There are ransoming angels who come for our deliverance. Angels who stand at the right hand of God and fight. They don't just fight but they stand in place for us. When we operate in this region, God will bring people to stand in place for us, like Judah was for his brother. This is a transmutation principle; enemies become friends. "When a man's ways are pleasing to the LORD, He makes even his enemies to be at peace with him" (Pro 16:7 NASB).

If Benjamin can find his equilibrium to operate in his dimension, then he has the capacity to turn anybody into a friend, even if that person was an enemy. But if he is a wolf, he is a problem. He had to transmute from being a wolf into a dog, to transmute from sorrow / weakness into strength, to transmute from loss into abundance and to have the capacity to move and turn things.

Benjamin is a laboratory, a dimension in Heaven, where we can transmute things. It is a place where we practice and get trained to move things from one place to another. In this dimension we can look at the nature of things and realize they are not as solid and as strong as we think they are. We can practice moving them, transmuting them. We are given a tree and we are told by God that the tree is a flowing river. In our mind a tree cannot be a flowing river. What God is doing is working on us so we can be a creative agent and can transmute things from one dimension to another. God says, "Look again." Depending on our perspective, it is either a tree or it is a flowing river. The capacity to transmute is our perception. The first gift of a born-again believer is the capacity to see, which is also the capacity to call forth and create. What we see, we can create.

Section 2: Benjamin : The Dimension Of Power

NAVIGATING THE FOURTH TRIAD

SEEING IN THE HEAVENS

We live in an open universe. The Temple of Ezekiel and all the gateways and doorways that are narrated within it (Ezekiel, chapters 40 to 48) show us how to use these paradigms to navigate the Heavens. This temple allows us to look at how God functions within us, how we develop ourselves and how we can move in the different spheres. In the Book of Revelation, when it talks about the Heavenly city, it is giving us a microcosm of how the universe functions. The Heavenly city has 12 foundations and 12 capstones, which is 12 below and 12 above. But there's always one that is left. In every 12 there is the 13th. The 13th does not change, because the 13 is the Messianic principle.

In the Old Testament, the '13' is a female. In the New Testament, the '13' is a male, but it is the feminine 'Shekinah'. In the Talmud it says, where two or three Jews are studying the scriptures, the Shekinah is present. Jesus says in Matthew 18:20 "where two or three are gathered in My name, there I am in the midst". He's making Himself equivalent to the Shekinah.

Christ was born of the Holy Spirit. The Holy Spirit is the progenitor of Christ in the physical form. He is the seed of the woman. In the woman, Mary, is a symbol of the Shekinah, the indwelling.

We have the capacity to leave our body and have out-of-body / supernatural experiences. How much of our religious upbringing are we willing to let go? I have trained myself not to remember my religious understanding when I walk in the Heavens. It was hard. Our memory and knowledge is our power and weakness. A part of training to move in the spirit is learning how to forget what is known. Our identity is intricately linked to what we know. Even when we think we are being free with the Lord, we are putting our so-called trained spirituality in front of what God wants to do for us.

One of the biggest problems spiritual people have is judging and releasing themselves. These are things we must work through, because our knowledge can be our greatest hindrance. If we want to know God, we must be willing to forget what we know about God! If we want to transform the world, we must overcome the formation. It is hard work, but it is also by grace. Grace imparts the knowledge that no matter how much we know, it is never enough. We must be willing to let go of what we know, allowing new revelation to take root.

"Yea doubtless and I count all things but loss for the excellency of the knowledge of Christ Jesus my Lord: for whom I have suffered the loss of all things and do count them but dung, that I may win Christ." (Philippians 3:8 KJV)

JUDGING AND COURTS

Give God permission to change the way He is viewed by you in order to get deeper. If we want to explore God we cannot be caught only in the washroom of God. A washroom is where we are constantly washing and cleaning our self. If we are spending most of our time in the courts of Heaven getting things judged, we have a wrong understanding. The judgment court is the lowest place in Heaven. Too many people are stuck in the lowest place in Heaven and they make that into a religion. If we went to natural court every month the judge will mark us as a troublemaker!

"Let your foot be seldom in your neighbor's house, lest he have his fill of you and hate you. (Pro 25:17 – ESV)

The Bible teaches that we should make peace with our enemy before we get to the courts. People are talking about going to the court of judgment, but nobody is talking about the peace we are supposed to make before we get to the judgment court. Scripture says to make peace with our enemies before we get to the courts so that when we get there he doesn't defeat us. We need to be able to move from that place of judgment to the place of celebration, intimacy and divine exploration. Explore God! Explore the chambers, channels, courtrooms or the different places, houses and divinity inside of God. We need to be able to shift from judgment to divine exploration.

The reason for judgment is for us to be set free. If we are set free, we are able to go into the different dimensions and spheres of God's inner being. There are some things that we need to just leave to the Lord and let Jesus deal with it. This allows us to go do what we are supposed to do.

Peter turned and saw that the disciple whom Jesus loved was following them. (This was the one who had leaned back against Jesus at the supper and had said, "Lord, who is going to betray you?") When Peter saw him, he asked, "Lord, what about him?" Jesus answered, "If I want him to remain alive until I return, what is that to you? You must follow me." (John 21:20-22)

Jesus told Peter to go do what he was supposed to do and not worry about the things that don't concern him. How many of the things that we have taken to the judgement court in Heaven have manifested on the face of the Earth? We have access. We do see results when we come to the throne of judgment, but judgment does not yield much. The purpose for judgment is to condemn the guilty and release the righteous.

If we are not going beyond the throne of judgment and experiencing the Temple of God in Heaven, joining God in worship before the throne, all we are doing is looking at one side. The judgment seat is in the gate where we can enter or not. Even the throne room that John saw in the book of Revelation is not where we stop. It is the gate to other dimensions. That is what the elders are doing - they are sitting in the gate. When we go into the throne room, don't stop there. Go through one of the gates, go behind the Father's throne, go into the tabernacle.

The Bible says God has a temple in Heaven. It says that a temple in Heaven was open. We have access and we need to use our access. Don't stop at the place of judgment. The Father has already decided we are not guilty before we get to the judgment room. If He didn't already make that decision, we wouldn't even be present. Our minds should move beyond the courts of judgment.

In the book of Ezekiel, there is mention of the chambers of the women, the chambers of the righteous, the chambers of the elders and different courts and places of interaction between people of equal status. It's not just a place of judgment. The king's court is a place where people dance. It's also a place where the jester is. There are soldiers and maidens in the king's court.

Maybe one of the reasons we don't get results is because we are trying to manifest things in the courts of judgment that should have been manifested in other courts in Heaven. We can be freed from judgment for some sin that we have committed before the throne, but we can't ask for financial breakthrough in the judgment room. We can ask for what we are owed, but we can't ask for what we are not owed.

We must go on and discover the depths and dimensions of the Heavens that are nested in God. Walking through the Lower 12 Dimensions of Heaven changes and prepares you to overcome and live in the benefits and position of sonship. To become like your Father!

THE LOWER KINGDOM DIMENSIONS: THE 12 SONS OF JACOB

STONES

"Seek ye first the kingdom of God and His righteousness and all these things shall be added unto you." (Matt 6:33 KJV)

If our focus is on God and on developing a connection, then everything we desire gets drawn to us.

There are stones in the various dimensions. The first three stones are mentioned in Genesis 2:11-12; "The name of the first is Pishon; it is the one which skirts the whole land of Havilah, where there is gold. And the gold of that land is good. Bdellium and the onyx stone are there." Stones and precious metals represent the four dimensions that are revealed in every cosmos. In every cosmos there are four dimensions, the four quadrants, which determine everything that happens.

No man is complete as a tri-dimensional being. Man must become 'four' in order to be full. It is at the fourth dimension that a human really begins to operate by power. Most people will never get there. Every cosmos has four dimensions and that is why the scriptures begin with four rivers (Gen 2).

Exodus 28:13 says that the cherubim were covered with

precious stones. When we look at the stones of the High Priests, they are supposed to mimic the placement of the stones in the different dimensions of Heaven. Consider the concept of 'parallel universes' as it is manifested in the stones. There are 12 stones that are in the breastplate, but there are two basic stones. The two onyx stones are the stones with the names of the sons of Israel.

"You shall take two onyx stones and engrave on them the names of the sons of Israel, six of their names on the one stone and the names of the remaining six on the other stone, according to their birth. "As a jeweler engraves a signet, you shall engrave the two stones according to the names of the sons of Israel; you shall set them in filigree settings of gold. "You shall put the two stones on the shoulder pieces of the ephod, as stones of memorial for the sons of Israel, and Aaron shall bear their names before the LORD on his two shoulders for a memorial. "You shall make filigree settings of gold, and two chains of pure gold; you shall make them of twisted cordage work, and you shall put the corded chains on the filigree settings. "You shall make a breastpiece of judgment, the work of a skillful workman; like the work of the ephod you shall make it: of gold, of blue and purple and scarlet material and fine twisted linen you shall make it." (Exo 28:9-15 NASB)

Within the dimensional Heavens there are stones related to every tribe. The stone colors represent a dimension of the Heavens. We are so familiar with the descriptions of the Heaven where the streets are gold are that we act like gold is the only thing that is there. Isn't platinum costlier than gold? Gold is not as rare as people think it is. Diamonds, for example, are all over the Earth. It is the market that keeps the prices high. A diamond is just like a stone, it is everywhere. Precious stones, trees and liquids are all important because they represent for us certain aspects of Heaven.

PARALLEL AND OPPOSITE

The tribe of Israel and the apostles based on the Book of Revelation are paradigms of dimensions of Heaven. One tribe becomes both the key to unlocking the other tribe and the boundary stone for the other tribe in its weakness.

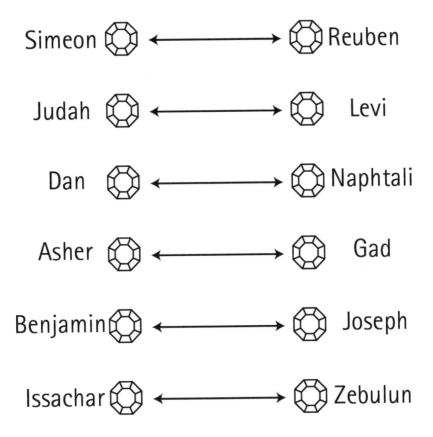

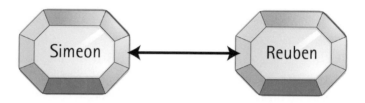

These two stones represent Reuben and Simeon. The world of water is parallel to the world of fire. Simeon is fire. Reuben is water. Reuben stops the fire.

If we set something on a fire long enough, moisture comes out. If we heat something long enough, it steams, which is water. Water and steam are not as separated as we think they are. They exist, one within the other, and they mutually affect each other. The worlds are like this. One is the opposite of the other, yet is the reflection of the other. The opposite is important, but within the opposite is a similarity. If we get this into our mind then we will understand how to deal with people and how to navigate the world. There is a way in which opposites either enhance the strength of each other or exaggerate the weakness of each other. When in opposition they become destructive to one another. When they are in harmony they enhance the strength of each other.

The shift between parallel universes is not really a quantum leap but a simple shift. Parallel universes are not that difficult to get into. What is difficult to get into are dimensions. We can shift easily into a parallel universe without realizing we have done so, but to consciously shift into dimensions requires intention.

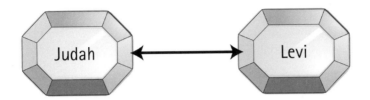

Levi and Judah are parallel universes of the priest and the king. They represent more than just the tribe of Israel. Ultimately, when the two are combined in harmony, something is created. This is the case of Christ. He is like Melchizedek; a priest and king. In most cultures the priest and the king are opposed to one another. Many wars have begun because kings want to control priests or vice versa.

Priests sacrifice animals. Kings sacrifice human beings. The priest must stand in the way of the king and his tendency to sacrifice other people for his purpose by creating a substitute in a sacrificial system. In the United States today there are many businessmen who are kings in their nature. However there are no priests in the companies, so they devour people. We should keep working these things out to find the deeper meanings.

In Israel, it was the king who was supposed to stop the priest from idolatry. The Bible always says "and the king did that which was evil." It does not say the priest, even though the priests were the ones who carried out most of the sacrifices. Scripture does not blame them. It always blames the king. The king was supposed to stop idolatry, because the priest had a tendency towards idolatry. The blame is put on the prophets and the priests for the bloodshed in the country. The Bible blames the priests for the bloodshed of the innocent when it should blame the kings, but it blames the kings for idolatry. One is supposed to balance out the other. Paul keeps saying "bear one another's burden" and give each other what they need. Bearing one another's burdens means becoming a strength in their weakness. It means becoming a balance to them and becoming a boundary to their weakness. It means to enhance their strength and help minimize their weakness. It is not about material help alone.

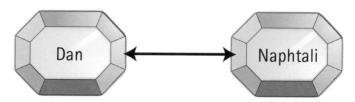

Dan is an aggressor who moves in judgment towards destruction. Naphtali is a wrestler. He holds back, wrestles and keeps Dan back. They are powerful because one is wrestling and the other is fighting. Dan is fighting in an underhanded way because he is a serpent. Wrestling however is not warfare. Wrestling is more to the ground than it is above. Only a wrestler can deal with a snake because his whole style is on the Earth. We can't be a good wrestler if we don't have an equilibrium, a center of gravity.

When I was growing up, wrestling was part of the way that African children were trained. During moonlight, young people were brought out to the square to wrestle with one another. We practiced wrestling and the person who won was considered the victor for that city. It wasn't a fight. We have a phrase in our language that "wrestling is not fighting". Wrestling is a training ground. Look at the power now between Dan and Naphtali. That's how the stones are placed, so they benefit and set limits on one another.

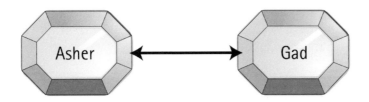

Gad is a "troop" and "good fortune." Gad is also the three-fold lion. Asher is happiness and joy. What is it that soldiers like to do? Drink, sing and shout (when they are not fighting). Every nation makes sure that they provide a bar and a dancing place for their soldiers. This is what keeps the warrior instinct in check. Both the passion for joy and celebration can be twisted into the passion for killing. The sexual centers come from the same place. When soldiers are not given a source of joy and happiness, they rape and destroy women.

If a nation wants to develop soldiers that are completely inhumane they simply need to deprive them of women and joy. The soldiers will channel all that sexual energy into destruction. The ultimate warrior that is going to arise is the antichrist. He will have no interest in sex. He will channel his whole sexual energy into destruction, not into joy. He will have no pleasure in the things that human beings enjoy.

"Neither shall he regard the God of his fathers, nor the desire of women, nor regard any god: for he shall magnify himself above all" (Daniel 11:37, KJV)

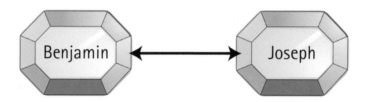

Joseph was a king. In fact, he was the only son who got a double portion from his father, Jacob. Judah did not get the double portion even though his father gave him many blessings. Joseph got the double portion of Israel because he had two inheritances; Ephraim and Manasseh. His father gave him a double portion as his firstborn. Joseph was the only one buried in two places; his skin was left in Egypt, but his bones were transplanted to the land of Israel.

The Bible describes Benjamin as a "ravenous wolf." Joseph is described as a "fruitful bough" - a provider of food. They are opposites, but similar. Each one needs the other. If one is without the other, they will become extreme in their weakness. As in all these pairings, the one serves to curtail the weakness of the other and to strengthen the strengths of the other.

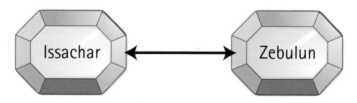

Issachar is a carrier of burdens and a diviner that sees. He is able to discern the times. Zebulun is the wayfarer who travels in ships, but he is also the one who dips his feet in oil. He is the one who produces wealth and who lives in a place of wealth. Why is he paired with Issachar? We need to understand times and seasons. It says that Issachar knows what Israel should do. A king and a merchant need to understand the times.

Economically, companies and CEO's who do not understand the season go bankrupt. This is why merchants are involved with psychics, tarot cards and similar activities. They need to find out what the season is. That is why kings call astrologers and magicians. It is all about making profit and having the wealth, to do what they need to do and to go to war.

Zebulun is dipped in oil. He is a merchant and an adventurer. He must go even when it is not warfare. He is moved to go everywhere. He can become a vagabond, so he needs Issachar to restrain him.

Issachar himself is one who creates wealth by not moving. They both create wealth, but Issachar is the tribe that didn't need to labor. They just threw their seed into the field and, because the field was so fertile, they didn't have to work like everybody else. They threw their seed into the ground and produced the greatest harvest because they knew how to discern the times. They would help Zebulun in his adventures as a merchant.

WORKING TOGETHER AND BALANCE

Our strength is our weakness. Sometimes our weakness, when harnessed, is our greatest strength. A problem is that we want to focus on our strength, because we are comfortable with it, and our weakness gets hampered. Our weakness is not the opposite of our strength. If we harness our weakness, look at it in the face until we develop it, it will make us stronger. Why does God say, "my strength is made perfect in weakness"? (2 Cor 12:9 KJV)

We have been taught to fear our weakness. What we should do is work on our weakness, face it, develop it and make sure we can deal with it until it becomes our strength. When our weakness becomes our strength we will put our whole intention into it. It is something we intentionally develop. Our strength is something we don't intentionally develop, it is simply part of our interaction with reality. We rejoice in it thinking it is something great but we didn't develop it. That which we develop intentionally is more powerful than that which we have been given. Most Christians are comfortable with their strength and never try to transmute their weakness into strength. As they are in our life so they are in the universe! The un-inhabitable universe is paralleled by those who are in the inhabitable. These bodies communicate with one another. The Sun is parallel to the Moon and they need one another. They can mutually destroy each other, but they also need one another. The man needs the woman. They can mutually destroy each other or they can come together and work and produce something. They are not as far apart as they think they are.

Gad is a force that holds back Dan. When moving in the Heavenly dimensions, with parallel universes (universes that are close enough to one another, linked together in one place), we will come to this place. Dan is a serpent, he represents a seraph in the Heavenly realm. The difference is Dan goes down and the seraphim fly above. The serpents in Heaven have no poison because it is impossible to have poison in Heaven. When they fall, they become poisonous. It has been proven in ordinary life. The higher a serpent goes the less capacity it has to bite. This is why eagles take a serpent up high, to keep it from being able to strike.

Judah is a three-fold lion. When we are in that dimension, the face of the Lord, according to the description of Judah, is a three-faced lion. Scripture speaks of Gad as a lion (a one-faced lion) because the Earthly lion has one face. Why does it describe Judah as a three-faced lion? Judah represents the Messiah.

"The scepter shall not depart from Judah...until Shiloh comes...and unto Him shall the gathering of the people be." (Gen 49:10 KJV)

If Judah is a representation of the one that comes to Shiloh, Christ really is a three-faced lion, the embodiment of the tribe Judah. When we look at the capacity of God to deal with the serpent, we will see a lion growling at the serpent on the ground. The lion vibrates the Earth so that the serpent can feel the vibrations. How does an eagle deal with a serpent? It takes it up high. The lion deals with it on the ground where it crawls; the eagle carries it up high.

There are four faces of God. Scripture describes the living creatures who have four faces and the name of God is four, "YHVH". The name represents the nature of the person in all dimensions. When we begin to deal in heavenly dimensions, it is easy to confuse the fallen serpent with other serpents. When Satan fell, he did not fall as a lion. One of the reasons why Satan is considered a serpent is, even though he is a cherubim, he also takes the form of a seraphim. He fell in the form of a serpent. What was he doing when he fell? There's one word for it: deception. The same thing he was doing in Heaven that made him fall is the same thing he used to make man fall. The serpent is the nature he took on while he was speaking to the angels. It was the same nature he took on when he was speaking to the woman. Why would Satan take the form of a serpent? The serpents are the guardians of the throne room (but not the coverers of the throne).

There were two points of the transmutation of the genetics of some of the children of Israel in the wilderness. When the snakes bit them and when Aaron made the golden calf. There is a reason why it is dangerous to traffic in angels. It is easy to be misled. We must be able to make a distinction between those who are fallen. Not all demons are gross looking. This is why human beings fall into demonic processes. They operate based on need. Therefore, it is easy for people to be misled by fallen angels.

THE BREASTPLATE, THE TRIBES AND THE ZODIAC

"You shall make the breastplate of judgment. Artistically woven according to the workmanship of the ephod you shall make it: of gold, blue, purple, and scarlet *thread,* and fine woven linen, you shall make it." (Exo 28:15)

How many colors? Four. God's four letter name. Four basic colors. Four faces. Four dimensions.

"It shall be doubled into a square: a span *shall* be its length, and a span shall be its width. And you shall put settings of stones in it, four rows of stones: *The first* row *shall be* a sardius, a topaz, and an emerald; *this shall be* the first row; the second row *shall be* a turquoise, a sapphire, and a diamond; the third row, a jacinth, an agate, and an amethyst" (Exo 28:16-19)

In the Hebrew, 'jacinth' is "shem," a precious colored stone described as reddish orange or red and white. There is a reason it is mixed like that. The color that is given to Dan is a mixture. There are snakes that have red and white markings. Why would God place this on the chest of the High Priest? Remember, Dan will not be saved until the final days and he will not be saved as a Jew. He will be saved as a Gentile. That is why his name is not in the Book of Revelation. In fact, it seems that Dan is the precise reason why Christ came!

The next stone in the third row is an agate. It is a precious stone and it is a hard stone. In the Hebrew it is called Shibot, Sibbot or Shebo. If we play around with the Hebrew gematria numbers, we will see that this forms an ark. Every stone in the breastplate of the High Priest represents a tuning of a gateway for travel from one dimension to another. Every gateway represents the nature of the children of Israel and the dimension we are going through. This is why people in the occult, in the church and in all religions use stones as a way of communication. We don't need to use the stones now because we have become the stones.

"And you are living stones that God is building into his spiritual temple. What's more, you are his holy priests. Through the mediation of Jesus Christ, you offer spiritual sacrifices that please God." (1 Peter 2:5 NLT)

These stones were alive. They were living entities. Dimensions opened when the High Priest wore the breastplate with these stones and entered the Holy of Holies. He went from one gate, took the people in that gateway and went through all the other dimensions. He wore it upon his heart, so that his soul went through these stones in the breastplate and went through the person or the tribe that had done wrong. (He was also moving through the tribe whose sign was in ascendancy).

The Zodiac changes because it is '13'. Thirteen tribes. There was always a day left. The Day of Atonement shifts. Not much, but it does shift. Now we have programmed the calendar but that does not mean that the Heavens are programmed. They move in ascendancy and descent. They are not always in ascendancy. It depends on which epoch it is. Leo is Judah, who is the one who bears the responsibility for what Israel does. Why is it that Jesus is called the Lamb of God even though He is from Judah? And whose ascendancy is that? If we understand that, then we understand why He came as a lamb and why a lamb is the gateway. The tribe is also the gateway.

When the goat was sacrificed, the lot fell upon the tribe to take the goat into the wilderness. The person who carries the goat into the wilderness is the tribe that becomes the gateway for the burden-bearer. They cast a lot for who would take the goat because it was more precise. The lot fell upon a certain tribe.

Different tribes had different times.

If these stones represent tuning instruments for dimensions, should they be tuned according to a particular tribe at a particular time, so that a person can go through them? The 24 dimensions represent the Heavenly dimension, a microcosm of the whole dimension. The 12 Tribes are half of that dimension. The priest, by wearing the stones, is able to go through those dimensions in order to make atonement as the basis for the whole world! Was the sacrifice of Israel just for Israel? No, it was for the world. They thought it was just for them, but they were making a sacrifice for the whole world and for the cosmos!

Whenever Israel wanted to do something, they would ask on which tribe does the lot fall. For example, if they wanted to go to war, who shall go first? How did they know that David wants to go to war and he calls for the ephod. If there is a sin in Israel, a lot is cast to find out whose sin it is. That is what Joshua did. If a tribe goes astray on the Day of Atonement, those stones light up in a certain pattern and this determines what the priest is going to do and who gets called first. The stones sparkled, they emitted light once a sacrifice was made. This is not about the atonement itself but which tribe the High Priest goes through in order to be able to bring to redemption.

Now the length of Leo lasted a long time. The end of the time of the tribe of Benjamin was when Saul came, so he couldn't last longer than that. No matter what he did, his time was over. It was not an issue of sin but an issue of timing. Saul is a Benjamite. Benjamin is a wolf. He needs Joseph. (Ephraim was not there. Every time we ascend, we need something to hold us up. Neither Ephraim or Manasseh had the power at that time).

The color of Dan's stone is amber (also called jacinth or ligure). If the President says "code amber", it is a warning sign. It is the next color before red. The next stone is amethyst, of Asher. Asher brings joy. Amethyst is purple, but it is not a real precious stone.

It is a semi-precious stone. This is not about price, but symbols. Most of the stones in this breastplate have no real monetary value. It is not about the value of the stone, but the color and the nature of the stone. (If diamond supply was not artificially controlled they would be cheaper than ordinary amethyst. They are expensive because of the world's control of diamonds. A diamond is not that precious).

RULING AND JUDGING

Gad is king. He is the king of Earth. This is the tier where we have the lion and the power. Gad needs the joy of Asher. A king, without joy, is a dangerous king. A warrior, without joy, is a dangerous warrior. Dan became what he was because of bitterness. He was bitter about his inheritance. He was mad at God and his brothers, so he spent four thousand years killing off his brothers and everything that came out of Israel. The greatest enemy of Israel today are the Europeans. Everything Israel does, they stand against. They have killed more Jews than any other group in the world.

In this dimension we will find the principle of judgment that is poisoned by the serpent because of bitterness. We need the warrior who stands against the serpent. This is Gad, the defender of Israel as a king. Then we find Asher, who infuses the warrior with joy.

We are called to be a judge. We must understand the danger of being a judge. The danger of being a judge is acting out of bitterness and allowing our bitterness to become the basis of our judgment. This is where the arsenals of God are. These arsenals are embedded in the prayers of the saints, which are embedded in their DNA code! Revelation 5 says that when they brought the book before the Lamb, they looked all around the world to see who was going to open the book. There was nobody to open the book. Only the Lamb was able to open the seal of the book. When the Lord Jesus Christ opens the book, there is a line in the scriptures that says, "and in it was the prayers of the saints" (Rev 5:8). When the seals are broken creatures come out. They are God's instruments of war, hidden in the DNA of man. Who opens the book? The Lord Jesus Christ. Who is the book? We are.

When the time comes, when our prayers begin to be answered and our DNA is split, new things will begin to come out of us that God has put inside of us. If we are a written epistle then we are a written code. God has placed so many things in us in relation to our being. Every part of our DNA contains something so powerful and vital that, when we become who we are supposed to become, we can produce out of our being weapons of warfare!

God is working to bring under subjection the serpent in us. We all have Dan in us. The serpent is there. The lion must ascend so that the serpent can be trampled. The way to trample the serpent is by the expressing the categories of gratitude - a joyful exuberance - an existential response of gratitude. The serpent's poison comes from lack of gratitude, satisfaction, contentment and joy in what God gives to other people. The serpent thrives in work, not grace. We can make our self god by thinking God is cheating us, like in the Garden. Also, we do this when we feel He is not giving us enough based on what we have done for Him. When we start saying such things we have already missed the mark and disqualified our self from what God is going to do for us. We are now saying God must bless us based on our work, capacity and faithfulness.

If we expect God to work according to our words and statutes and He doesn't do it for the few minutes we are in friendship with Him, we get angry. We are no different from Dan because it started when he was not given what he thought belonged to him. He was offended and found himself another god.

The reason most people in church are not blessed is because

they disqualify themselves. The blessings of God in their lives are based on their own faithfulness. Whenever we think God should bless us because of our faithfulness we disqualify our self. Everything God does is a gift. If we must work for a gift, we are already disqualified for it. When we try to work for something and don't get it, we get bitter.

We want God to bless us based on the 10% we give for tithes. God wants to bless us out of His riches. By sticking to our 10% we have limited what God can do for us. When that 10% blessing doesn't come, we get angry. We are always comparing ourselves with other people, disqualifying our self from being blessed.

In this dimension of gratitude, while we have this capacity to be a warrior, this capacity to live in joyful exuberance and to enjoy God, we also have the tendency to live in hubris where we sit in judgment over God. If we sit in judgment over God, how is the blessing going to come? Blessings flow downward, not upward. If we are above God, what happens? How do we purify this? How did Isaiah purify this? By the coal touching the mouth and burning the tongue of the serpent. Now the tongue is cleansed!

Asher represents joy. When the king is joyful he has mercy on his captives. When the king is joyful he shows mercy in judgment. Dan's problem is serpentine by nature. Serpents don't show mercy unless their tongue has been burned. We bring a lot of things on our self and others with our mouth. We must be very careful when we say certain things or we end up projecting our self on to other people. Dan thinks he knows what God is thinking, that somehow God's intent is not pure. A person who misjudges God will misjudge other people.

God says that Ephraim is a snake that will not be charmed. A snake that will not be charmed has a problem because it will strike us. We can charm a snake through sound and vibration. They respond to vibration.

The ontology of gratitude is fueled by worship and praise. There is no dimension of Heaven where praise is not heard. Angels are attracted to praise. Snakes are even attracted to praise and they lose their poison. That is why David was such a powerful person. He could play music and charm serpents. It is all over the mythology of Apollo through the ancient world.

We lose and dissipate our energy by focusing on things we are not supposed to focus on, and by constantly agitating, using our energy to worry. We should not be reactionary to our circumstances, but intentional. We should not be moved by the so-called needs of human beings (like Reuben and Simeon). When we do something, we must do it out of intention. If we are so agitated because the things we want aren't happening, we only postpone what is supposed to happen.

Paul says knowledge puffs up (1 Cor 8:1). One of the things that we must learn as God's people is to take the knowledge that we have with a grain of salt. It is so easy to sit in judgment over other people when we know certain things. We must develop a level of humility before our brethren because we can be messed up by what we know. Celebrate everyone that stands in front of God's people. There is not a person who speaks that we cannot learn from.

We should never think someone else can not teach us or we cannot celebrate the Word of God, even when it comes out of the mouth of a donkey. It is hard. God must deal with us at a certain level for us to be able to do that. The Word of God is that deep. We could live a thousand lifetimes and not know the Word of God completely. We should never get to a place where we think we know everything. The things we know should show us how much we don't know. Never use knowledge to beat people over the head. This is what happens to a lot of academics.

When the Lord moved me from academia to do ministry I met people who didn't know much academically. When they opened their mouths, God always said something. So, I am always listening for God because He is always there, especially among His people.

Don't ever underestimate God's people. We should never think we are the only one who is doing what we are doing. (It may be true but that is only by God's discretion. If we die being the only one who can do what we do, then we haven't done our job!)

DEALING WITH THE SOUL

Moving through the Lower 12 Dimensions is not a simple matter of understanding the principles or even memorizing this book. It is a walk with the Godhead, to transmute your DNA into your true nature. This is not an intellectual exercise. It is not a solo exercise. We need the church in Heaven and Earth to help us, challenge us, encourage us and to strengthen our weaknesses.

All of Heaven wants you to mature, to experience these dimensions, so you can rule, judge and manifest the desires of Heaven into this realm. The lives of the Tribes of Israel are there to reveal what is possible in the heart of God and what is restricting in the heart of Man.

Be patient. Cry aloud for help. Rest in knowing you had it before you asked. God is a good Father. Mature sons was His idea! He has made provision through Christ for your every need in overcoming.

ABOUT THE AUTHOR

AACTEV8 International was founded by Adonijah Ogbonnaya (ATC, BA, MA Theol, MA, PhD Theol, PhD Bus. Publishing) and Benedicta Ogbonnaya as a Church Planting and Christian Education Service located in Venice, California. After twenty-five years in ministry, the Lord called Dr. Ogbonnaya in 2001 to expand his Ministry to allow full participation in the Fivefold Ministry by the total body of Christ. In 2003, Dr. Ogbonnaya moved into Apostolic Ministry by opening congregations and ministerial centers and holding meetings around the globe. Dr. Ogbonnaya is the founder and CEO of AACTEV8 International and is recognized as one of the foremost revelational Biblical teachers of our time. He has impacted the lives of hundreds of thousands of people nationally and internationally. AACTEV8's founder has published books and multi-media collections that have transformed many around the world.

HASHAMAYIM 2A AND 2B

After decades of cultivation and living in the secret place, Dr. O continues releasing this precious revelation upon the Earth. Hashamayim 2A and 2B will continue the discussions of the Nested Heavens by addressing the "12 Upper Kingdom Dimensions." These dimensions reveal how the Messiah fulfills the scriptures and, through the symbolic nature of the 12 apostles, how we can unlock the Upper Heaven.

SeraphCreative

Heaven's Heart for Earth

Seraph Creative is a collective of artists, writers, theologians
& illustrators who desire to see the body of Christ grow
into full maturity, walking in their inheritance as
Sons Of God on the Earth.

Sign up to our newsletter to know about the release of the
next book in the series, as well as other exciting releases.

Visit our website :
www.seraphcreative.org

ALTERNATE VIEWS OF THE ECOLOGY OF THE NESTED HEAVENS

The New Jerusalem
Revelation 21

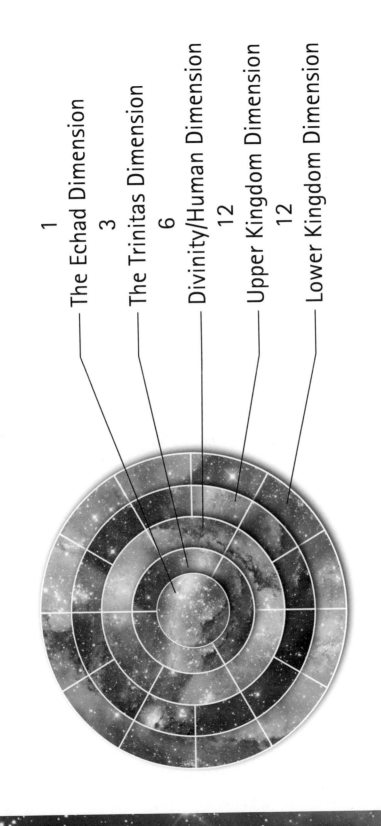

1
The Echad Dimension

3
The Trinitas Dimension

6
Divinity/Human Dimension

12
Upper Kingdom Dimension

12
Lower Kingdom Dimension

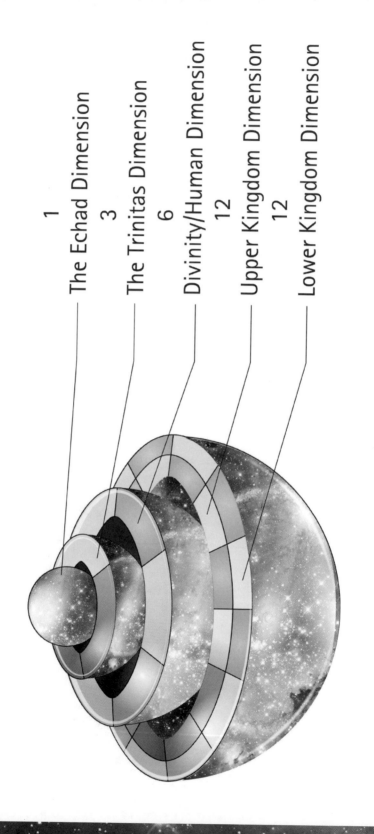

1
The Echad Dimension

3
The Trinitas Dimension

6
Divinity/Human Dimension

12
Upper Kingdom Dimension

12
Lower Kingdom Dimension

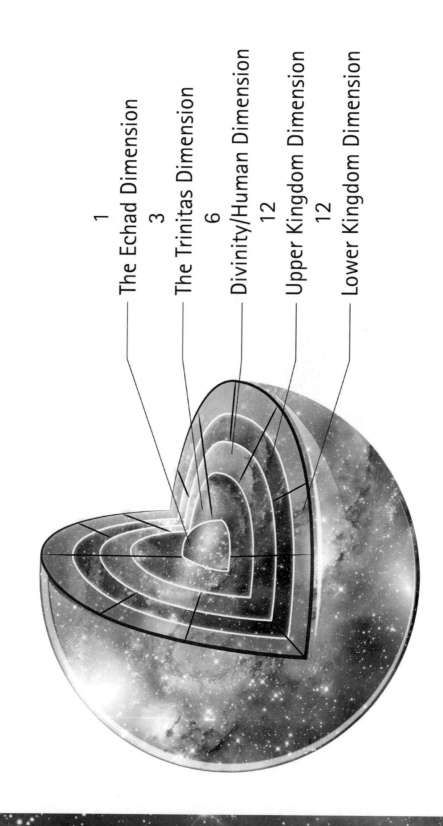

1
The Echad Dimension

3
The Trinitas Dimension

6
Divinity/Human Dimension

12
Upper Kingdom Dimension

12
Lower Kingdom Dimension

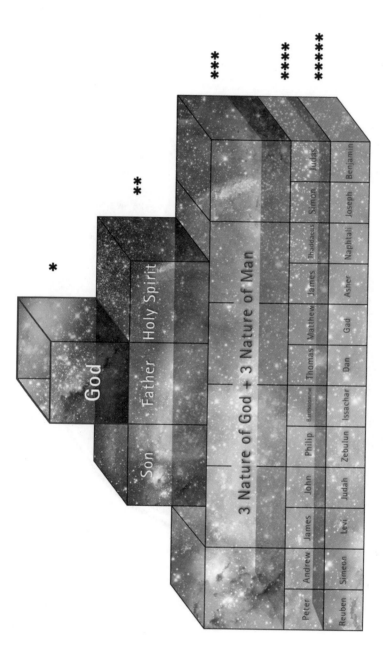

God

Son | Father | Holy Spirit

3 Nature of God + 3 Nature of Man

| Peter | Andrew | James | John | Philip | Bartholomew | Thomas | Matthew | James | Thaddaeus | Simon | Judas |
| Reuben | Simeon | Levi | Judah | Zebulun | Issachar | Dan | Gad | Asher | Naphtali | Joseph | Benjamin |

*   – The Echad Dimension: The Person of God (not a heaven) Deut 6:4

**   – The Trinitias Dimension: God in 3 Persons (not a heaven)

***   – The Divinity / Human Intersection Dimension: The Embodiment of God in Man (a created heaven of 6 dimensions)

**** – The Upper Kingdom Intersection Dimension: The Sons Of God (a created heaven of 12 dimensions)

***** – The Lower Kingdom Intersection Dimension: The Sons of Israel (a created heaven of 12 dimensions)

CW00558075

Who Writes the Rules?

… For Living in an Over-Populated,
Multi-Cultural, Dying Society

A novel by

Norman George

Copyright © 2022 by Norman George

All rights reserved. No part of this book may be reproduced or
used in any manner without written permission of the copyright
owner except for the use of quotations in a book review.

All characters in this publication are ficticious. Any resemblance
to real persons , living or dead, is purely coincidental.

FIRST EDITION: December 2022
Cover Art and Photography: Norman George

Paperback ISBN: 978-1-7392330-0-6

To Scientific Reasoning and Common Sense

"Nothing in biology makes sense except in the light of evolution."
- Theodosius Dobzhansky

"When the soul of a man is born in this country there are nets flung at it to hold it back from flight. You talk to me of nationality, language, religion. I shall try to fly by those nets."
- James Joyce

"Imagine there's no countries - It isn't hard to do.
Nothing to kill or die for - And no religion too."
- John Lennon

"$e=mc^2$."
- Albert Einstein

"Greenhouse gas emissions keep growing. Global temperatures keep rising. And our planet is fast approaching tipping points that will make climate chaos irreversible. We are on a highway to climate hell with our foot on the accelerator … Humanity has a choice: cooperate or perish."
- UN Secretary-General António Guterres
COP27 Climate Change Summit, November 2022

Acknowledgements

Nearly two decades ago, the spark of an idea was triggered by events in the early 2000s, including melting glaciers, rainforest and habitat destruction, exponential human population growth, refusal to accept man-made causes of climate change, wars, the plight of refugees, terrorist atrocities driven by fundamentalist hatred … The idea was a desire to embed scientific arguments and debate into a novel, thereby encouraging people who wouldn't normally read scientific literature to reflect on those thoughts. The spark became a slow-burning passion, gradually spreading until the opportunity arose to feed the flames.

For the first cells in Thera's chemical pools to flourish and evolve into modern, complex life forms, it was sex and oxygen which eventually provided the impetus. Retirement in 2021 provided me with the time and opportunity to develop the spark into *Who Writes the Rules*. However, like evolution, that spark was driven by an environmental change that fed and steered it until it became a completed book.

I owe a debt of gratitude to the following people who have provided nourishment and direction through their comments, reviews and constructive feedback.

Marty Kennedy, a trusted friend since our

schooldays, had to suffer the initial versions of the earlier chapters: heavy on science and lacking a plot. Marty's opinions convinced me that I needed to keep the science simple and readable while concentrating the focus on the interactions of the protagonists.

As the story developed, the honest opinions of my children, Alex, Louise and Chris, were encouraging. Reviews from Alastair MacDowell, Geoff Thornton and Anna Thornton reassured me that the science was on the right track, while the plot was reasonably engaging.

Thanks are due to my wife, Mags, for remaining patient while my head was stuck in the clouds around Thera, being a soundboard for ideas and debates, and suggesting the Python-esque epilogue title.

I am indebted to Julie Helliwell, who reviewed and copy-edited the later versions of the text, refining it into the structured and hopefully readable, finished novel.

At the time of writing (November 2022), earth and humanity are teetering on the brink of a precipice, over which lies catastrophic environmental disaster and the potential annihilation of life from starvation and nuclear war. We can only hope that the social and political leaders of all our cultural divisions will embrace the Scientific Reasoning and Common Sense that will lead them to work towards consensus and harmony.

Who Writes the Rules

Chapter 1. Thera and the Majans

From a mountain ridge, a figure regarded the glaciers across the valley. Extending tongues of luminous white, blue and grey flowed imperceptibly downward, grating the mountains which bore them. The creeping ice scoured away rock fragments, reshaping the terrain. Powdered remnants of millions of years of rock crystallisation leaked into rivulets, cascades and torrents, which merged into ever-growing rivers. The seas were eventually fed with sediment that would one day be sucked back into the bowels of the planet. The figure was known as Mosse within his society: a cultural group that called their species Majans and their planet Thera.

There were many cultural groups among the Majans. Their cultures were separated by the languages they spoke, the geographical areas they inhabited, and the social, moral and political frameworks within which their societies functioned. However, all shared a common biology and species identity. A common original region in which their species had evolved before migrating around their planet. Over the course of thousands of generations, their populations had grown, spread, clashed, mixed, fought, interbred and competed. Their differences had diverged while their biology remained virtually unchanged. When different cultures met, they competed for land, food and the planet's resources. This often resulted in wars, carnage, and either disappearance, suppression or assimilation of the defeated group.

Mosse lived during a time when there was little room left for the expansion of his species. A time of famine, food shortage and social tension. A time when the environment and the habitats of other species were in a state of steady deterioration and impending destruction. Many Majan societies possessed weapons so powerful that to use them would assure annihilation – not just of their enemies but also of the planetary resources upon which they themselves depended. Only the necessary but usually reluctant cooperation with other cultures allowed the major political groups to coexist in an uneasy truce, which could not be called harmony.

Individual Majans were quite varied in appearance. Some very distinctive differences exaggerated the divergence between cultural groups, which had been geographically separated for many generations. However, they shared a common anatomy, physiology and biochemistry. Their bodies were constructed from many cell types. In each cell, oxidation of carbohydrates provided the energy required by biochemical processes. Their development from single fertilised eggs into adults was coded by the base sequence of deoxyribonucleic acid (DNA) molecules. The DNA base sequence was arranged into genes. The genes coded for unique proteins and how they interacted in the biochemical pathways inside each cell type.

Adults ranged from below 1.5 metres to more than 2 metres in height. Their body structure was based on a central trunk, carried above two locomotory appendages. Two additional appendages on the upper trunk were used for the manipulation of external devices. At the top of the

9

Who Writes the Rules

trunk was a control and coordination centre. The control centre processed electronic signals from many sensory devices. These were triggered by external changes in light, sound, pressure, temperature and environmental chemistry. The signals were interpreted into complex maps of the environment, which triggered subconscious control instructions. Carried to organs and muscles by nerves, the instructions managed movements and changes in body chemistry. In the control centre, the instructions governed the analytic and decision-making processes, which the Majans believed defined their distinctive intelligence as a species.

The Majans regarded themselves as the most advanced of the many species that shared their planet. In reality, it was only in mental and physical manipulation and communication that they were particularly gifted. They couldn't fly. They couldn't breathe underwater. They couldn't photosynthesise or perform various other tasks at which numerous species excelled. Yet their arrogance led them to believe that they were a superior species. The criterion for justifying their superiority was their complex reasoning ability. Unfortunately, this wasn't always put to optimal use.

At 1.75 metres, Mosse was a male of average height, lightly built and moderately athletic. He might be regarded as moderately handsome by a female of his species. He was 40 years old, approximately half the lifespan of a healthy Majan. He had piercing grey-blue eyes and dirty-blond hair. His skin had a reddish-gold tan from spending much of his time outdoors. In his leisure time, he trekked on the mountains, whose grandeur inspired a love of the nature which surrounded him.

He had once lived in a crowded city, where he had worked as an engineer in IT communications support. Working in an office, he had become disillusioned by the selfish, competitive and predatory behaviour of many peers. While IT support had provided an income, it had always been a means to an end. His real love had always been natural science and life. He had moved recently to what was previously a holiday house in the mountains. Here, he could enjoy an outdoor life and pursue the study of natural history. The physical formation of his planet. The history and interactions of the living entities that covered it, including his own species.

Mosse observed the creatures who shared his adopted homeland. Green plants and shrubs adorned sloping meadows, which climbed out of dark green forests. Grey crags and glaciers spilled from the sky. In summer, a multitude of yellow, white and blue flowers transformed the hillsides into a colourful carpet. On the meadows, insects danced while domesticated and wild grazing animals feasted on the seasonal growth. Silhouetted against the deep blue sky, feathered hunters glided on rising thermals. Their sharp eyes focussed below to catch the slightest plant movement that would betray the final location of a small grazer.

The dramatic landscape presented a varied and beautiful but delicate tapestry containing a wealth of habitats. Variations in altitude, aspect, exposure, geology and microclimate all housed their own particular group of specialist populations. Each diverse locality supported a specific niche. The populations within each interacted as components of a dynamic machine. Fuelled by radiant energy, the machine rolled forward over seasons and years, adapting to long-term environmental changes.

Over recent years, Mosse had witnessed the glaciers recede upwards, leaving tell-tale grey-black plumes of moraine debris. Ridges of broken rock dropped at the sides and ends of the ice tongues too recently to support more than a few annual plant species.

For billions of years, the surface of the planet Thera had functioned as an integrated, complex system rolling slowly forward through time. Now, the machine was shuddering. Weather patterns had always varied, usually over long periods of time. However, all over the planet was evidence that the atmosphere was now warming rapidly. The receding glaciers were just one of many consequences.

Most of his contemporaries saw their environment as a static picture. Their current visual images had permanence in their perceptions. They struggled to imagine the future. They failed to notice the continuous re-sculpting of the landscape by nature's elemental forces.

They considered their kind to be at the top of an evolutionary ladder. At a pinnacle below which all other species showed increasing inferiority as their degree of relationship to the Majans diminished. They failed to recognise that their species, like every other on the planet, was just an eddy in the grand flow of life. A swirl that had rippled out of the main flow and would roll and twist with it for a short distance. It interacted with all surrounding ripples, but would soon dissipate as a definable entity. The Majans were no more highly evolved than any other creature. From the tiniest cell to the most complex animal, all were about three billion years downstream from their earliest common ancestor.

Mosse's studies had taught him that the planet was a dynamic system in a perpetual state of motion. A machine with solid, aquatic, atmospheric and living components resonating in harmony as the entirety rolled along. Mountains grew in response to movements and pressures from deep within. They eventually eroded as ice and water ate their way through the surface layers. Landmasses and seas were continually reshaped by natural forces over many years. The ocean currents set the wind and rain in motion. Air and water distributed the heat absorbed from the radiation of Sol – the star around which Thera orbited.

He could see that the activities of his species were causing changes in climate that accelerated parts of the machine. Now, the glaciers across the valley were melting faster than any frozen precipitation could be accumulated into new glacial ice. Eventually, they would disappear – maybe even within his lifetime. The spectacular beauty he witnessed today would be lost to future generations.

It frustrated him that his species were divided into many groups by cultural boundaries. They were obsessed with their own differences and power struggles. They failed to heed warnings or take actions that might save the environment which had produced them. The mechanism upon which they were dependent for their existence was now being disrupted and fragmented. The continued presence of life on Thera was threatened.

From his rocky vantage point, he thought about how this dynamic world had flowed smoothly along a natural progression. The flow now disturbed since the

Who Writes the Rules

arrival of modern Majan society. How could his species be made aware of the reality of their flickering existence in the enormity of time? An existence that might be quickly snuffed out by their own destructive actions.

Some distance along the ridge, Mosse could see a figure. Dressed in red and black, they were easily visible against the pale yellow-green of a flower-covered meadow. Another individual was sharing the beauty of the mountain vista. Possibly a female Majan? The distance between them made it impossible to tell.

Female Majans were generally a little smaller than males. They were usually physically less powerful, yet they often compensated with their powers of intelligent manipulation and persuasion. Skills by which they could frequently encourage the males to bend to their will.

Heelia was a tourist from a neighbouring country, taking a short break in the mountains. She liked exploring the trails where mountain flowers bloom in the early summer. An attractive, fairly young adult in her early 30s, Heelia stood at 1.60 tall. She had almost black hair, olive-brown skin, and deep brown, engaging eyes. Her dark complexion contrasted with a bright red tee-shirt, complemented by black shorts. The combination tightly hugged a curvaceous but athletic torso, emphasising a healthy, elegant figure.

Originating from a different nation and culture, Heelia spoke a different first language. She had a different perspective of life on the planet Thera from Mosse. Their worldviews contrasted; however, the pair shared a love of the outdoors, the natural environment and the dramatic scenery of the mountains.

Mosse's fascination with nature and the mountain environment stimulated his innate curiosity. How had the landscape come into existence over the aeons of time?

Thera was a world born from a nebular cloud of spinning gases and debris. This had been produced by the supernova explosion of a star five billion years earlier.

The process of planet formation followed the natural rules of chemistry and physics. There were laws of nature which drove the inevitable march of chemical evolution along thermodynamically predefined pathways. A continual flow of cosmic energy cooked elements into ever more complex chemical compounds. Natural processes were driven by the need to absorb and dissipate free energy in search of a state of equilibrium.

The Majan astronomers and mathematicians had determined that the known Universe began 14 billion years earlier. The Universe is energy, and energy is the Universe. It started with a big bang, releasing all that energy in the biggest explosion ever. The Universe is an inconceivably large pulse of immense heat and radiation rushing out from the smallest point unimaginable. It wants to spread, to cool down, to fill any void. To reach equilibrium where all instability will have been reduced to stable particles of equal temperature.

Some of the Majans believe the Universe was created and set in motion by an intelligent super-being. That would suffice to explain how it all began. While this may satisfy their curiosity, it leaves the origin of the super-being unexplained. Unless he, too, was created by a super-being,

Who Writes the Rules

who was created by a super-being, who was … ad infinitum.

Mosse did not accept theories of super-beings creating the Universe. Everything he had learned about science convinced him that the Universe *is* outwardly spreading energy. Heat flows forward through time, cooling down as it goes.

Heelia preferred to appreciate and admire, without feeling any need to find explanations. Mysteries in life could be attributed to divine creation.

As it spreads and cools, energy condenses into particulate matter, detectable as elemental atoms. It becomes hydrogen, oxygen, nitrogen, carbon, and all those many substances that unite to make the stars, the planets and everything on and between them. Stars are chemical factories that combine elements into more complex ones. But when they do, one plus one in elemental mass is less than two. The mass that is lost during this fusion of elements is released as more pulses of energy. The Majans knew this to be true. A very clever scientist had predicted that these mass differences would be replaced by bursts of radiant energy. This was the energy they could sense from Sol, or convert to electricity in a nuclear reactor. The energy which they could release from an atomic explosion above a population centre of an adversary culture.

As the Universal energy races outwards, coalescing particles attract one another due to electrostatic and gravitational forces. As growing masses of matter are formed, all of the weight of an accumulating mass presses inwards towards its centre. When one of these masses reaches a certain size, its internal temperature and pressure climb above a threshold. The processes that combine elements and release more energy are triggered. This is known as the burning of nuclear fuel. It causes stars to shine brightly.

Once a star has used all of its nuclear fuel, much of its matter will cool rapidly and contract. As it collapses inwards under its own gravity, the collapse ends with an explosion called a supernova. A supernova explosion is another part of the cycle of element production. It results in the formation of metals and heavy elements, many of which are unstable and release energy as radioactivity.

Nearly five billion years before the Majan species emerged on Thera, a star exploded into a supernova. It scattered a massive swirling cloud of all the elements it had produced during its existence. For perhaps half a billion years, the cloud contents condensed into larger and larger bodies. These merged and continued to swirl around the centre. Most of the material accumulated in a central mass. When it reached the threshold which ignited its nuclear fuel, a new star, Sol, was born. The remaining material in the cloud formed smaller bodies. These orbited Sol in the form of planets and their satellite moons. Each planet was different in character, size and surface temperature.

On one planet, the surface conditions were perfectly tuned to support the evolution of complex chemicals into living organisms. The organisms would gradually subdivide into separate, individual species. Eventually, one species with specialised manipulative and communicative abilities would name the planet Thera and themselves Majans. The Majans strove to understand the planet which they inhabited. However, their misuse and misunderstanding of the universal energy from which they were derived threatened to destroy themselves and all other life forms.

Heelia admired the mountain panoramas. The walk to the ridge had been tough but worth the effort. All around her, aesthetically pleasing images, dramatic peaks, colourful flowers and the distant glaciers excited her sense of wonder. The high forests must be havens of strange, mythical creatures, dangerous animals, reclusive wizards and witches – never to be entered after sunset. But in the daytime, the fairies could fly, and children pick flowers. Resting trekkers like herself could amuse themselves by conjuring up childhood story scenes. It seemed that the mountains had been there forever, or at least since the creation of the planet Thera.

Thera was roughly 6.5 thousand kilometres from centre to surface. It had a tilted axis around which it rotated as it orbited Sol. The spinning and orbiting were quite fast, to begin with, slowing gradually. By the emergence of the Majans, a day was about 20-something Earth hours. A year was about 300 and something Theran days. The tilt of its axis meant that it had an exposure to radiation from Sol that was fairly constant around its equatorial belt. However, it had increasing seasonal extremes towards each pole. This resulted in a northern hemisphere summer during southern hemisphere winter, and vice-versa.

Thera's single moon, Luna, produced a gravitational pull which interacted with that of Sol. This caused tidal flows of the large water masses, which would later develop on its surface. Gradual changes in the tilt and the shape of Thera's orbit meant that seasonal differences were not constant. They followed cyclical variations in extremes, lasting for tens of thousands of years.

The material of Thera was a mixture of around 90 elements; oxygen and silicon were the most abundant. There were various metals, including aluminium, iron, sodium, calcium, magnesium and potassium. Other non-metallic elements such as sulphur, nitrogen and carbon would be important for the evolution of life. These elements usually reacted to form the molecules that were often found in silicate minerals, metal oxides and complex gases. The young planet had much water vapour, nitrogen and gaseous compounds mixed into a hot, acidic atmosphere.

The mountain landscape that Heelia was admiring had not been created in a moment. In the early years, most of Thera was molten, pitted, rutted and bubbling. Magma flowed over a surface bombarded by asteroids, meteorites and comets. Planetary gravity sucked in the remaining masses of material from space. The surface and atmosphere gradually cooled sufficiently for water vapour to form clouds. These released torrential acidic rain onto the hot surface. All recesses were slowly filled until embryonic oceans spread on a thin but solid crust. The interior of the planet was primarily a hot, extremely viscous fluid. Heavier minerals sank towards the centre, displacing lighter ones. These were carried slowly up towards the surface by convection currents. This carried immense heat from the central core towards the surface, melting and fracturing the crust.

Have you ever slowly boiled a pan of soup or maybe custard? Heat does not spread evenly through the pan. It is carried upwards in globules or cells of warm

19

substance. The heat is dispersed as it rises to the surface. It releases a bubble of vapour when it gets there. Now imagine the pan is 6500 km deep and spherical, with its main heat source right at the centre. The blobs rise, slowly, slowly, eventually approaching a cool surface on which a thin skin has formed. Blobs first make contact with the lowest-lying part of the skin, warming it from below and causing it to stretch and rupture.

Some of the hotter, liquid custard may emerge at the surface, pushing the broken skin sideways. Since the skin rests on liquid custard, it doesn't crumple but is displaced. It flows as a flat unit across the surface. In a saucepan, it would crumple against the edges of the pan, as it has nowhere else to go. In a spherical mass of convecting custard, globules would rise at different places. Each would break the surface and produce some displacement of the skin.

For each area of displacement by new, rising custard, an equal area will be lost. It must either crumple or sink back into the underlying liquid.

And thus, it was on Thera. As the planet's surface began to form its first crust, rising cells of magma caused breaches in this. These were usually in the deepest part of the oceans, where the crust was thinnest and closest to the planet's core. At its surface, the crust eventually developed into a patchwork of plates. These slid very, very slowly over a hotter and more fluid mantle layer. In some places, displaced plates pressed together, causing crumpling of the surface. This pushed up mountains over tens of millions of years. In other places, a plate would slide under an adjacent one, causing earthquakes and volcanic eruptions. This plate collision caused lifting of the overlying plate to a higher altitude, thereby producing volcanic mountains.

The crustal skin on the planet Thera was formed by rising magma breaching the crust along ocean floor ridges. Ocean crust spread away in a continuous plate of basalt rock formed from the cooling magma. As the basalt moved away from a ridge, it slowly cooled and became denser. Oceans would gradually widen as the crust extended from the ridge.

Where plates collided, as they spread away from ridges, the volcanic minerals that were ejected were lighter. These formed rocks which floated on the basalt like whipped cream on top of the custard. The heavier basalt plate would sink downwards, back towards the mantle from which it had originated. The lighter minerals accumulated to form continental landmasses, separated by ocean basins.

From when plates had first been set in motion, the lighter, floating masses slowly began to accumulate into continents. These were carried around the planet like ocean islands held up by the heavier, underlying crustal mass. In the course of time, the continental mountains would be eroded by atmospheric conditions and weather. They would be washed back to the sea in river sediments. The sediments would ultimately be carried under colliding plates and then regurgitated in the volcanic output at colliding plate bound- aries in another cycle of mountain building. The planet Thera was a complex, interacting system. The motion of oceans and continents fuelled by the immense heat of its core was a continual process.

The ridge where Heelia stood and the scenery she was admiring had not been there since the creation of the

Who Writes the Rules

planet. The oceans, continents and mountain ranges had been in perpetual motion for the past four billion years. The vista before her had been lifted, tilted and constantly re-sculpted during the last few million years of this period. It continued to change imperceptibly slowly.

Sol was a cog in the expansion of the Universe, formed by the coalescence of elements since the Big Bang. Thera was a smaller cog, carrying energy from a hot, radioactive interior to a surface and atmosphere. From there it could be lost to space.

In the few billion years after its initial formation, the surface of Thera had provided a canvas. A canvas upon which the radiance of Sol rearranged the simplest elements to paint a colourful picture of harmonious nature. A picture the Majans would eventually scorch, dissolve and trample upon.

Mosse's world was that scorched, dissolved, trampled planet. To begin to reverse the damage, the Majans must comprehend how their planet functioned as a system. They needed to recognise the limits of their relevance within the Universe.

Majan societies were governed by rules that divided them according to religions, nationalities, and political and linguistic barriers. These divisions created rivalries and power struggles: conflicts which had only detrimental effects on the planet. Their cultural rules and the barriers they created were the fundamental cause of the planet's problems.

The problems affecting life on the planet Thera would not be easily resolved. Mosse believed that all nations and cultures needed to endorse a common set of principles. A doctrine which would unite them as one species sharing a planet that they must protect for their own self-preservation. However, it seemed more likely that the depth of divisions between Majan societies would likely lead to global conflict.

Already, leaders of nations with almost irreconcilably opposed views had their fingers close to buttons which could set loose a nuclear holocaust. Would any of them attempt a pre-emptive strike?

The grandeur of the mountains had initiated Mosse's curiosity about their origin and the processes that had shaped and governed his planet. They harboured a great diversity of life. They included many delicately balanced niches and habitats. Once, they had presented a wilderness. Now Majan habitation and activities pushed ever deeper and higher, displacing the wild.

Mosse liked to climb on footpaths to a high point on a favourite ridge. From here, he could survey a panoramic landscape for many miles around. He could imagine how it had come to take its current form over millions of years. At 2,500 metres above sea level, he found fossils of creatures that had swum in deep oceans more than 100 million years earlier. Their skeletal or shelly remains had been preserved in ocean sediments. These were subsequently compressed into rock strata.

The rocks would eventually be lifted and tilted by the dynamics of moving crustal plates. They would finally be exposed by erosion of the scree slope on a mountain ridge. The rocks themselves told a story of hundreds of millions of years of history of the planet's surface.

23

Who Writes the Rules

The Majans might destroy many habitats in the coming years, but one day, their own history would be compressed into a thin layer of rock on a mountain somewhere.

Chapter 2. The Thunderstorm

Heelia breathed deeply from the effort of trekking up the steep track to the ridge. Expecting only sunshine during her climb, she had dressed lightly in a tee-shirt and shorts. She wore sturdy walking boots and carried a small backpack containing money, a snack and a bottle of water. When she had left the hotel that morning, the air temperature was warmer than expected, if a little humid. Sol was shining brightly from a cloudless sky. She had seen no need to prepare for adverse weather.

She had hiked along a mud and gravel trail, wide enough to drive up in an off-road vehicle. The trail was used mainly as a ski piste in winter and a walking track the rest of the year.

Many Majans liked to participate in winter sports that involved strapping plastic and metal, low-friction planks to their feet. They would then hurl themselves down slopes covered in compacted snow, sometimes reaching quite high speeds. This was despite the fact that their bodies were formed from soft tissues encasing their bony skeletal structure. A body type which did not fare well when they impacted hard objects at high speed.

The trail had been suggested to her by Mila, the receptionist at the hotel in Carina where she had arrived the previous day. Mila had arranged for a taxi to drop Heelia off at a parking area at 1,450 metres altitude. There was an adjacent, recommended mountain restaurant where she might choose to have lunch. Since she didn't know what time she might return from walking, Heelia had told Mila that she would find her own way back to the hotel, but she took a contact number as a precaution.

The trail had risen gently, zig-zagging around hairpins as it had ascended through forest. It bridged several small streams which gurgled downslope towards larger torrents below, draining the hillside. Emerging from the forest after an hour's ascent to 1,700 metres, Heelia had crossed a flower-covered meadow traversing a wide ridge. There were open mountain vistas to either side. The ridge climbed steadily in front of her for about one kilometre to an altitude of 1,900 metres. It then rose quite steeply to 2,100 metres over the next 500 metres of trail. Heelia's destination was a viewing point at 2,100 metres, offering a magnificent view of the ice cap and glaciers coating the White Mountain and the massif of peaks and ridges that surrounded it.

Arriving at 1,900 metres, Heelia gazed up the path which ascended to the viewpoint. Her legs were already tired from the ascent. The path would be difficult. The irregular terrain was as steep as a staircase, which would force her to use her arms and legs. The trail, cut by rainwater and the regular pressure from walking boots, was an obstacle course of rocks, boulders and wet mud. It was not quite a rock climb, but a very difficult walk, requiring both hands and feet where the gradient was steepest.

Having come this far, Heelia was determined not to be beaten by the ascent. As she approached it, several other walkers had descended past her. Some were much older than her.

"If they can do it, I can do it," Heelia had assured herself. And she did. Methodically moving between the boulders, she used whatever leverage was available to assist her progress. She pushed herself upwards until she emerged at the 2,100-metre vantage point. As she looked over the top of the path, the scene that had been obscured by the sloping mountainside opened up in front of her.

The ice cap at the summit of the White Mountain was 15 kilometres away, but somehow looked as if she could reach out and touch it. Sweeping towards her from the summit was an array of ice-covered peaks and ridges. Glaciers were pouring off them like icing on a badly made cake. The top of the White Mountain was nearly 5,000 metres above sea level. She stood at 2,100 metres altitude. Steep slopes and sheer cliffs dropped downwards in front of her into a deep, linear valley that separated her from the icy massif to the east.

Heelia's vantage point offered an open panorama totalling about 300 degrees on three sides. Running southwards from her position, the trail continued along a flat ridge for 500 metres. It then climbed over the following 500 metres to an altitude of 2,500. Mila had told her that she could continue beyond the first vantage point to the 2,500-metre summit. However, she knew that might be pushing herself too far on her first day up the mountain.

She decided to rest and enjoy the view for a while. Choosing the least uncomfortable dry boulder she could find, she sat down to eat her snack. Hypnotised by the breathtaking scenery across the valley to the east, Heelia failed to notice the dark storm clouds creeping towards her from the western horizon.

As Mosse climbed higher, the atmosphere became

Who Writes the Rules

clearer, holding less dust and moisture. The radiation from Sol included deadly levels of high-frequency ultraviolet, but most of the ultraviolet was absorbed by an upper layer of ozone in the atmosphere. Fortunately, this offered some protection to those creatures that lived on the planet's surface.

The pigmentation of Mosse's weather-beaten complexion helped prevent some of the potential damage to his skin cells from the high energy of solar radiation. It was prudent to use sunscreen for additional protection, particularly at altitudes where ultraviolet light was intense in the clear mountain air.

For more than an hour, Mosse had strolled along the ridge. Now he was watching the sky darkening above the peaks to the west. Towering, purple-blue clouds engulfed distant mountaintops as warm, humid air ascended. Mingling with colder air at higher altitudes, moisture condensed into billowing expanses of heavy droplets. He began to descend at a brisk and determined pace. He was sufficiently familiar with the deadly power of lightning. It would be very wise to seek refuge from the approaching storm.

In early summer, the heat and humidity would frequently generate dramatic thunderstorms. Their spectacle thrilled Mosse. Since childhood, he had watched for the flashes, then counted the delay before the thunder arrived. As the delay became shorter, signalling the approach of the storm, the urgency of finding refuge indoors would increase.

There was nothing unusual about the occurrence of a thunderstorm. However, to Mosse, it seemed that they had become more dramatic, more powerful and more damaging in recent years. The thunder and lightning would often be accompanied by a deluge of torrential rain. This could cause sudden, localised flooding. Sometimes large hailstones tore the leaves from trees. Occasionally, on steeper slopes, waterlogged soil and stones would be destabilised by the deluge. A fluid mass might free itself from the bedrock, chasing gravity until it came to rest at a lower position. Everything in its path would be flattened and destroyed. Obliterated!

In many areas, the natural forest vegetation had been cleared. Historically this was for animal grazing. In more recent years, this clearance was accelerated for use by habitation and winter sports development. Forest had been replaced by open meadows. Removal of natural barriers increased the risk of flooding, landslips and avalanches. Only recently had the Majans learned to pay attention to such hazards when choosing the sites for the construction of new habitations. Yet still, they made mistakes in their choices: mistakes which would become apparent following deadly avalanches.

Mosse did not intend to wait on the mountainside to discover the strength of the storm. He could sense the increasing humidity. His shirt began to cling to his skin. Despite its sultry warmth, the air was too wet to evaporate his sweat. Occasional gusts of warm, damp air rushed up the mountainside, attacking the growing storm clouds and carrying moisture into the angry sky. He quickened his movements. A rugged track led towards a lodge at the bottom of a cirque a good 800 metres below him. The rough path had been carved into the mountain meadow by the flow from previous rainfall. Concentration was needed to

Who Writes the Rules

negotiate it carefully to avoid twisting a limb.

Several trails converged at the lodge as they dropped from different viewpoints on the ridge above the cirque. Scanning the mountainside, Mosse could see a number of figures making their way quickly down the hillside. Driven on by the rumbling of distant thunder, they were all heading for the shelter offered by the lodge. A solitary figure trailed far above the others, easily visible in a bright red top and black shorts.

The humidity condensed into droplets as it rose. These then chilled at high altitude, forming ice crystals, which collided and mingled in the swirling mass of cloud. Their friction shifted electrons, producing electrostatic charge gradients. Electrical energy would accumulate, with differing polarities between cloud faces and between cloud and ground. At a certain threshold, the charge difference would ionise a pathway in the air. An electrical pulse would dash through the pathway in a split second to seek equilibrium. The pulse of electric discharge released heat, light and a reverberating shock wave. The shock wave boomed and rumbled into the ears of those creatures whose auditory senses could detect it.

Heelia, a visitor to the area, was unused to the mountain climate. She had been taken by surprise by the rapidity of the change in weather conditions. That morning, she had left her hotel dressed in light summer clothes. Sol shone brightly, and the sky was a clear, azure blue. She had brought a small backpack containing a few necessities, but no waterproof overclothes.

She had spent the morning walking up a long,

undulating path. This took her to a position on the same ridge from where Mosse had started his descent. Admiring the panorama from the top, she had paid little attention to the clouds building on the horizon until she noticed the temperature drop and heard the faintly echoing grumbling of thunder in the distance.

Then she had started along the nearest trail towards the valley bottom, zig-zagging downwards into the cirque. Her heartbeat and breathing quickened as she tried to descend a rocky, slippery footpath.

Nature is governed by irrevocable physical laws, which always seek stability and equilibrium. As the energy of the Universe spread ever outward, particulate matter formed, seeking equilibrium by creating stable molecular products. In storm clouds, electrical discharge reduces polarisation to seek electrostatic equilibrium. Electrical storms reduce charge differences. Excited atoms and molecules redistribute their energy, cooling themselves while warming those previously colder. The most fundamental law of nature was that energy would flow down a gradient, flowing from hotter to colder, until stability was achieved.

For half a billion years after its initial formation, Thera had been bombarded by asteroids and comets. Additional materials accumulated as the hot surface was cratered. Gradually the bombardment had diminished. The surface had formed a crust of slowly moving plates. The dust-filled atmosphere consisted mainly of gases which belched from volcanoes. Nitrogen and ammonia, hydrogen and methane, water vapour, carbon dioxide and hydrogen sulphide accumulated. Fast rotation around the planet's axis

Who Writes the Rules

produced rapid and powerful winds that whipped dust and water vapour into heavy clouds. Transported violently upwards by convection, their mass became illuminated by dramatic lightning bolts discharging immense electrostatic forces.

The electrical storm that was approaching Mosse and Heelia would be considerably less energetic than those which had ionised Thera's atmosphere in the early years after the planet's formation. At that time, the atmosphere lacked oxygen. This would not be able to accumulate until there were sufficient photosynthesising life forms to release it. Any free oxygen would quickly react with hydrogen to produce water vapour, or would combine with metals in their oxidation at the planet's surface. Lack of oxygen meant that there was no ozone layer to block the full intensity of ultraviolet radiation from Sol. Ultraviolet radiation supplemented the energy of electrical discharges. This assisted the ionisation of atmospheric gases, enabling their rearrangement into new molecular products.

Elements produced by a star such as Sol may exist as individual ions in a plasma while they remain entrapped at the high temperatures associated with thermo-nuclear reactions. However, those basic laws of physics meant that atoms would seek the most stable configuration they could achieve within their environment. At the lower temperatures found on the planet Thera, most elements formed molecular complexes by reacting with other elements.

The intense ultraviolet radiation and electrical pulses energised atmospheric gas molecules to form charged ions. These were then free to react with ions from other gases. New, more complex molecules were produced, including amino acids and nucleotides. These were the precursor building blocks of proteins and nucleic acids: the fundamental components in the construction of organic, carbon-based life forms.

The intense storms in the early Theran atmosphere produced torrential rain. Dust particles and organic molecules were washed to the hot surface of the planet. As the surface cooled to below 100°C, water began to accumulate in pools on the planet's surface. These eventually grew into oceans covering three-quarters of the planet. The atmospheric conditions and the chemistry of the planet's surface gradually led to increasing concentrations of the molecules fundamental to living organisms.

As Mosse descended the trail towards the lodge, intermittent thunderclaps increased in volume and frequency. They bellowed with growing anger from the flickering dark clouds pouring across the sky from the west. He quickened his pace, careful to avoid slipping as he shuffled down the muddy trail. As his feet fell on the steep path, he was forced to fight with tensed calves against gravity. The pull of gravity, teamed with his momentum, tried to pull him over as he skipped between large stones and vegetation clumps.

On a converging path from higher up the mountainside, Heelia concentrated on finding safe footfalls on a difficult track. Her heart racing, adrenaline flowing, she tried not to panic, but was becoming increasingly anxious as the thunder grew louder. The lodge below seemed a long way off, but she knew she needed to reach it before the rain

Who Writes the Rules

arrived. It was difficult to run on the downhill slope. The path zig-zagged, crossing the hillside, then hair-pinning around bends to change direction. Heelia could speed up on short traverses, but had to manoeuvre carefully on steeper sections. As she ran, she silently prayed that she would get to the lodge before the lightning struck. Life was precious.

For a billion years after the early Theran thunderstorms, organic molecular mixes accumulated. Where local conditions permitted, organic building blocks were held close together. Molecular chain sequences would grow from monomer building blocks. RNA chain sequences would be constructed from nucleotide units. These replicated themselves by attaching to the building blocks of complementary RNA chains. Occasionally, a chain would be formed that was more efficient than its neighbours at replicating itself. This replicator would be better at copying itself than other RNA sequences with which it must compete for monomers. Eventually, the more efficient molecule would replace its neighbours. Its faster replication rate would mean it was naturally selected in competition with neighbouring RNA molecules constructed from different nucleotide sequences.

For millions of generations, the organic components evolved. Complexity increased from basic RNA sequences to associations of RNA and protein. Interacting protein and RNA combinations eventually became packaged inside membrane structures across which metabolic reactions could be managed. The first living cells had emerged. The cellular chemical processes worked best in salt-water pools containing organic building blocks.

34

Every biochemical reaction and process was naturally adapted to function in a liquid pool containing all the ions and salts of the ocean. The cell membrane acted as a semi-impermeable barrier. The flow of molecules in and out of the cell was managed by the electrostatic properties of enzyme proteins embedded in the membrane. As long as there was an energy source and building materials in the environment, the cell could live. The enclosed cellular structure maintained the pH gradient between the inside and outside, ensuring the continued transfer of materials in and out.

The first rudimentary cells had evolved. These were capable of ingesting nutrients from their surrounding environment, which provided energy and constituents for their own growth and reproduction. Each cell was a self-perpetuating unit containing simple metabolic processes. These processes were driven by electrical or pH gradients between the inside and outside of the unit.

Life had begun on Thera. The living entities occupying the shallow waters of Theran oceans had been assembled, step-by-step, over a billion years. Carbon, hydrogen, nitrogen, oxygen and sulphur originating from the volcanic gases, complemented by phosphorus and metal salts that bubbled into the seas, when combined, were fundamental. Together they formed the molecules which comprised life's building blocks. Living cells had been assembled from the dissolved salty residues of the solid planet.

When did life begin? There was no sudden spark. No complex creature rising phoenix-like from the volcanic flames. No helping hand had been needed to set the ball rolling. No push to spin the wheel of life. Natural thermal and chemical gradients had split, reassembled and moulded chemical constituents. These spawned the nutrients from which the replicator complexes grew.

The replicators could only begin to develop and accumulate when atmospheric and surface temperatures allowed the accumulation of liquid water. The slow dissipation of universal energy created circumstances that led to the gradual evolution of basic chemical building blocks.

These evolved into self-contained replicating machines, which could pass their encoded genetic instructions on to following generations.

The trail was uneven. Heelia's boots gripped well, but it was some effort to navigate between boulders. The path sometimes descended steeply over slippery ground. She had trotted as quickly as she could. She was still a few hundred metres above the lodge when an explosive boom erupted to one side of the cirque. It reverberated its way around her, filling the air with a menacing, echoing rumble. The first large drops of rain began to find her face and the bare skin of her arms and legs. She tried to quicken her pace, but had to concentrate on negotiating the rough terrain to avoid falling.

A blinding flash and almost simultaneous crack of thunder startled Mosse as he reached the lodge. The lightning had struck a tree barely 100 metres away. As it seared down the trunk, the heat vaporised its sap, causing a burst of pressure. The wood split into slithers, the upper section now tumbling downwards with a crash.

The tree had been a majestic specimen more than 150 years old. A product of three billion years of evolution since the earliest cells had been formed. It had provided sanctuary to many smaller creatures. Tiny bacteria, already much more complex than the earliest replication complexes. Small animals whose anatomy, physiology and metabolic processes were as organically sophisticated as those of the Majans.

Ducking for shelter under a covered porch, Mosse pondered the fragility of life. Stability and continuity of energy flow engendered growth and progressive development. During the lifetime of an individual, and throughout the lives of generation after generation across millions of years of evolution, constancy of energy supply was needed. But raw energy concentrated and focussed instantaneously against the constancy of a living environment brought only death and destruction. The power of lightning had initiated the chemical march toward life. It chopped the ingredients for the molecular soup, but life itself was delicately balanced. A burst of energy could destroy it.

Electricity was critical to the Majan way of life, but for many creatures, its production meant death. Majan society derived most of its energy from fossil fuels. Coal and oil reserves had been buried and accumulated over hundreds of millions of years. These trapped organic molecules and the energy that bound them were originally derived from solar radiation. The Majans now burned those reserves to release that energy. They used it to produce electricity, power transport and drive their industries.

Who Writes the Rules

They relied on the energy of ancient solar radiation, which had been stored underground. Now they consumed that huge store of energy to fuel their economies. Power-hungry cultures changed atmospheric chemistry by burning organic materials. Combustion of organic fuels released residual carbon dioxide into the atmosphere. The Majans also cleared forests that had been generating oxygen and trapping carbon in solid structures.

Electricity powered their industries and their dwellings. They could have trapped and used the current radiation of Sol for its production without changing atmospheric chemistry. However, it was simpler and cheaper to continue releasing ancient, trapped energy than to convert Sol's current output.

The division of Majan society into different nations and cultures meant that each culture strove to improve its economic status by maximum utilisation of fossil fuels. Economic superiority meant cultural and military dominance. For several hundred years, the energy obtained from fossil fuels had been used to generate new products, from machinery to services and weapons. In the political battle to remain globally powerful or to advance national status, nations were sacrificing the health of everything living on the planet Thera.

The recent history of Majan culture was a catalogue of wars, disputes and power struggles. All driven by the urge to control territory, which would allow them to extract and utilise more fossil fuels. Abundant energy shone on them every day from Sol, more than enough to empower all of their activities. However, they could focus only on expending energy to unearth buried fuels. Combustion of carbon-based fuels caused further harm to the atmosphere.

The receding glaciers and strengthening storms were a consequence of the activities of Majan industry. The chemical properties of carbon dioxide meant that it trapped solar energy.

Increasing carbon dioxide concentration was warming the atmosphere causing ice to melt, both on mountain glaciers and at the polar ice-caps. Melting ice fed the oceans, raising their levels little by little, threatening low-lying cities and communities.

In recent years, powerful storms and floods were more frequently reported. Seemingly ever-strengthening winds driven by captured solar heat caused widespread destruction. Perhaps today's downpour was just another summer thunderstorm?

Looking up briefly, Heelia spotted a figure reaching the door of the lodge about 400m ahead of her. At that instant, a flash lit up the silhouette of the tree that it hit, the crash of thunder deafening her a split second later.

Mosse turned the door handle and entered the dry warmth of the lodge as the deluge began behind him. He closed the door to shut it out.

Heelia saw Mosse close the lodge door behind himself, oblivious to her plight. Immediately the sky poured its contents onto her, soaking her in seconds. She ran as fast as she reasonably could along the wet, muddy track through a curtain of rain, which almost obscured the lodge completely.

Arriving in front of the door, she ducked under an overhanging chalet roof, which sheltered her from the

Who Writes the Rules

downpour. Streams of water dripped from her long, dark hair. She squeezed locks of hair to wring out the water. She tried to wring the rain from her soaked shorts. She had no choice but to enter the lodge sopping wet and hope that she could dry out inside. Reaching for the door handle, she turned it and entered, embarrassed at her sodden state.

Chapter 3. The Complexity of Life

The timing of Mosse's descent had been good. He had felt the first warm splashes of the impending deluge just a few seconds before reaching the lodge. The sky had split open with a passion as he had raced to the door. A downpour, which would soak in seconds, was poised to drench him. It arrived in the instant the lightning bolt had struck the tree. He had glanced fleetingly as the flashing brightness illuminated a multitude of large globules pounding onto the lodge terrace, exploding up crowns of droplets. Escaping from the storm, Mosse had stepped into the lodge closing the door behind him.

Inside, a dozen or so walkers had taken refuge. The storm was a good excuse to select a table close to a glowing log fire. Here they could take some nourishment and rest weary limbs. The sky roared out a noisy message. A sheet of corrugated metal covering an insulated wooden roof rattled with the beat of a thousand drummers, accompanied by an occasional discordant rumbling bass. Below it, Mosse was safe and dry.

Hungry after his walk, Mosse ordered lunch from the lodge-keeper. He was quickly brought a plate of salad with cheese, bread, a few slices of cold, smoked meat, and a jug of water. He ate slowly, savouring the flavours of the cheese and meats. A sweet stimulating drink after his lunch would help him restore strength and give him energy for the descent back to his home.

The lodge was at 1,600 metres. Today he had

Who Writes the Rules

ascended to a favourite vantage point at 2,500 metres, a high point on the ridge. From there, he could enjoy an unobstructed 360° panorama of the surrounding mountains. An unbeatable view of the adjacent rugged massif from which the glaciers streamed imperceptibly down from the ice sheet that topped the White Mountain.

On occasions, he had climbed higher into the mountains, up to about 3,800 metres. Ascending from sea-level, the air pressure would drop off, unnoticeably at first, but eventually thinning exponentially. Above 3,000 metres, the amount of available oxygen would become appreciably lower. It would become necessary to breathe more deeply and move more slowly. His body would become fatigued more easily by the effort. Oxygen was critical to almost every living creature on Thera. Without it, their metabolisms would cease to function.

There were two principal types of living creatures found on Thera. There were those that absorbed solar energy and used it to combine water, carbon dioxide and other necessary nutrients from their environments. They used light energy to combine these substances into the building blocks of their own bodies.

The second type of creature fabricated their body constituents by eating other organisms. Food components were broken down to produce energy for their metabolisms and to provide building blocks to construct new body parts. The Majans belonged to the second type of creature. They needed to digest food organisms to provide the nutrients for their own body maintenance and growth. In order to ignite and maintain the metabolic processes of their most basic functions, they required oxygen.

Like most other complex living organisms, the body of every Majan was composed of billions of microscopic cells. These were combined in a vast alliance to form an integrated system. Within every cell, an intricate network of tiny components formed a miniature factory. Interlinked metabolic processes performed vital biochemical tasks that needed oxygen in order to function. Every cell was itself a complete system. Each was far more sophisticated than those complexes of RNA, protein and phospholipid membranes that had appeared three billion years earlier.

One billion years of molecular evolution followed by two billion years of cellular evolution had produced a type of cell that was an association of components. A DNA database carried the architectural instructions. These were translated via RNA into all of the proteins and enzymes needed for cell life. Enzymes would catalyse many chemical reactions in an intricate metabolic mesh.

The cell contained specialist organelles for energy production, the synthesis of proteins, and internal digestive processes. The original phospholipid membrane had developed into an intricate protective barrier. It managed the transfer of substances into and out of the cell, maintaining differences between the interior and the outside environment.

The DNA contained the gene code for many functions. It was wrapped by specialist proteins into one or more chromosomes. Each chromosome would be copied and then separated during cell division into daughter cells. Each daughter cell contained a replica of the parental gene code.

For hundreds of millions of years, evolution had

Who Writes the Rules

crawled forward by a slow process of DNA mutations in some individual cells. These produced new features that, if advantageous to the cells containing them, would be selected for future generations of offspring. Most of the DNA of most cells in any population was identical. The replication process was protected against errors by a suite of security proteins. However, mutations sometimes crept through, and the most useful ones were selected for future generations.

For evolution to gain pace, there needed to be genetic variation between the individuals of any given population. Variation was the source of different characteristics upon which natural selection could act. The evolution of sexual reproduction provided the required impetus. Sex meant faster reshuffling of genes. Sex ensured more variation between individuals, providing more choices upon which natural selection could act. Sex would become the foot on the accelerator of evolution.

In the cells of some early organisms, replication of chromosomes produced new cells with duplicate chromosomes. These duplicates remained in close contact with each other and sometimes swapped segments. A mutation in one chromosome would not be reflected in its complementary partner. Changes to the cell division process eventually resulted in complementary chromosomes being separated into new cells. Each new cell contained just one chromosome from each pair. Occasionally, the new cells would merge. In merged cells, the chromosomes could pair and swap material again before separating to form the next cell generation.

After many generations of genetic swapping, the

44

cell populations included many variations. This led to faster selection of the cells that were the most efficient reproducers. Eventually, certain species of single-celled organism became totally dependent upon a mechanism of genetic shuffling during the course of their reproduction process. Sexual exchange of genetic material had commenced, and because of sex, evolution would accelerate. These sexually reproducing cells included the common ancestors of both plants and animals.

An early consequence of sexual reproduction was the appearance of two complementary types of individual cells: a male and a female type. Thus began the need for sexual partners to find each other in order to reproduce.

The simple, regular swapping of genes from different parental cells would evolve into a potent force. This became the basis of the most powerful instincts controlling the behaviour and destiny of nearly all living creatures. The importance of sex as a producer of heredity variation would dictate the course of evolutionary change. The most efficient variations in all subsequent biological progress would be those most likely to guarantee the sexual success of their possessors. The better an individual was at sexual reproduction, the more likely they would outrun their competitors in the evolutionary race.

It had taken three billion years for single-celled, sexually reproducing organisms to evolve. During the fourth billion-year period, the cellular units would join forces. They united to form larger complexes. At first, they formed colonies of similar cells. Then organisms evolved, containing many different specialised cells in various types of tissue. However, each individual in each generation would be

45

Who Writes the Rules

derived from one initial single cell: a pollinated seed or a fertilised egg. The embryo would embark on a voyage of division, growth, development and differentiation into different tissue types. This culminated in a mature body ready to engage in another cycle of sexual reproduction.

Mosse's body comprised many types of tissue, all constructed from specialised cells. His weather-beaten skin covered a muscular, skeletal frame. Blood cells carried oxygen from his lungs, pumped through a network of tubes by beating heart muscle. Oxygen maintained the metabolism in every cell within each of his distributed tissues. Nerve cells carried stimuli from sensory organs - from eyes, ears, nose, tongue and skin to his brain. Signals from his brain caused his muscles to react according to the stimuli they received.

The continued existence of Mosse as a living entity was driven by the laws of thermodynamics and chemistry. These laws demanded the continual supply of chemical energy to be released from the molecular bonds of nutrients. Hydrocarbon fuel was oxidised within mitochondria, the microscopic engines providing the power to every cell of his body. Just as a motor vehicle oxidises hydrocarbons to release the energy to keep its engine running, cells need oxygen and fuel. The cellular metabolism in all of his body cells would be extinguished rapidly if the oxygen and nutrient supplies were cut. Lack of oxygen to vital organs, in particular his brain, would kill him within minutes.

Nearly all his cell types carried two sets of chromosomes, one set from each parent. There was a very important exception. In a specialised organ between his legs, chromosome separation and gene reshuffling were constantly occurring. This process generated sperm cells, each containing just one chromosome from each of the parental pairs found in all his other body cells. Every sperm cell contained a new gene arrangement. A new variety ready to encode the development of a unique, individual Majan. Like the majority of other male Majans, Mosse was constantly subconsciously driven by instinct to achieve life's goal of reproducing by sexual union with a female of his species.

Nature's intent was the remixing of chromosomes to form a fertilised egg. The egg would contain two sets of genes, one set from the egg and one from the sperm cell. This would provide a unique genetic fingerprint derived by reshuffling the genes from two parents into a new combination. Majan behaviour was driven not by the desire to create new Majans but by the lust to release sexual urges.

Monogamous by culture but polygamous by instinct, Mosse was compelled to glance at any female in his proximity. His senses would sample the scent of pheromones, examine the curvature of form, and note the attractiveness of hair and facial features. His control centre performed an instant analysis and assessment of sexual compatibility.

Female Majans tended to be less polygamous. They were more influenced by indications of the social status of a male than simply by his physical attractiveness. The Majan female had evolved to carry a developing child throughout pregnancy. She had consequently become the principal child raiser following its birth. Subconsciously and instinctively, she sought a partner who could provide support and protection in return for the release of sexual urges within a long-term relationship.

Who Writes the Rules

She usually had less instinctive desire for sexual release than a male. However, she might respond to the appropriate caresses from a partner who could potentially offer social status above whatever threshold she would willingly accept. In most Majan cultures, socially acceptable behaviour demanded that both partners would develop an emotional bond. This relationship, supported by mutual sexual pleasure, would usually cause each to lose interest in seeking that pleasure with any other partner.

Majan sexual contact frequently began as a form of cat and mouse game. The subconscious analysis, a furtive glance, fleeting eye contact, a concealed smile. A change in posture or stance to emphasise features of gender difference. Senses and body language all tested the water from a safe distance. A wrong choice would provoke a frown, a stern expression, or a cold shoulder. Occasionally, the eye contact might last longer, a lingering smile and relaxed posture betraying a willingness to extend that initial interest to flirting chat. Subconscious analysis would drift into increasing awareness and attraction.

While Mosse had been ordering his food, a lady had entered the lodge. Dripping wet, she had evidently been too late to have escaped the rain. She panted, her breast rising to catch her breath as her dark hair dripped onto shining, dark olive-coloured skin. She was vaguely familiar. The figure he had spotted in the distance on the mountain. Her wet clothes gripped the curves of an athletic body, at which Mosse had tried hard not to stare. The same red tee-shirt and black shorts he had seen in the distance on the mountain. She sat down at a table close to his, within reach of the fire's warmth.

Mosse glanced indirectly from time to time as the lady warmed herself with a bowl of soup and a hot drink. She was attractive, with deep brown eyes, a sweet, friendly face, a little younger and slightly smaller than him. He guessed that she was a tourist, a visitor from another region or a different country. He felt himself flush nervously as she caught his sideways glance, but relaxed as she smiled amicably before continuing to finish her lunch.

When she had finished eating, Mosse braved himself for an attempted introduction. "You were caught by the storm?" he queried.

She turned to regard him, then smiled warmly. "Yes, I was too far from shelter when it started. I was going to hide under a tree, but it was hit by the lightning just before I got to it. Lucky I wasn't killed! So, I ran here – very wet! I saw you close the door before I could get here."

"Oh. I'm very sorry. I think I spotted you up the mountain before the storm, but I didn't see you when I was at the door."

"It's OK. I was still too far away to escape the rain."

She spoke his language very well, but a lilt in her accent betrayed her foreign origin. Her eyes shone brightly. He was relieved that her cheerful response suggested that she was happy to talk to him.

"Are you from Perali?" Mosse enquired.

Perali was the country on the other side of the mountain chain, to the south. A country with a warmer, drier climate, where the language was different from his but sufficiently similar to betray a common origin in the past thousand years.

49

Who Writes the Rules

"Yes. I came to walk in the mountains for some days. It's so beautiful here. Do you live here?"

Mosse was pleased that she had chosen to pursue the conversation with him, as he answered, "I have a chalet in Carina. Yes, it's a beautiful environment around here. I like to get out and enjoy it when I have a chance to."

She tilted her head in interest, giving him an inquisitive smile. "You are so lucky to live in such a wonderful place! You must have an interesting life. Do you work here?"

"I work in the tourist industry during the peak summer and winter seasons. I also work freelance in remote IT support, which I can do online via the global network. I'm also studying part-time for an ecology qualification. I can do most of the academic bits online when I'm not working on other things. And you?" Mosse enquired.

"Wow, you're such a busy person! I work as a language translator. Mostly government work for refugees. I also teach some adult classes part-time in different languages, including yours."

"That's why you speak it so well! Can I ask what your name is? I'm Mosse."

"I'm Heelia. Nice to meet you, Mosse," Heelia replied, smiling radiantly.

After several more exchanges, Mosse invited Heelia to join him closer to the fire, where she could enjoy the warmth and dry off more quickly. They chatted for a good hour, discussing their work, their lives, the mountains and the weather. Occasionally a furtive glance would reinforce their initial eye contact. Seemingly from very different backgrounds, they had much in common. Neither had children, and both were single, having separated from a partner in the past year. Both enjoyed relaxing in the grandeur of the mountains. Each was now enjoying the other's company.

By the time the rain had stopped, Heelia's clothes had almost dried. It was a long descent through the forest to the village below. Heelia was happy to accept Mosse's offer to accompany her. They left the lodge together. The sky had cleared, and Sol returned from behind the clouds. It was now late afternoon. The temperature had dropped a few degrees. They would walk briskly down the hillside to keep warm.

They trekked for more than an hour downhill, discussing the forest and mountain wildlife. Mosse explained how holiday activities and tourism were damaging the local environment. Heelia listened closely, respecting his knowledge of the countryside and wildlife. She shared his concerns about the impacts of climate change.

As they passed by his chalet, he suppressed a desire to invite her inside for coffee. It would be impolite to make the suggestion to a lady he had known for barely three hours. They continued for another fifteen minutes down into the village. Mosse walked her to the door of the hotel where she was staying.

"Is your chalet near here?" she asked him, not wishing to part company too quickly.

"We passed it a little while back up the hill," he said, gesturing approximately towards his home further up the hillside from where they had just descended.

"But you didn't need to come all the way down

here. You could have stopped back there!" She was quietly content that he had chosen to escort her past his own home to her village hotel.

"That's alright. I was enjoying talking to you."

He reddened a little, realising she must see he was flirting with her, but also wanting to find a way to continue their acquaintance.

"Have you been up to the glaciers yet? There are some nice walks up there."

"No. This is my first visit to Carina. I would love to go there, but I don't know my way around or the best places to go," she replied, looking directly into his eyes.

Grabbing the opportunity that she had presented him, he offered, "If you like, I could take you up there tomorrow. I have some data I want to collect, so I need to go there anyway."

He could have told her that her company was of much greater interest than any ecological data he might note on their outing. However, it was prudent to give her a reason other than romantic interest for taking her to the glaciers.

"Oh! That would be kind of you. I've not decided what to do tomorrow, so I would love to come with you. Maybe I will learn something about mountain ecology."

Mosse was thrilled at her acceptance. He felt tempted to hug her before parting but suppressed the urge. He wanted her company and looked forward to meeting again. He did not want to betray that his motivation was anything more than being kind and helpful to a visiting stranger.

"I'll drive down here after breakfast, then. We can

get by car up to about 1,300 metres and then take a path up into a very spectacular valley. I'll bring some food for lunch. If I pick you up at 9:30, would that be OK?"

"That will be perfect. I'll be ready."

She didn't want him to leave, but at least she would see him again tomorrow. She grinned happily at him as they began to move apart. He smiled back at her as he turned towards the path back up to the chalet.

"And you'd better make sure you have some waterproof clothes with you," he added, "just in case we have another downpour. Have a nice evening."

Mosse strolled happily back along the path towards home. The spring in his step reflected his happy mood, pleased with himself at the new acquaintance he had just made and excited in anticipation of what the next day might bring.

In her hotel room, Heelia explored her baggage, trying to decide what she should wear for her next day's outing. She had expected to explore the mountain meadows alone on her visit to Carina, but now she was anticipating an exciting day with an interesting male companion.

She wanted to look her best.

Who Writes the Rules

Chapter 4. In the Garden

Mosse's home was 1,000 metres above the level of the oceans. It overlooked the town of Carina from the west side of a V-shaped valley. A central gorge split the valley, deeply excavated over millennia by fast-flowing, glacial meltwater. Carina began as a trading post above the east side of the gorge on a trail leading to a mountain pass. It developed over centuries into a market town for agricultural communities. In recent years, the advent of mountain sports and tourism had led to extensive construction. Traditional farming hamlets and communities of modern chalet buildings stretched along and up both sides of the valley. Access roads wound up into the forest and meadows, connecting valley life to mountain meadows, tracks and sports facilities.

Carina was popular with tourists; most visited from their places of work in larger towns and cities to benefit from the clean mountain environment. They came to hike or relax in the warm summer months, or enjoy sports on snow-covered slopes during the winter.

Having spent many years working in cities as a technical specialist supporting computer networks, Mosse had recently chosen to move to his mountain chalet. Career disillusionment and the breakdown of a romantic relationship had steered him in a new personal direction the previous year. The chalet was a retreat from which he could work remotely. It allowed him to escape the petty office politics, competition, predation and dishonesty that he had witnessed where he had previously offered his services.

For Mosse, business IT support had always been a means to an end – a way of financing his lifestyle. His deeper interest was the environment in which he lived, life, evolution, ecosystems and natural science. Relocating had given him more opportunities to observe and experience nature. From his mountain retreat, he liked to reflect on how the Majan species had affected natural systems throughout their history.

The chalet that Mosse called home was typical of the traditional mountainside buildings, such as the lodge where he had met Heelia. The structure was constructed from blocks of a hard, concrete-like material covered by elongate planks. Cut from tree wood and stained a rich, golden-brown, these presented a decorative façade. The result was aesthetically pleasing while solidly fabricated to give shelter from the extremes of mountain weather conditions. An overhanging chalet roof offered covered shelter for an external, tiled deck terrace. This served as a perfect observation and relaxation platform for dining, and sun-bathing. Or for simply drinking in the ever-changing colours of the panorama across the open valley beyond. Below the platform, a sizeable garden stepped down through a series of paths and terraced growing beds. Sculpted into a sloping hillside, the terraces contained plots in which a range of edible vegetables was growing. Below the decking platform a glasshouse provided a nursery environment for early germination, and for protection of seedlings.

Arriving back at the chalet, Mosse passed his vehicle, which was parked on a hard forecourt. He walked around the side of the building to the garden. Climbing up a few steps, he emerged onto the deck above the garden. Passing a table and exterior seating, he arrived at a door that gave access to his kitchen. He entered the house and opened a refrigeration cabinet, browsing the contents for possible sandwich ingredients.

The chalet would have easily accommodated a small family. Several accesses radiated to different rooms from an open hallway behind the kitchen. There was an open lounge and dining room on one side of the kitchen, and a bedroom on the other. All had windows facing the panorama across the valley. A bathroom, a second bedroom, and a stairwell were across the hallway. Stairways led up to a third bedroom and an office, plus down to several cellars and store rooms. A downstairs door led through the glasshouse and into the garden. Two of the bedrooms had private ensuite showers and toilets, which Mosse retained empty as occasional guestrooms.

All of the rooms were spacious. The walls sported framed images of mountain scenery, maps, or information sheets showing flora and fauna. On the wall in the central hallway, a large relief map of the White Mountain massif and surrounding areas had pride of place.

Trotting down the stairs from the hallway, Mosse entered the glasshouse and checked some plants that produced red globular fruits. These could usually be put to use in salads or sandwiches. Today some of the leaves were drying and turning brown. The fruits had dull blotches and looked ready to rot. This was a blight - a microbial infection by which the fruit of these plants would be rendered inedible. It was probably too late to save them. He tried to control the environment and ensure nutrient availability for the plants that grew in the glasshouse and in his garden plots. Unfortunately, it was not easy to prevent infections.

Plants require water, light, nutrients and sufficient space to grow. The amount of each depends on the species. However, plants provide sustenance for many other creatures, from microbes to herbivorous creatures of different sizes and voracity. In nature, water, light, nutrients and space are not controlled. Nor are the myriad of lifeforms that obtain their sustenance, directly or indirectly, from the plants. All organisms had evolved in constant competition with their own and other species. They had to sustain a perpetual effort to obtain necessary resources while avoiding predation.

Mosse could ensure water and nutrients were supplied to his garden; however, continued maintenance was needed to remove competing wild plants and suppress infestations. The availability of solar energy was weather dependent. Plants combine carbon dioxide from the atmosphere with water from the soil, using solar energy to photosynthesise hydrocarbons from these components. The absorbed energy would be locked into the plants in the chemical glue that bound together carbon and hydrogen atoms. This formed the building blocks from which living tissues would be constructed. Addition of nitrates, sulphates, potassium and small amounts of other elements from soil nutrients provided everything the plant would need. Plants grew to maturity from basic organic building blocks such as carbohydrates, proteins and nucleic acids.

Sexual reproduction of plants required pollination of ovules by pollen grains. The result was fertilised seeds that would grow into new, genetically unique plants. In Mosse's glasshouse, as in nature, pollination was usually aided by small insects that flitted between flowers.

However, the price of this pollination was sometimes loss of leaf material to the pollinators. Or to the larvae that emerged from their eggs after these were laid on the plants. Chewed leaves or fruit were often an entry point for infections such as the blight that he had observed.

The vegetable cultures in the glasshouse and garden are examples of controlled ecosystems. An ecosystem can be described as a particular, defined physical environment, and all of the organisms and resources it contains. Ecology is the study of how these organisms interact with each other and with the environment itself. Energy flow through the system drives the cycling of nutrients and resources to change the populations and relative biomasses of each component species.

It is convenient to think of individual ecosystems as comprising specific environmental characteristics and niches. Studying and describing the interactions within these systems can help us to understand how natural interactions work. However, in nature, environments are very dynamic. It is rare to find easily definable, closed boundaries. In reality, every local environment is meshed with its adjacent neighbours. Species may migrate in and out of localities as populations grow and available nutrient resources change. Ultimately there is one large, interacting biosphere – a single ecosystem comprising the planet's surface and all of the living creatures inhabiting it.

Mosse salvaged one or two of the red, globular fruits that were least blighted. He picked a handful of succulent green leaves that would complement these in tomorrow's sandwiches. Returning to the kitchen, he placed these in the fridge. He poured a cold, carbonated, slightly-intoxicating drink, which he carried back to a table on the deck. Sitting down, he reclined and gazed across the valley at the panorama before him.

The centre of Carina sat about two kilometres away from him at 850 metres altitude. A small town, it spread on either side of the gorge of a mountain stream that cut the valley. Carina was a market town on a trade route, which had developed over several thousand years. It guarded trails that circuited the large massif to the east. A granite pluton rose majestically at the centre of the massif to form the White Mountain – an ice-covered peak rising to nearly 5,000 metres.

Flowing from the summit, a sheet of white gripped the upper ridges like a claw from which talons of glacial ice descended. The flowing ice cut deep valleys and gorges between rugged cliffs. White, blue, grey, and then brown gradually merged into shades of green as slopes rolled downwards into increasingly dense vegetation. Scrub and moorland of the upper slopes gave way to dark forest, then paler, greener mixed forest and pastureland.

At the base of the forest, isolated chalets emerged. Their frequency grew as they united to form the town of Carina.

Heelia dined in the restaurant of a moderately-priced hotel by the market square in the town centre. Her meal was simple but tasted good, cooked from fresh, local produce direct from the market stalls. The hotel was comfortable and adequate as a base for exploring the trails in the surrounding valley.

Heelia had told Mosse that she was from Perali, the adjacent country on the south side of the mountain chain. She lived in Perali, but her background was more complex than she had chosen to explain to a stranger in a mountain restaurant. She had been born in a country much further to the East. It was a country governed by an oligarchy of tribal leaders who followed a system of strict control. An authoritarian and patriarchal regime in which females were allowed very few rights.

Typically, young females were married to selected husbands. Families effectively bought females from their parents, often while still sexually and emotionally immature. They would then be considered to be the property of their husbands. This system followed traditions intended by the perpetrators to maintain their tribal integrities. Cultural hierarchies could be preserved, supporting their established familial and tribal relationships.

For many in the tribal society, this system worked to maintain their extended social, political and religious relationships. However, for others, the marriage procedures were a cruel imposition. A system that prevented people from taking the life partners of their choice.

A husband had been chosen for Heelia before she was ten years old. The match was agreed upon between the would-be husband's parents and the tribal elders in the extended community where Heelia's family lived. Between her tenth and twelfth birthdays, wedding plans were already in discussion, to the horror of her parents. They could not refuse the will of the tribal elders, who would consider the price being offered as more than reasonable for the families involved. This was a commitment that Heelia must honour. If she were to refuse, she might be stoned to death. Her father would be obliged to lead the stoning and finish it by casting the stone that would kill her. The family would be disgraced, losing their status within the tribal hierarchy.

Heelia's parents were intelligent, generous and loving people. They would not subject their daughter to a marriage that they knew was not going to be a happy one. They chose what they considered their only option: to flee their country as political refugees. Before Heelia's twelfth birthday, they discretely left their home, taking the minimum quantity of belongings with which they could travel. They began a long journey that finished after several months at a refugee camp in Perali. Here they applied, eventually successfully, for asylum.

Heelia attended school and university in Perali, eventually qualifying as a language teacher. Although reasonably well integrated with local Perali culture, she remained a partial outsider with close links to a large immigrant community. Most of that community shared a similar background derived from Eastern cultures.

Integrating into their new society was more difficult for her parents than for Heelia. Language and cultural barriers made it easier to remain in a close community with fellow refugees. As parents of an attractive and intelligent daughter, they were frequently approached with respect to choosing an appropriate husband for Heelia. While many of the attitudes and traditions of their mother nation had travelled with the refugee community, life was freer in Perali. Here the threats of violent punishment and disgrace

Who Writes the Rules

were much reduced, but some cultural pressure remained.

Heelia could freely refuse arranged marriage proposals in Perali. However, through her late teens, several eligible young males were suggested. Eventually, she agreed to accept one such introduction, with whom she found herself forming a close friendship. A relationship developed, which culminated in a marriage ceremony.

While still at university, Heelia was married in a colourful wedding. A celebration and feast attended mainly by associates from the Eastern immigrant community. The marriage began with hope for a long and happy future together. However, both partners were still young with no experience of co-habiting. Neither had known the closeness of having a romantic and emotional personal relationship. As they got to know each other, rather than their partnership strengthening, cracks appeared in the fabric of their marriage. An early pregnancy, which had held the promise of a future happy family, tragically miscarried. This brought sadness, disappointment, questions and blame. Personalities clashed, and arguments became louder and more frequent. When physical violence began to threaten, Heelia decided the only option was divorce. Although disappointed, her parents were supportive and understanding. Heelia returned to her parental home to pursue a career.

Heelia had settled into a role as a language translator and part-time teacher of adult evening classes in Perali. Although she had had a few brief relationships in the years since her divorce, none had resulted in a serious romance. She had come to Carina for a short break. To escape the hustle and bustle of daily life in Perali. To enjoy the splendour of the mountain scenery.

This was the last place she had expected to find romance. She had no presumptions of such from her meeting with Mosse. However, she had enjoyed their initial meeting and looked forward to seeing him again. After dinner, as she prepared for the morning excursion with new company, she felt pleasant anticipation that the day would bring some happiness into her life.

Chapter 5. The Spirit of the Ice

Mosse awoke before dawn. His mind too active to permit him to slip back into slumber, he wrapped himself in a warm bathrobe and prepared a hot drink. Carrying his drink to the outside table, he took in a deep breath of cool, morning air, settled into a cushioned garden chair and relaxed. From the edges of his garden and hidden in the vegetation beyond, a battalion of feathered creatures sang and whistled, declaring their presence to potential partners and competitors. Across the valley the White Mountain slept under ice sheets, still hidden by a purple-black night blanket, the boundary of which formed a sharp silhouette against a yellow outline. An orange halo was diluted into the darkness as it merged with a pre-dawn, deep purple-blue sky. A few high clouds along the upper ridges stained the sky with splashes of dark red-grey-brown.

Clasping his hands around the hot cup, Mosse watched the slow transformations as beams of yellow began to radiate from a point on the ridge. The beams strengthened and brightened rapidly as their source slowly emerged from behind the mountain until he had to avert his eye in deference to the power of Sol. The radiance of the first rays warmed his skin while the sky was repainted with a coat of azure blue, predicting perfect weather for exploring mountain trails.

Sounds of distant traffic infiltrated the dawn chorus, announcing a new day in Carina. Mosse returned inside the chalet and showered. He dressed in lightweight, but weatherproof clothes, designed for summer trekking. He had a large bowl of cereal, a mixture of grains, seeds and nuts in a pool of milk, washed down with fruit juice. This was quick and easy to prepare and consume, yet sufficient sustenance until lunchtime.

Opening the fridge Mosse removed the salad vegetables and fruits he had selected from the garden the previous evening. He combined these with cold meats in a container, which he put, along with bottles of fruit juice and water, into a small backpack. To complement these, he included a bottle of alcoholic drink produced by fermentation of bunches of a red fruit. Some napkins, cutlery, disposable plates, cups and a pair of robust drinking glasses completed his picnic assembly.

Taking two pairs of telescopic walking sticks and a waterproof picnic blanket from a cupboard, he tied these beneath the backpack. After donning a lightweight walking jacket, he pushed his feet into a pair of tough but light trekking shoes. To prevent the laces from loosening while he walked, he tied them in double bows.

Shortly before the pre-arranged meeting, time Mosse left the chalet, locking the door as he departed. He unlocked the doors of his vehicle and placed the backpack and walking sticks on the rear seat. As he started the engine, he released the break and then manoeuvred from his parking area onto the access road that wound downhill. The access road joined a larger road, on which he descended a kilometre towards Carina.

Arriving at the edge of the old market town area, he parked at the roadside. The aroma of freshly baked bread emanating from a shop at the roadside stimulated glands in his mouth to produce saliva. The occupants had spent the last few hours busily baking a range of bread and cakes. Selecting freshly baked rolls with which to make sandwiches, and cakes for a sweet dessert, he paid the shopkeeper. Returning to the vehicle, he put his purchases into his backpack.

From the bakery, Mosse followed the main road over a bridge across the gorge and uphill into the centre of Carina. At 9:30, the business day was already well underway, and the town was bustling, but it was still pre-tourist season. Children had already been delivered to their schools, so traffic was fairly light. He had no trouble parking outside the hotel where Heelia was staying.

Mosse left the vehicle, crossed a pavement and mounted the few steps to the hotel entrance. He entered the door and was approaching the reception desk when he recognised Heelia's voice calling behind him.

"Good morning, Mosse!"

Mosse turned to the beaming face that greeted him. Heelia had been sat not far from the door, a small backpack by her feet. Keen to join him for a mountain trek, she had been ready early. She had used some face makeup. Not excessively, but enough to add a little colour and definition to her features. His face reddened slightly as he thought to himself that she was even more attractive than he remembered from the day before. A bright, beautiful face, with laughing eyes and a warm smile.

Today she wore a cream tee-shirt and matching showerproof trousers. Good quality, tough but lightweight walking boots and soft, thick socks protected her feet. She placed a pale-blue, weatherproof jacket over her arm as she rose to join him. Although the weather was expected to be warm and dry, she would not be caught out so easily if it rained.

Appropriate for unpredictable summer weather in the mountains, Mosse thought. "Morning, Heelia," Mosse smiled back. "Have you had breakfast already?"

"Yes. I'm ready to go trekking – unless you'd like a drink or something to eat before we go?"

"I'm fine. Best if we get to the base car park on the mountain in case it fills up," Mosse responded.

Heelia picked up her backpack, and they left the hotel together. Crossing to the parked vehicle, Mosse opened the front passenger door for Heelia. She smiled, catching his eye as she climbed through the door into the seat. He moved round to the driver's door, sat down and started the engine. The vehicle moved slowly into the traffic. They turned onto a road which would take them along the top of the gorge towards the southern end of the valley.

While he drove, they chatted about how they'd spent their respective evenings and Heelia's hotel. She told Mosse that she had enjoyed her evening meal at the hotel and had slept well in a comfortable bed. She didn't mention how much she had been looking forward to their outing.

A few kilometres from Carina, Mosse turned to the left, away from the main valley road. They continued uphill past open meadows, then through a hamlet of chalets. At a junction where several valleys converged, he selected a narrow road that rose into the forest. Climbing steeply uphill, they negotiated a series of narrow, straight road sections inter-linked by sharp, hairpin bends with limited visibility beyond.

Who Writes the Rules

Heelia took a deep breath. "I don't know how you can drive on these roads. What if something comes the other way?"

Smiling, Mosse dropped to a low gear as he approached a bend. He took a wide trajectory, then accelerated out of the bend before changing up a gear again. "You get used to it. There's very little traffic up here. If anybody comes down the other way, they should pull in to let me pass. Best if the ascending driver can keep the momentum to avoid stalling. There are enough passing places to allow descending traffic to stop."

As the road exited from the forest, the vehicle emerged onto a straight section of road. They climbed less steeply through pastures toward another hamlet of chalets. Historically, they had been built as shelter cabins for those who tended grazing animals on summer pastureland.

Some way downhill from the hamlet, Mosse turned off the road onto a parking area. It had been constructed to allow tourists to access the mountain trails, which radiated from this location on the west side of the massif.

Exiting the vehicle, Mosse collected the backpack and walking sticks from the rear seat. He handed a pair of walking sticks to Heelia, demonstrating how to use them.

"There are three segments. Twist the joints anticlockwise to loosen them. Pull them to the correct length and then twist clockwise to lock them in place. To get the correct length, grip the stick with your fist around the handle. Put the tip on the ground and your arm at right angles to your body, then tighten the joints in that position. These will make it much easier to walk both up and downhill. It'll take the stress off your knees and help you grip where the path is steep or slippery."

They set off up a steep path leading to the hamlet. The cluster of wood-faced chalets, some of them modernised farm buildings, dated back many generations. In recent years, the hamlet had been extended by newer chalets that were used mainly as holiday homes. Most of these were unoccupied for much of the year.

They stopped at the entrance to the hamlet to recover their breath and turned to observe the scene behind them. The community rested 100 metres above the car park and 400 metres above Carina. The mountain massif rose behind them to the north and east. To the west was an uninterrupted panorama of about 120°. Looking out across the vista to the west and south, Heelia drank in the scene of settlements reaching up from the valley bottoms.

Holiday villages were dotted along access routes leading to meadows adorning the middle sections of the surrounding mountains. Chalets and apartment blocks were clustered in developments around the old farming communities in the summer pasturelands. Thin, dark lines climbing through forests and up meadows marked the routes of power lines and cables that carried passenger transport equipment for winter sports. A few of these also operated in summer to take walkers up to the higher meadows. As the slopes stretched upwards, forests thinned out and disappeared into the lighter greens of flower-covered mountain meadow. The meadows gave way on steeper slopes to grey scree escarpments and cliffs. The boundaries of many of the pastures were straight-edged or shaped to follow descending pistes and tracks. Clearly marked areas which had been deliberately cut for snow

69

Who Writes the Rules

sports.

"This view is magnificent! Is this where you planned to take me?"

Mosse glanced towards Heelia, revealing a bemused smile as she absorbed the view. "This is just the starting point! I'm taking you to one of my favourite places. A valley that will make you feel a world away from this tourist vista."

"Wow, this is already a stunning view, so it must be a special place."

"It is!" Mosse assured her confidently.

They walked gradually uphill past a number of chalet buildings, brightly adorned with flower displays of reds, blues and yellows in window boxes and hanging baskets. They emerged after 200 metres onto a meadow, from where a signposted footpath directed them onto a trail that circuited the massif for nearly 200 kilometres.

They followed a well-worn path across the meadow, joining the circuit trail on undulating terrain, traversing alternating meadow and woodland. In places, the path entered thick, dark forest, where sections were sometimes steep and quite slippery. As they climbed, they chatted, occasionally stopping to recover their breathing after steeper sections.

"Now I understand why you brought the walking sticks. This would be difficult without them."

Mosse replied, "The leverage helps you keep your balance on the steeper sections. Without the support, it's easy to slip."

For about an hour, they continued, mostly on gently undulating paths. Occasionally steep, but gradually taking them up through dark coniferous forest. Sometimes they emerged into short clearings where small rivulets drained water down across the path, making the ground muddy and slippery. Stopping to admire the view at every clearing, they chatted between deep breaths as they ascended the route.

As the trail turned a bend on the hillside, they entered a clearing where a small waterfall trickled down the uphill embankment on their left side. It crossed the trail swirling through a short series of stepping stones, then dropped downwards on their right side.

Mosse stopped and put his hand beneath the water, where it dropped into a pool at the side of the path. He raised a handful of water to his mouth, slurping quietly. "Taste the water. It's pure and clean. Spring water filtered through the mountainside."

Heelia mirrored his action. "Oh. It's very cold and so good to drink."

Continuing along the trail, they emerged from the forest onto a traverse across a steeply sloping meadow. The meadow stretched uphill on their left to grey cliff faces several hundred metres above. To the right side of the path, the meadow declined steeply for a few hundred metres, then dropped around a steep curve into a river gorge. Near vertical faces fell into the gorge, more than a hundred meters deep. As they moved away from the forest, the panorama opened up on the downhill, western side. A spectacle of peaks, ridges, valleys, meadows and forests stretched to the horizon.

Heelia sighed in wonder. "This is so beautiful! But you need to have a head for heights here! I'd be worried without the sticks for support."

71

Who Writes the Rules

Mosse smiled. "It's not as steep as it looks. The path is fairly wide and flat, cut across the gradient of the hill. It's completely safe. Even if you fell off the path, it isn't steep enough for you to slide downhill, so don't worry about the gorge. The trail is well away from the edge all the way round the hillside."

The path climbed gently around a curving mountainside for about a kilometre, traversing the slope as it rose. The meadows to either side were awash with flowers. Pinks, blues, purples, yellows and whites splashed the rich green foliage, which consisted mainly of coarse grasses and small scrub plants. A multitude of insects with brightly coloured wings flashed patterns of blues, browns or oranges as they fluttered around flowers.

Heelia noted that a particular insect species seemed to favour a particular plant species. Natural partners! She watched one insect alight on a favoured light purple flower, its wings fluttering slowly. It flashed bright orange and brown upper sides, then folded these vertically to display dark brown-black undersides. Underneath, there were black and white spots arranged to resemble large spider eyes to deter predating birds.

Complex pink and purple flowers curved their petals around openings. Coloured caverns enticing specific insects to come and feed, pollinating the flower as they did so. Over millions of years, particular pairs of flowers and insects had co-evolved. They had marched together along the trail of time, step-by-step, generation by generation. Synchronously changing their form to keep in step with each other until their stride was totally interdependent. An environmental change reducing the viability of either

72

species would automatically affect the other.

As they walked, Mosse and Heelia discussed the creatures that lived on the mountainside. The plants and insects that they could see, and other species they hoped to see. The furry, red-brown animals that burrowed under rocks and kept watch for each other, whistling to warn of the arrival of predatory hunting birds. The wild grazers that were sure-footed enough to climb the cliff faces in search of salt-licks and fresh springs.

Mutual admiration was growing between them. Heelia was more than just an attractive female. She was witty, warm, intelligent, curious and fascinated by the nature that they were admiring. Mosse was knowledgeable and helpful. Strong and charming. Serious but keen to make Heelia's experience enjoyable and educational. Their eye contact was becoming more frequent, and their posture more open towards each other as they both sensed an increasing connection.

A butterfly alighted on the thigh of Heelia's shorts. She stopped and exclaimed with delight. "Look, Mosse! I have a passenger!"

Heelia stretched out her hand in front of the insect. It touched an outstretched finger with antennae and the front pair of six legs. Gingerly it stepped the remaining four legs onto the finger, its rich colours contrasting with a pale pink painted fingernail. Lifting her hand slowly to chest height, Heelia held it before Mosse, gasping excitedly. The wings closed to a vertical position. The passenger had found a new flower on which it was content. It stepped mechanically and slowly to the back of her hand, exploring Heelia's skin with a long thin proboscis, tasting the surface.

73

Who Writes the Rules

"It's enjoying your taste. Probably the salts in your perspiration." Mosse then added, slightly embarrassed, "Sorry if that sounds a bit personal."

Laughing, Heelia replied, "Not at all. That's the truth. I'm probably horribly sweaty after climbing up this hill."

"I hope it's not too much for you. Maybe I should have chosen something less steep?"

"No, of course not. This is spectacular and not too difficult. Anyway, I need the exercise."

The insect fluttered its wings slowly a few times, flashing the colour pattern with interjections of cold, dark eye spots.

"If I could talk to you, what would you tell me?" Heelia spoke gently to the insect, jubilant that it had chosen her as a travel companion.

Already enchanted by his new acquaintance and now touched by her admiration for the butterfly, Mosse felt his heart grow warmer as their familiarity slowly grew.

The insect rode Heelia's hand for a further five minutes. They continued along the path as it gradually rose around the curved hillside to a highpoint at about 1,600 metres.

As they arrived around the curve, Heelia gasped at the view that opened up before her. "Wow! What can I say? This is amazing!"

Mosse hesitated a few seconds, scanning the scenery. "Now you understand why this is one of my favourite places," Mosse responded, pleased that Heelia appreciated the magnificence of the landscape.

From the highpoint on the trail, a spectacle had

come into view. The path ran gently downhill for about 500 metres to a fairly flat expanse of yellow-green, flower-rich grassland. A basin about 500 metres wide, below a horseshoe of crags and ridges, stretched away from them across a flat valley for about 1,000 metres. The meadow then slowly curved uphill, transforming to darker, broken forest, then scrubland, then scree slopes. Steep, rocky slopes rose from the scree to rugged grey ridges that were cut by fingers of glacier ice. Fingers pointed into the bowl as they descended from a fist of ice sheet that gripped the top of the ridge above. The scrub and scree slopes carried distinct ridged mounds of debris, deposited in walls that curved downhill. These were lateral moraines defining the edges of the now-melted glaciers, which had dropped them in the fairly recent past. The upper reaches of the moraines were pure grey scree. Green patches appeared progressively as the moraine descended towards the lower reaches. At the bottom, the vegetation was mature and dense, bordering the meadow which stretched across the bowl.

A dozen meltwater streams cascaded down the distant slopes beyond the meadow. They fed several larger streams, which wound their way across the grassland, converging to a focal point at the near end of the valley. Here, in the foreground, they joined into a single mountain torrent – a confluence – which dropped down a series of cascades and waterfalls into the gorge below the trail that they had just ascended.

Large granitic blocks were randomly distributed around the meadow, interspersed by mounds and ridges of smaller blocks and rock debris. Where the slope merged with meadow at the far end of the valley bottom, groups of

Who Writes the Rules

fairly mature conifers provided shelter on the flanks of the streams. A few dozen domesticated animals grazed on sections of the meadow, partly walled in by stone barriers that had been constructed from glacial debris.

At the entrance to the valley, above the top of the gorge and the confluence of the torrents, was a cluster of dark brown chalet buildings. Wooden cabins with silver-grey roofs suggested that a small community lived in this remote high valley. However, apart from a lodge providing meals and some accommodation for climbers and walkers, the buildings were mainly unused. The windows were shuttered. The chalets were remnants of a past when the meadow was more actively used for summer grazing.

"This valley is a glaciologist's dream," Mosse told Heelia. "Less than 10,000 years ago, this entire valley and all the land below, down to about 400 metres altitude, was filled with ice. You can see the valley is like a bowl with sides that were carved by descending ice as the glaciers flowed down from the ice cap above."

"It's so picturesque. Such a beautiful mountain scene," Heelia responded, awestruck.

"This valley is a great illustration of just about every textbook glaciation feature. Do you know much about glaciers?" Mosse asked.

"Only what I learned at school. Glaciers are like rivers of ice, moving very slowly. As they move, they cut the land. They pick up bits of rock and move them around, dropping them as perched blocks, and moraines and things," Heelia replied.

"And the Ice Age?" he continued.

"Of course," Heelia responded. "Thousands of

years ago, the planet was much colder. A lot of the land was covered in ice. There were many glaciers that shaped the land, but it's warmer now. The ice melted, and we can just see the features which they left when they melted."

"That's right. The ice used to fill this bowl. When we look at the features, we can see where past glaciers have melted away. You know what moraines are?"

"Yes, of course. They're like walls of rock dropped at the side or the end of a glacier." Heelia confirmed.

"Excellent!" replied Mosse. "The moraines and other features tell us the history of how ice eroded this valley. But not just at the end of the Ice Age. The ice is melting rapidly now because of climate change. What you see in front of you is living proof of that."

"That's interesting," Heelia responded. "We were taught about glaciation as if it was something from very ancient history, not linked to what's happening today."

"Climate is changing all the time. But never as fast as it has been in the last couple of centuries, especially in the last few decades. What is happening today is just like at the end of the Ice Age, but much faster."

"Should we be worried about that?" asked Heelia.

"Yes. For lots of reasons. Loss of stored fresh water; rising sea levels; mountain erosion … But first of all, think about what the glaciers are telling us. The ice has gradually melted back as climate became warmer in the past. Sometimes quickly, but other times with reversals, depending on how the climate was responding to the influence of planetary and lunar orbits, which vary over time. Every glacier has an equilibrium point. Above that point, ice is accumulating, and below it, it is melting. If the climate gets warmer, then the equilibrium point moves back up the glacier. The glacier shrinks backwards as the snout melts away, dropping a trail of rocky debris along its path and walls of moraine debris where its sides were."

"So, the bottom of the glacier moves uphill," observed Heelia.

"Exactly! If the temperature stays the same, but the climate gets wetter, the equilibrium point may also move downwards as more ice accumulates. The dynamics are quite complex. But in general, the glaciers have been receding upwards for most of the last 10,000 years. Glacier melting has accelerated significantly in the last 200 years. This is because we Majans as a species have been changing the gases in the atmosphere, mainly by burning coal and oil!"

"We hear a lot about climate change," noted Heelia, "but when people don't see big changes in their day-to-day lives, they don't really think about it."

"Absolutely true," Mosse agreed. "This valley tells a lot of stories about how the landscape has changed. Not just over thousands of years, but also in recent decades."

"At one point, the bowl probably held a lake behind a wall of debris that blocked the entrance to the gorge. As the glacier melted, the water pressure must have washed through the debris at some point. The lake drained down the gorge, which would likely have caused a serious mudslide and flood below. It must have been several thousand years ago, maybe before anybody lived in these mountain valleys."

"That would have been dramatic," Heelia observed.

"If you look at the current glaciers above this

valley, you can see that they have completely melted below about 2,000 metres altitude. The lateral moraines below them are very prominent." Mosse pointed to a prominent grey wall of rock on the right-hand side of the scree slope. "Look over there, about two kilometres ahead of us. There is a grey ridge with steep sides, like an upside-down V, which forms a wall descending down the slope. Can you see that?"

"Yes," replied Heelia. "It's quite prominent."

Mosse continued, "As you look down the slope, it gets greener. That's where the vegetation has been able to colonise the rocks without being disturbed by glacier ice. Coming downhill, along the ridge, the vegetation gets more mature. This moraine shows how the influence of the ice is moving quickly uphill. The end of the glacier has moved up by about 200 metres in altitude in the last 100 years or so. If you see old paintings of the glaciers around this massif, they all tell the same story. The glaciers have all melted back significantly in the last 100 years."

Heelia gazed with awe at the valley and the features that enclosed it.

"It's amazing; the power of Mother Nature, to have shaped all of this! And it's such a beautiful place. A real paradise."

"But climate change is destroying this scene and disturbing the creatures that live here," Mosse replied.

"That's so sad," Heelia responded. "It will be a lost paradise."

The insect that had been tasting Heelia's skin fluttered its wings and took off.

"Ah, the Spirit of the Ice!" Heelia called out. "You

Who Writes the Rules

welcomed us into your kingdom, and now you leave us to explore your world!"

Mosse laughed, "It does look a bit like a fairy-tale kingdom down there. Let's go down and see if we can find a pot of gold."

"We have to spot the rainbow first," said Heelia as they set off down the trail towards the climber's lodge in the chalet cluster.

Chapter 6. Sense, Sensuality and Sensibility

Mosse and Heelia wound their way along the trail for a few hundred metres of undulating hillside, descending slightly into the bowl that had been shaped by the ice sheet and vacated by receding glaciers. As Mosse had said, this was a world apart from the modernised tourist developments scattered across the mountains and valleys to the outside, none of which were now visible.

They arrived at the small cluster of chalet buildings on the north side of the torrent that drained all of the glaciers and meltwater from above the valley into the gorge below. The gurgling and splashing sound of cascades and fast-running water pervaded the area around the climber's refuge and café, which provided meals and drinks to passing walkers.

"I think we should stop here for a drink and toilet break," Mosse suggested.

"Yes, that's fine with me," replied Heelia. "We can rest our legs for a little while."

"The walk back will be a bit easier," said Mosse. "All downhill. The meadow in this bowl is fairly flat, depending on how far you want to go up at the far end. But we can decide when we're ready to turn back."

"Not until after our picnic, of course," laughed Heelia.

They ordered a hot drink each, chatted for a while, and then took it in turns to use an outside toilet that seemed to hang precariously close to the torrent at the top of a cascade that plunged into the gorge below. It was still only

81

Who Writes the Rules

about midday. The early summer radiance from Sol was strong at close to 1,600 metres altitude, promising to maintain a pleasantly warm temperature throughout the afternoon.

They strolled along a lightly used track adjacent to the largest of three streams that converged into a single torrent above the cascade near the refuge. The stream bed was covered by a trail of rock debris, which had been dropped from glacial ice and washed downstream. The bed was about 25 metres wide, but today the stream level was relatively low, meandering rapidly down a central channel of two to three metres. Beaches of granite and gneiss pebbles, rounded by constant battering in fast-flowing water, formed on the longer side of each meander.

"Can we walk in the water?" Heelia asked.

"If you want to, but you may have a bit of a shock," laughed Mosse.

They dropped their packs on the grassy bank, removed their boots and socks, and gingerly slid from the bank onto the pebble-beach surface beside a meander. The water ran fast through the central channel, but the stones in the channel were smooth enough to stand on. As they reached the side of the channel, Heelia stretched pink painted toenails above the water and dipped them below the surface.

"Wow! It's freezing," she yelled, pulling her toes back out of the water.

"I warned you that you might have a shock," laughed Mosse. "This is glacial meltwater that has flowed rapidly for a couple of kilometres since it melted, so it's not had a lot of time to warm up. Bet you haven't got the courage to step in," Mosse dared her.

"Neither have you!" Heelia responded defiantly. "But I will if you do it first," she challenged, laughing.

"No problem," Mosse retorted, immediately taking a step forward.

Within seconds, Mosse could feel the cold biting his feet as Heelia hesitated on the edge. "That's not fair," he complained to Heelia. "You were supposed to come too!"

Giggling, Heelia took a step into the freezing water until both feet were submerged above her ankles. Her eyes widened, and she gasped deeply as the cold bit her feet. With a horrified expression, she rapidly turned to look directly at Mosse and pushed her hand towards him.

"Arrgh! Help me get out!" she exclaimed in a suppressed scream.

Mosse grabbed her hand and stepped back out of the water onto the pebble beach, pulling Heelia towards him.

Their eyes met as they almost collided. They laughed together while still gasping from the shock of the freezing water on their feet. Mosse suppressed an urge to pull Heelia closer, releasing her hand but still holding her gaze. Heelia wiped a tear of laughter from the corner of her eye. She had enjoyed the shock of the water. And she had enjoyed the handholding - if all too brief. She would not have objected if Mosse had pulled her closer.

"I have a small towel in my bag," Mosse told Heelia. "Better dry your feet quickly and get them warmed up."

They sat on the grassy bank, dried their feet and let them warm in the sun for some minutes before putting their

Who Writes the Rules

footwear back on.

"Ready to continue up the valley?" Mosse suggested.

"Yes, please. Let's go and find a nice picnic spot."

Heelia would have liked Mosse to take her hand again. He was tempted, but wanted to avoid offending her.

"How are your feet?" Mosse asked.

"Still freezing, but they'll be ok when we've walked a bit."

Although there had been a few other walkers at the refuge, they had diverged on different paths, leaving Mosse and Heelia alone in what felt like their own private mountain meadow. The sounds were of nature: fast-flowing water, occasional animal calls, bleating, lowing, cawing, chirping, the buzz of an insect. As they strolled along the path that followed the riverbank towards the slope at the far end of the valley, they were oblivious to the world outside their local paradise.

About a kilometre from the refuge, a copse of conifers guarded a clearing where the grassland merged into patches of thicket and denser scrubland. A cuboid block of granitic rock almost two metres in each dimension, with several smaller blocks close to it, formed a partial wall around which they entered the clearing. At the sunnier side of the wall, the ground was level and covered with tall grass and flowering plants. Beyond this, another stream skirted the opposite side of the clearing. Above the stream, a dense thicket obscured the base of a moraine, which curved up the hillside for more than 500 metres. The climbing ridgeline of the moraine guided their eyes to the bottom of a prominent glacier that dominated the upper slope.

"I think we've found a perfect, sheltered picnic spot," Mosse suggested.

"Yes, this looks great. I'm hungry after all that walking uphill," Heelia smiled, indicatively patting her abdomen.

Mosse untied the picnic blanket and laid it across the grass at the base of the large block of migmatite, a granite-like rock with large crystals of black, white and grey mixed with swirling bands of mainly pink feldspar crystals. He sat on one edge and patted down the vegetation below to flatten it.

Inviting Heelia to join him, he said, "If you sit on that side, we can put the food in the middle and lean back against the rock as a backrest."

Heelia joined him on the blanket as he opened the backpack and began to remove the contents. Placing four disposable plates in the centre, he put salad items on one, cheeses and meats on another, and one plate each in front of himself and Heelia. He took out two bread rolls from the bag, placing each on a serviette, and poured water into two disposable cups.

"Wow, you're very organised! This looks like a well-planned picnic," Heelia complimented.

Mosse smiled, extracting the glasses, drinks and wine bottle. "The easiest way to deal with this is to build your own sandwiches," said Mosse as he tore open a bread roll and filled it with a mix of cheese, meat and salad.

Heelia followed suit, took a bite and savoured the mixed flavours of her sandwich. She had become hungry as they had walked. Now she salivated, induced by the rich smell and taste of the food. "Delicious, Mosse. I was ready

Who Writes the Rules

for this."

"Would you like some wine?" asked Mosse, opening the bottle and arranging two glasses, ready to pour.

Heelia hesitated before answering. In her family's culture, alcohol was forbidden, although many people, including her parents, would ignore this within the privacy of their family homes. She had drunk alcohol before and enjoyed it, but the moment suddenly reminded her that she and Mosse came from different backgrounds, where the rules were different in many ways.

"Yes, please," she answered after a brief moment.

Mosse poured two glasses of wine. Picking up the wine glasses, he reached one out to Heelia. As she took it from him, their fingers touched. They caught each other's eye, both tensing for a moment, each wanting the contact to endure.

"Cheers!" said Mosse, releasing the connection, raising his glass and relieving the building tension.

"Good health!" replied Heelia, holding his gaze as their eyes locked.

Mosse looked down, embarrassed, and raised the wine glass to his lips. Heelia could see his embarrassment but somehow didn't share it. She felt a growing warmth between them. They hardly knew each other, but she sensed strong chemistry between them – an attraction that was physical, intellectual, emotional and sexual.

There was a short silence as both were unsure how to continue the conversation. Heelia sipped the wine. It was sweet, spicy, aromatic and fruity, warming as it descended to her stomach.

"This is very nice wine, Mosse," she said, breaking

the silence.

"Glad you like it," he replied. "It's one of my favourites."

They finished eating their sandwiches and chatted while they sipped another glass of wine each. They then packed the items from their picnic back into the backpack. Heelia glanced up at the large block that had formed their backrest.

"Let's climb the block, Mosse!" she proclaimed, like a playful child.

The block was about two metres tall, but the sides were sub-vertical, with sufficient footholds to make it an easy ascent.

"Come on then," agreed Mosse. "Let's do it!"

They scrambled up from the blanket. Heelia placed her right foot on a suitable step to start the climb. Finding handholds, she pulled herself up and positioned her left foot on a higher support point. As she struggled to reach the top, Mosse assisted from behind by placing his hands under her buttocks and pushing her upwards.

On reaching the top, Heelia stood upright, scanning the view of the clearing and the valley beyond from her new vantage point. As Mosse emerged beside her, she turned towards him.

"I think you enjoyed that," she mocked accusingly.

"I was only trying to be helpful," he responded before adding, "but since you've mentioned it, I'd be happy to help again anytime."

Heelia giggled in response. Feeling the effect of the wine, she swayed slightly before grabbing Mosse's left arm for support. Mosse placed his right arm on the back of her waist.

"You're not drunk, are you, Heelia?"

"No, just a tiny bit wobbly," she laughed, catching his eye with a longing gaze.

Mosse had held back his instinctive desires, but he could no longer resist. He pulled her gently towards him. She reached her arms around his back and lifted her face towards his, their lips meeting – briefly, at first, barely touching each other, then merging into a long, passionate kiss.

Heelia had been a gift to Mosse's senses. Her visual beauty had grabbed his attention. Her sweet smell, enhanced by a faint, aromatic perfume, transfixed him. The gentle singing of her voice enchanted him. Her touch had excited him, and now her taste aroused him.

Since the first living cells evolved, their existence, growth and reproduction depended on their ability to sense the details and changes in their environment. Changes of temperature, pressure, chemical gradients, light intensity and wavelength all provided external stimuli to which an organism could react. Cells and organisms that could respond to any of these variable environmental factors were favoured by evolution. The capability to react to environmental changes could result in finding nutrients, energy or reproductive partners.

Simple photosynthesisers would have benefited from any new ability to move towards light sources. Everything that is edible gets eaten eventually – photosynthesisers by herbivores, prey animals by predators, and dead organisms by fungi and bacteria. Hydrocarbon energy sources and nutrients are continually recycled through ecosystems, through food chains, and generation by generation of each component species. Constant changes in the external stimuli drove the continual evolution of sensory systems and the capabilities of organisms to act upon the effectiveness of these.

As organisms evolved into more complex, multi-tissue, multi-organ species, sensory systems increased in sophistication. They functioned by informing a central coordinating organ, a nerve ganglion or a brain, via a nervous system. The brain reacted, consciously or subconsciously, to sensory stimuli by controlling movement of the organism to allow it to respond to or exploit external conditions. As predators improved their predation capabilities, prey would evolve improved predation avoidance techniques. At any stage in the history of life, within every ecosystem was a dynamic interaction of species responding to and evolving to move harmoniously with environmental changes.

All life on the surface of the planet Thera was fuelled by the continual influx of solar energy. Evolution was driven by sex. Without sexual reproduction and intergenerational death, there could be no evolution. Sexual reproduction created a range of new genetic blueprints in every generation of every species in every ecosystem. As organisms evolved complexity, their sensory systems were not just focussed on survival by finding shelter and nourishment, but also on ensuring that they found sexual partners to ensure the continuation of the life of their own genes, carried into the next generation.

Many species developed complex courtship behaviours, often using visual displays, vivid colours, songs, dances or routines. One gender would perform while the other decided whether the performer was a good biological bet with whom to share genes in the production of the next generation.

In the Majan species, sex had become more than a means of procreation. The male genitalia produced a constant supply of sperm cells from when an individual was a young teenager until he was an elderly gentleman. His instinctive sexual desire created a perpetual need to release the supply of sperm as it accumulated, like removing shipments of goods from the loading bay at the end of a production line. The female produced a mature egg once a month, which would wait several days for the arrival of sperm to fertilise it.

However, the Majans had a complex family life. Families usually had anything up to about a dozen children, with a year or more between siblings, none of whom could easily live independently until they were at least in their late teenage years. It was important that more than one parent, or an extended family, were involved in child-rearing.

While biologically, sex had always been the driver of evolutionary change, it had also become a source of pleasure used to cement the relationship between adult individuals. Enhanced touch associated with erogenous areas of the body, combined with chemical hormone release during sexual activity, produced sensations that led to the experience of sexual orgasm. In the case of the male, this was associated with ejaculation of sperm from the production line, temporarily freeing the loading bay for the next batch.

For the Majan female, the sexual process was not so

simple. In the event of pregnancy, she must carry at least one growing foetus for nine months before the birth of a highly dependent infant. Her role in reproduction was much more significant than that of the male, who might be regarded simply as a sperm donor. However, since families usually needed two parents, it was important that the mother retain and cement the relationship with the father. The pleasure of sex was instrumental in most couples for the happy continuity of this relationship.

As a consequence of the Majan social structure, while sex was still the evolutionary driver, it had become almost more important as a source of pleasure and bonding. This had reached the extent that most sexual activity was purely for pleasure, not necessarily for reproduction. Throughout Majan history, sexual desire had affected many aspects of the behaviour and regulation of different societies.

Desire was constantly present, particularly among males. For females, establishing trusting and loving relationships, usually enhanced by sex, was of higher priority. That sex had become more important among Majans than reproduction was exemplified by the existence of many same-sex couples, who could not reproduce biologically together, but could mutually satisfy what had become their basic instincts.

Neither Mosse nor Heelia had gone to the glacial valley intending to reproduce, or even to perform sex acts which potentially could lead to reproduction. They were instinctively attracted to each other, initially visually, but had become increasingly linked emotionally and psychologically. Natural pheromones may have added to the

91

attraction, possibly enhanced by manufactured perfumes. They had been enjoying each other's company, but had both been stimulated by brief touches that they instinctively wanted to prolong. Their interactions and body language had drawn them closer. When their lips met and their bodies locked together on top of the rock, they were both slipping into a state of sexual arousal.

Mosse traced the curve of Heelia's back with his fingertips. One hand placed on her upper back pulled her towards him, while the other moved down her back and over her buttocks and hips, caressing and pulling their bodies together. Both hearts beat faster. Heelia felt a flush of warmth in her face and genitals as her nipples hardened in response to Mosse's caress. They continued a long deep kiss, tasting each other, losing all thoughts of anything beyond their own bodies. A gentle purr of pleasure emanated from Heelia as she allowed herself to be absorbed by the kiss.

A noise in the distance distracted them.

"Some people coming this way," said Mosse, breaking the kiss.

Some other visitors to the valley were walking along the path towards the clearing, just a few minutes away.

"Maybe we should get down before we fall off our perch," joked Heelia.

Mosse scrambled down the rock and reached back to help Heelia descend. As she dropped to the ground, he put his arms around her once more, and they embraced again for a repeat kiss. Heelia trembled. For an instant, she imagined lying naked with Mosse, making love on the picnic blanket, then lying flat on the rock exposed to the mountains, like a sexual, sacrificial offering to the Spirit of the Ice.

They broke off as the voices came close by, staring deep into each other's eyes.

Heelia had wanted to go to the glaciers with Mosse today and enjoy his company, but this passionate, sexual chemistry was unforeseen. What was she doing? Was this just a holiday fling, or was there something stronger here? This was a male from a different culture, who drank alcohol, and probably didn't share her religion … if he had a religion! She liked him, and her heart wanted to go further, but her sensible side was telling her to cool down the contact. She hardly knew him, but wanted to know more.

"Hello."

"Good afternoon."

Two people approached, walking a pet, which ran to Heelia happily, tail wagging, as they came to the clearing.

"Hello! You're very friendly. What's your name?" Heelia asked the animal.

"His name is Pepper," came a reply from his owner as Heelia scratched behind his ears.

"You're lovely," Heelia informed Pepper.

"Nice picnic spot," Pepper's owner observed. "Enjoy it."

"Thanks, enjoy your walk," responded Mosse as the walkers headed on up the streamside path.

Mosse turned to Heelia, feeling a little sheepish.

"I hope you don't think I planned this," he ventured.

"You certainly produced a nice picnic … perfectly planned. And you brought a bottle of wine! Maybe you

Who Writes the Rules

wanted to get me drunk ..." Heelia joked.

Slightly taken aback, Mosse asserted, "I wanted you to have nice food washed down with a nice glass of wine. I didn't expect you to be drunk on two glasses!"

"I'm not drunk, maybe a little bit tipsy. I don't drink alcohol very often." Heelia giggled and smiled at Mosse.

"I was joking. Don't be so serious. I know you didn't intend this, and neither did I, but I enjoyed every second and can't wait to do it again," she assured him. "I can see you're a gentleman who wouldn't want to take advantage of a lady … especially one who's drunk too much!"

Warmed by her response, Mosse smiled back. "I enjoyed every second too. I'm flattered that such a lovely lady would permit me to hold and kiss her. Can we try again to make sure it was as good as we imagined?"

Heelia swayed into Mosse's arms once more, and they kissed again, slowly and warmly, enjoying the close, sensual contact. Heelia was becoming conscious of their mutual excitement and decided it was time to break off again.

"I'm not sure this is the right time or place for this. It was our valley until those people came along, but now it's been invaded. Maybe we should walk a little further up the moraine."

Mosse sighed, "Yes, I was supposed to be showing you nature in the valley."

"What we just did seemed natural enough to me," laughed Heelia, picking up her pack while Mosse retied the picnic blanket beneath his backpack.

The couple crossed the clearing and followed a

track along the second stream until they found a suitable point to cross towards the moraine. They picked their way through scrub as they worked their way up the slope for several hundred metres. Ascending the side of the moraine, they emerged from the scrub. They clambered up a bank of rock debris to the ridge that ran along the length of the moraine. Around their feet, small colonising mountain plants were establishing a foothold on the moraine debris. As they proceeded up the sloping ridge, the plants disappeared, and the surface of the rocks was coated green with algae and small mosses. Further up the moraine, they could see the rock was grey. On the upper reaches, plants had not yet been able to coat the rock. On the right-hand side of the moraine, glacier ice was still present, covered by a layer of blue-grey rock dust.

"It's so easy to visualise how the glacier used to be lower but is melting back up the mountainside, allowing the vegetation to progressively colonise the moraine," Mosse pointed out.

From their position on the moraine, they could scan the valley sides around them. Everywhere they looked, they could detect the ghosts of past glaciers, which had shaped the terrain, gouging out their tracks and depositing the materials that would tell their story long after their demise.

"This has been so interesting, Mosse. Thank you for showing me nature in this magical valley," beamed Heelia, eyes twinkling.

Mosse responded by hugging her to him once more and resuming the kisses they had shared in the clearing.

When they eventually surfaced and locked eyes again, Mosse added, "I think it's time to head back now while the sunshine is still on the valley. We can have a little dessert stop on the way back."

They retraced their steps back to the clearing and alongside the stream towards the climber's refuge. Stopping at the site of their earlier paddle in the stream, they sat on the bank and shared the cakes and fruit juice from Mosse's backpack before continuing the return trek.

After finishing their dessert, they walked back past the chalet cluster, out of the valley and along the trail through the butterfly meadow. Happily chattering and laughing as they descended through the forest and meadows, they passed through the village where they had joined the trail and arrived back at the parking area. They exchanged few words on the drive back to the hotel, both slightly fatigued from the trek and pondering the physical and emotional contacts that they had shared.

Mosse parked outside Heelia's hotel and exited the vehicle before moving to open the passenger door.

"How many more days are you here for?" asked Mosse.

"Four nights, including tonight. Then I have to catch a coach back to Perali."

"Why don't you come and stay with me for a few days?"

"Maybe you just want to get me into your bed?" returned Heelia with an inquiring smile.

"I have a guest room," Mosse responded genuinely.

Heelia gave Mosse an engaging look. Tilting her head to one side, she appeared to reflect on the suggestion.

"Well, if I can have my own room … I could stay here tonight and check out in the morning. That will give me a chance to get organised," she replied, imagining that Mosse's room may be more interesting than the guest room.

She wanted to be with him, to continue their kissing and intimacy as far as they felt appropriate, but she still harboured the inhibitions presented by their cultural differences. In the worst case, she could always insist on using the guest room, but her heart wanted otherwise.

"Fine," Mosse replied. "I can come and get you in the morning … About 9:30 again? Then we'll have time to explore somewhere else. Do you like swimming?"

"As long as it isn't in glacial meltwater!" laughed Heelia.

"There's a shallow lake in the valley below us. It warms up fairly quickly, and the weather's been sunny the last few weeks. Still a bit early in the year, but I'm sure we can risk it."

"That sounds nice," Heelia affirmed with a smile. "I'll look forward to you picking me up tomorrow."

"Just one thing Mosse … You told me you were going up the mountain to gather some data when you invited me to join you, but I didn't even see a notebook. Did you get your data?" Heelia teased, her eyes glinting.

Mosse reddened. "I keep it all in my head. I got everything I needed," he responded with a nervous laugh.

They hugged once more and parted with a brief kiss on the cheek. Heelia entered the hotel door, glancing back at Mosse with a radiant smile.

Mosse returned to his vehicle and headed for home, elated that the day's events had progressed as they had, and jubilantly anticipating the next few days.

Who Writes the Rules

Chapter 7. Going Swimmingly

Reflecting on the day's events as he drove back to his chalet, Mosse realised he needed to prepare for the arrival of an important guest. He diverted from the route home to visit a large food store at which he stocked up on some essential items, as well as purchasing fresh meats, fruits and vegetables, sweet and savoury snacks, wines and a mixture of alcoholic and soft drinks. Returning to his chalet, he unloaded his purchases, placing perishable items into refrigeration cabinets, and drinks into a cellar.

Once the shopping had been organised, he prepared a casserole containing red meat and the white fruiting bodies of a fungus in a mix of meat stock and red wine, flavoured by some spices and a pungent plant bulb that made his eyes water. He set the casserole to cook slowly for several hours.

From a laundry cupboard, he took two sets of bedding covers: one for the guest room and one for his own room. After making up both beds with fresh bedding, he turned his attention to cleaning the bathroom, guestroom shower and kitchen more thoroughly than he had done for months.

Finishing the spring clean, Mosse threw together a few snack items and poured himself a sparkling, alcoholic drink, which he consumed slowly, sitting at the terrace table as the sky darkened. There were few lights to the south, down the valley, away from the Carina communal centre. He gazed into the night sky above, where the curtains of air pollution, dust and light had been drawn back to reveal the

98

history of the Universe, told by the billions of stars and galaxies, whose light could now reach his eyes. The clear night sky presented another spectacular scene, hidden to most of the Majans by the light and dust pollution that cloaked their urban societies, clouding their eyes to the faint lights from distant heavenly bodies.

Mosse finished his drink, washed and cleared away the items he had used, and showered before going off to bed.

Shortly after returning to her hotel, Heelia informed Mila, the receptionist, that she would be checking out the next morning, cutting her stay by three days.

"Did you have a problem with your room?" asked the receptionist.

"No, the room and the hotel have been perfect, but I've met an old friend who has invited me to stay with her," Heelia lied.

Mila raised one eyebrow a little and replied with a knowing smile. "I see. That's fine; you can check out after breakfast tomorrow."

"Thank you," Heelia said, blushing, feeling that the receptionist had intuitively seen through her.

She returned to her room, where she organised her bags for a quick exit the following day, and then dined in the hotel restaurant. After dinner, she soaked in a bath of warm water and perfumed oils before taking to bed. Sleep didn't come quickly, pushed back by the recollection of the embraces and kisses she had enjoyed earlier in the day. Surely there would be much more of the same tomorrow.

Who Writes the Rules

In the morning, Mosse woke, dressed, had breakfast and sat on the terrace counting down the seconds before it was time to descend into Carina, where he arrived considerably earlier than intended. He stopped at the bakery for fresh bread, then drove to the hotel, where he parked outside. Walking to a nearby café, he ordered a hot drink to kill time until his 9:30 appointment.

Mosse entered the hotel at the agreed time to find Heelia sitting next to her baggage in the reception area, impatient as he had been to spend more time together.

"Morning, Mosse!" beamed Heelia.

"Morning, Heelia!" he responded, smiling.

From the reception desk, Mila looked up at Mosse, then grinned knowingly at Heelia. "I hope you've enjoyed your stay with us?" she queried.

"Yes, very much," Heelia assured her, her face reddening a little with embarrassment.

Heelia had one medium-sized suitcase and the small backpack that she had carried the previous day. Mosse collected both and took them to his vehicle, placing them in the back.

Heelia followed him out of the hotel and into the car. As soon as they were sitting down, they turned to look each other in the eye, both smiling blissfully, excited to be sharing each other's company again. They turned their faces together and exchanged a long kiss.

"I've been dying to do that again," said Heelia.

"Me too. But I thought it best to wait until we were out of the reception," Mosse laughed.

They drove out of Carina and a kilometre uphill, where Mosse turned onto the access road that led to his chalet. After parking, he exited the car and helped Heelia from the passenger seat before picking up her bags from the back seat.

"This way," he indicated, turning around the side of the house, and stepping up to the terrace. He strode to the door at the back of the kitchen, unlocked it and entered.

Heelia followed, hesitating on the terrace as she scanned the view of Carina and the mountain massif beyond on the east side of the valley.

"This view is wonderful, Mosse. I bet you could just sit here all day looking across the valley."

Mosse smiled, "Yes, I sometimes do. I was lucky to have found this house. If you look across the valley, a little to your right, you can see where we were yesterday. You can even make out the moraine we climbed up. You can see the darker grey ridge rising up towards the glacier above."

Mosse pointed his outstretched hand towards the moraine.

Looking along his arm, Heelia declared, "Oh yes. I can see it now. How far is it from here?"

"About eight kilometres in a straight line," Mosse answered. "Let's get you settled in; then we can come back out with a drink."

Mosse deposited Heelia's bags in the guest room, then showed her around his chalet. "Nice house. Too big for just one person," she smiled.

"I hope the guestroom is ok for you?" Mosse enquired.

"It'll be perfect," answered Heelia, wondering how likely it was that she would sleep in the guest room. When Mosse had shown her the room, they had both held back from embracing again, apprehensive of what that would probably lead to.

Mosse prepared a hot drink, which they took to the terrace table, where they sat together on a two-person cushioned garden lounge seat. Heelia shuffled closer to Mosse and laid her head against his shoulder.

"I like it here," she said softly. "So peaceful … And magnificent views."

"Unfortunately, you can hear constant traffic noise in the distance. It never seems to go away. Constant noise pollution!"

Mosse referred to a major transport route in the valley below, 400 metres altitude below them, and about four kilometres away. A perpetual reminder that they were still part of a noisy, polluting, civilised society. He returned to the kitchen, picked up a portable loudspeaker and switched on another device that transmitted music to the speaker.

"That should drown out the traffic noise," he smiled, returning close to Heelia and setting the loudspeaker on the table.

"Do you have a swimsuit with you?" he asked Heelia.

"Yes, but are you sure I'm not going to freeze again?" she demanded.

"It'll be fine. It's sunny, so you can warm up on the beach," he laughed.

"A beach in the mountains?" she asked in disbelief.

"Yes, it's at a lake in another flat valley, much lower than here, about 500 metres above sea level with a fabricated beach. It's very popular in the peak summertime, but it should be quiet today."

After finishing their drinks, they changed into swimwear in their respective rooms and redressed. Mosse took two sun lounger chairs and beach towels from a store room. He put these into the back of his vehicle. Heelia climbed into the passenger seat, and they set off for the beach.

Mosse followed a minor road shortcut through local farming communities, allowing them to drop quickly into the valley, bypassing Carina town. Once in the valley bottom, they drove to an access road that took them to a car park adjacent to an oblong lake of about 200 metres in width and 1,000 metres in length. A beach of coarse sand curved around one end of the lake. The beach sloped gently into the water, so the adjacent end of the lake was fairly shallow and warmed quickly in sunny weather. A striking feature of the lake was that when there was no wind, the surface mirrored the reflection of the White Mountain massif that rose behind it. It provided a stunning backdrop.

Admiring the reflection of the mountain, Heelia noted, "You keep taking me to these fantastic views, Mosse. Another lovely place!"

They carried the sun loungers and towels to a flat, grassy area by the edge of the beach. There were several dozen other lake visitors on the verges behind the beach, but it was far from crowded. They had easily managed to find a private area shaded by an embankment.

Stripping down to their swimwear, they settled onto the sunloungers, holding hands and exchanging conversation while they relaxed and enjoyed the warmth of the midday sun.

Who Writes the Rules

"So, what exactly are you studying, Mosse, that allows you to keep all the data in your head?" Heelia joked.

"At the moment, I'm just finishing some self-study courses and a couple of projects. Afterwards, I'd like to get into research in evolutionary ecology. I'm interested in how environmental variations, such as climate changes, influence evolution."

"That sounds very clever."

"Unfortunately, the current rate of climate change isn't very clever. Climate is continuously changing, and always has been, but the things we have done in the last couple of hundred years have caused changes at an unprecedented rate."

"And you think that has some effect on evolution?" Heelia asked.

"Evolution is driven by environmental change, which organisms must respond to by adapting, but if the changes are too fast for adaptation to be possible, then that is likely to lead to extinctions and changes in the geographical ranges that species can occupy."

"I'm not sure what you mean by "driven by environmental change." I thought evolution was driven by mutations and competition. Isn't it survival of the fittest?"

Mosse was impressed by Heelia's understanding and interest. Trying to elaborate, he continued, "Organisms don't just evolve in isolation. They inhabit niches within ecosystems, and those individuals that are most successful in having fertile offspring will be the ones whose genes are passed on to the next generation within their niche. But if something changes in the environment, temperature, water availability, nutrients etc., then any individuals that are metabolically better suited to the new conditions will be the ones more likely to pass on their genes. Does that make sense?"

"Yes, I think so. That's natural selection, isn't it? Survival of the fittest?" Heelia responded.

Mosse continued. "It's not about the biggest and best keep winning the race. It's the ones that work best in the changed conditions, which will pass on their genes. Evolution just means that the total gene pool for the species is constantly changing in order to adapt to the prevailing conditions. The characteristics or the metabolism of the species adjusts over multiple generations to keep in step with environmental changes. Species don't just evolve on their own, but advance in the context of the environment around them. Their gene pool responds to environmental change. That's natural selection of the best adaptations. Do you see that?"

"I think so, but shouldn't that also mean the species will get bigger and better as it evolves?"

"For most organisms, that seems to have been the case over millions of years, maybe because they're competing with each other or with other species, always trying to find food, find breeding partners and avoid being eaten. So over time, there is a tendency towards increasing sophistication. But short-term changes among a population may be just selection of variations in the gene pool in response to environmental change. Some of these may be reversed in the longer-term, depending on changes in the environment."

Heelia listened carefully as Mosse tried to elaborate.

Who Writes the Rules

"A characteristic that seems to be advantageous in some circumstances may be less advantageous or even deleterious after an environmental change. Most of what I'm talking about happens at a level that you can't easily see. Like in the metabolic processes of cells, or in development of a growing foetus, for example. Can you imagine that?"

"I'm not sure what you mean. You're saying I can't see this. I have to imagine it?" Heelia was struggling to follow his logic.

"If you think of flightless birds, their ancestors evolved from ancient lizard-like animals and learned to fly. But as they continued to evolve in their local niches, they didn't need to fly, so they gradually lost the ability. They didn't need to become better flyers. They lost the ability, but still have residual wings. I hope I haven't lost you yet?" Mosse asked.

"No, it's interesting, but it's still not clear to me how environmental change drives evolution. From what you're saying, evolution should happen anyway because mutations happen; so there is always selection, even if the environment stays the same." Heelia questioned.

Mosse laughed and admitted, "I think you're right, Heelia. Evolution would happen anyway because of selection of variations between individuals. But change happens – day changes to night, summer to winter, hot to cold. Climate and weather are changing all the time over various time cycles. The faster a change happens, the more pressure there is to adapt to it.

"I did a study project for an exam recently, where I put out a bird table with red and yellow dough "bugs" on it.

I had to see whether the birds showed a colour preference. So, I pointed a video camera at the bird table and then played back the bird predation scenes. I did this over a period of three months from late spring to mid-summer, an hour after sunrise every morning, and then analysed the results. In the video, I could not only see the order in which the "bugs" were eaten. I could also see what bird species ate each "bug."

"What I found was that selection of red or yellow was fairly random in the first month, but it became more specifically skewed by the third month. I also noted that nearly all of the predation in the first month was by common brown birds who were happy to eat any colour. They were joined by a few blue-green species in the second month, and by a blue-grey species with an orange breast in the third month. So, the environment was changing. The predators changed from month to month. A red bug variant that was around in the first month would be less likely to be eaten than a red bug that was active in the third month."

"What if the bugs live more than three months?" Heelia asked. "Maybe they'll all get eaten sooner or later?"

"That was just meant to be an illustration. The point is that environments are constantly changing. In this case, the predators vary, and the direction of evolution will vary. Individuals are selected according to current conditions. In this example, red bugs are more likely to survive in late spring, but yellow bugs are better adapted to mid-summer. If something happens to affect the bird populations, then this may change."

"But wasn't that just about selection of red or yellow, not evolution? Doesn't that mean environmental change drives selection, not evolution?" Heelia suggested.

Mosse was impressed that Heelia was actually interested in continuing a technical discussion on the topic. He had expected her to switch off more quickly.

"You're not wrong. The change I described illustrates how a short-term external change affects selection of individuals in a particular generation. The bugs that don't get eaten are the ones whose genes get passed on. But environmental changes are happening on many different scales, affecting multiple generations. Evolution is the cumulative effect of selection over multiple generations. If the environment stayed constant, there would still be background genetic variation due to simple mutations within a population, which might be more randomly selected. But environmental variation creates a driving force to determine which individuals are selected. Is that a bit clearer?"

"Yes, I think I see what you mean."

"At school, were you taught about predator and prey cycles?"

"Yes, I know about that," replied Heelia. "When there are lots of prey animals, the predators eat them, and their population gets bigger. But then they eat too many prey animals, so they have less food. When there are less prey animals, the predators starve, and their population falls, so less prey get eaten, and their population can get bigger again, and so on."

"Exactly!" declared Mosse, surprised and impressed by Heelia's understanding of the subject. "That sounds like a nice straightforward process, but life's not so simple. That picture treats the prey and predator as if they are independent of the rest of the ecological environment.

Consider this. Everything alive is fuelled by solar energy. It gets trapped by plants, which synthesise hydrocarbons. The plants are eaten by herbivores, which are eaten by carnivores, which are recycled by detritivores when they die. That creates more soil nutrients that plants need in order to grow. This picture is a bit simpler than most actual ecosystems, but imagine there is plenty of vegetation because it's been a good year for plants to grow. The prey animals do very well, and the population goes up. Then the predators are able to eat well, and their population grows. The prey can now be badly affected by either poor grass growth or by increasing predator numbers.

"Now, are you with me on that? Solar energy fuels the system, plants grow, herbivores eat plants, carnivores eat herbivores, and all dead stuff goes back to nutrient supply," Mosse summarised.

"Yes, I can see that," replied Heelia.

"Good, that brings me to a key point that is a bit complicated. For a period of more than a hundred years ending about 50 years ago, records were kept by fur pelt gatherers on a northern landmass with a temperate climate. They found that there were peaks in prey population size, each followed within a year or so by a peak in predator population size. All of the research papers refer to this as a ten-year cycle, but if you look at the graphs, the cycle average is actually between nine and ten years. They are usually explained as the consequence of the population dynamics of these two species. Occasionally they mention vegetation quality affecting the prey population. I have a better explanation for these cycles. Are you still with me?"

Who Writes the Rules

"Yes. Please tell me your theory," said Heelia, although she was starting to lose interest.

Mosse pondered. Since before the dawn of life, Thera had danced hand-in-hand with Luna, performing a cyclical waltz through the heavens. Their mutual attraction swung them around each other in a moon dance as they orbited Sol. This produced a gravitational force that pulled oceans and atmosphere, stamping longer-term beats on the rhythm of daily and seasonal weather patterns, to which life was continually adapting.

"This is caused by the 18.6-year lunar declination cycle. Once every 18.6 years, the moon orbits between 28°N and 28°S. This range drops to 18°N to 18°S in the middle of the cycle. Twice during the 18.6-year period, the orbit hits the midpoint, orbiting between 23°N to 23°S – i.e. once every 9.3 years. There are cycles in air pressure systems over the oceans, which influence weather in the adjacent continents. In particular, the average positions of areas of high atmospheric pressure and low atmospheric pressure get shifted. These shifts have been linked to the variation in the orbiting of Luna."

"So, you're going to tell me Luna causes the weather to vary?"

"Exactly! There are relatively warmer, wetter years and colder, drier years in the landmasses adjacent to the oceans. The weather varies in a cyclic way. Atmospheric pressure systems move around in a manner that is influenced by the phase of the 18.6-year cycle. But there are two midpoints in the cycle, so the most common weather patterns are likely to be around these midpoints, which happen every 9.3 years. That means that over the course of the 18.6-year cycle, the strongest selection of plant genetic variation will be for those individual plants best adapted to these most common conditions. Because plant metabolism selection will tend to be toward the most common climatic conditions, plant biomass production is likely to be highest during two optimal periods of the cycles."

"And I guess that means more food for animals?"

"Yes. More plant production means more food for animals. This will trigger an increase in the herbivore population, which then triggers the predator population increase. Decline in prey population will be partly due to predation, but also to less optimal weather conditions for plant biomass production in the few years that follow the peak. In this case, the population changes are a consequence of planetary dynamics and their effects on climate. It's not just predation."

"So, you're saying Luna causes population changes? But that's not evolution. Sounds like lunacy," Heelia laughed.

"Maybe it does a bit. Yes, the moon is changing population dynamics. Evolution is not necessarily immediately detectable. But, over a number of generations, selection of particular plant metabolism functions, for example, will result in evolution. The main point is that evolution of a species does not happen in isolation. Life is fuelled by solar energy, while ecosystems are affected by many cyclic, varying factors. Of these, the 18.6-year cycle is an important one since it causes climatic cycling in a time frame that affects many living organisms. Just like annual seasons, but longer term. By creating cyclic environmental variation, planetary dynamics result in selection of

111

Who Writes the Rules

particular genetic variants. This, in turn, results in evolution."

"So, do you have a big experiment to prove that population changes are linked to 18.6-year lunar cycles? That's going to take an awfully long time!"

"That's not easy. You have to analyse historical records of weather. These can then be compared to recorded data like the fur pelt details or tree ring thickness over long periods. But while available weather data has become more detailed and comprehensive in recent years, there is less evidence of population cycling. I think this is because of climate change. The weather has been changing so rapidly for the last 50 or 60 years that ecosystem dynamics and energy flow have been disrupted. The data is becoming obscured by this. It seems that global warming is overriding or having a stronger effect than the impact of the weather cycles in previous centuries. The challenge will be to find statistically significant data from past records," Mosse mused.

"Should we go for a swim?" suggested Heelia.

"I've bored you to tears now, haven't I?" replied Mosse.

"No, I am interested in what you were saying, but I can't easily follow all these details about lunar cycles and things. My little brain has just collapsed!" Turning to face Mosse, Heelia leaned over and put her arm across his chest, commenting, "It all sounds very clever to me. And you are extremely passionate about this, so it must be true."

He turned in response and kissed her softly on the lips. She reciprocated warmly, emotional excitement rising, despite their awkward embrace across the sun loungers.

After a minute, Heelia rose quickly, taking Mosse's hand and pulling her to join him.

"Time to cool down. Let's go in the water," she commanded.

Holding hands, they walked about ten metres down the beach to where the water lapped around the mix of coarse sand and small round pebbles at the edge of the lake.

Heelia cautiously stretched her toes forward, dipping them below the water's surface. "Seems ok. Not like up the mountain," she said, giggling nervously.

Mosse stepped into the water, walking forward and pulling her hand behind him. "Come in! It's warm."

"Don't pull me!" Heelia screamed. "I'll walk myself in," she added, finding herself trotting into the water, which was soon above her knees.

It was cold at first, but not biting like the mountain stream had been. Her legs quickly became accustomed to the temperature as they continued into deeper water.

"Best to duck in quickly. The initial shock will soon go," said Mosse reassuringly. He dropped into the water until his head was covered, then resurfaced, trying to hide his reaction to the cold.

Heelia slowly lowered herself until the bottom half of her swimsuit was immersed. She gasped at Mosse. "You said it was warm. It's freezing!" She lowered the rest of her body down until the water lapped her face, breathing deeply and slowly.

"Swimming will warm you," Mosse told her, starting to swim away from her towards the deeper centre of the lake.

Heelia followed, swimming quickly and breathing

113

deeply, slowly becoming accustomed to the water temperature. Mosse slowed down, treading water where it was too deep to stand.

"Maybe it's not freezing, but it's not warm!" Heelia complained.

Mosse swam behind her and advised her to lie back, gently pulling the back of her shoulders into his chest and swimming slowly on his back.

"How does that feel? A bit warmer?" He asked her, wrapping one arm across her abdomen beneath her breasts.

"Much better. I can feel the climate getting warmer in my new niche."

Mosse laughed as they swam slowly in circles, enjoying the closeness and contact of their wet skin.

"I could stay like this for a long time, but you must be getting cold, Heelia?"

"It's worth the sacrifice," she replied, desiring to kiss him again but facing the wrong way in the water.

"We should go back and warm up. There's a café halfway along the lakeside, which is good for lunch. We can go there once we've warmed up again."

"Can't you just hold me here until the sun goes down?" asked Heelia playfully.

"I'd love to, but that's about another seven hours, and we'll probably have hypothermia in about another seven minutes!"

"Ok then. Let's go back," she moaned, pouting her lips with mock disappointment.

Mosse swam her backwards into the shallower, warmer water close to the beach. He retained his arm hold under her breasts as though absolutely necessary until they reached the shallows where they needed to stand up to move out of the water.

"Ahh. The water is warmer here," Heelia observed.

"Yes, and the sun is warmer over this way," Mosse replied, heading for the sun loungers.

As Heelia trotted up the beach, he took her hand once more, and they strolled together to where they'd laid their pitch.

After drying off excess water and massaging sun cream into exposed skin, they settled onto the loungers, soaking up the warm rays of Sol. They positioned themselves as close together as they could, touching hands, occasionally kissing. They looked into each other's eyes frequently, warming themselves while reinforcing their growing relationship, happy in each other's company.

Once warmed, they made their way to the café, where they had a light lunch before returning to the loungers. Later, they cooled themselves again in the lake before drying off and relaxing in the afternoon sun, exchanging non-technical, easy conversation, swimming willingly into each other's nets.

Who Writes the Rules

Chapter 8. Inseparable

At the end of the afternoon, as the temperature began to cool slightly, Mosse and Heelia dressed again over almost dry swimwear. They carried the loungers and towels to the car before driving back up the mountainside to the chalet.

On arrival, Mosse poured them both cold drinks, and they settled into cushioned lounge seats on the terrace.

"I can cook dinner for you, maybe," suggested Heelia.

"No need," replied Mosse. "I cooked a casserole last night. Just need to prepare some vegetables."

"I should have known you would have everything organised!" she observed.

"What sort of host would I be if you had to cook your own dinner?" Mosse retorted. "Maybe you're worth the effort," he added, looking Heelia in the eye and giving a suggestive smile.

"Maybe you don't know what you're letting yourself in for," Heelia countered, giggling and returning his gaze.

Mosse leaned towards her, putting his hand behind her head, and stroking her hair while their lips connected in another passionate kiss.

Eventually, breaking off again, Heelia added, "My hair must feel horrible. I'm covered in lake water and sand. Can I go take a shower now, please?"

"Of course, and I should do the same before I finish preparing dinner."

Heelia gave him an apprehensive look, "Not at the same time?" she enquired.

"Sounds like a nice idea, but I mean I'll use the bathroom while you use the shower in the guestroom."

Heelia wasn't sure whether to be relieved or disappointed, but she knew that Mosse was gentlemanly enough to suggest the polite option.

They finished their drinks and retired to their respective rooms to clean themselves up after their day at the lake.

Mosse showered and shaved, dressing in one of his best casual shirts, new jeans and clean trainers, more appropriate for an evening out at a restaurant than for preparing food in his own kitchen. He sprayed some perfumed aftershave lotion, which he rarely used, onto his hand, and wiped it around his face, neck and upper chest area.

After finishing his self-preparation, he returned to the kitchen and peeled half a dozen quasi-spherical, carbohydrate-rich root vegetables. Warming oil in an oven dish, he rolled the root vegetables in this and sprinkled them with salt and an aromatic spice before returning the dish to the oven.

Heelia had taken a little longer than Mosse to prepare for dinner, using moisturiser and make-up items to enhance the tone of her skin and exaggerate what she considered her best facial features. She sparingly used a perfume spray, lightly enough to give her a pleasant, exotic aura without being overpowering.

Searching through the minimal clothing in her baggage, she selected what she considered to be the best quality and most attractive outfit she had available. This consisted of a light, V-necked top of a cream-coloured silky fabric, with matching knee-length skirt and open toe sandals, which revealed the curve and warm, olive-brown tone of her legs and the contrasting pale pink varnish of her toenails. As a finishing touch, she added a favourite silver necklace with an amber pendant and matching earrings.

Once satisfied with her appearance, Heelia returned to the kitchen to join Mosse.

"Wow! You look lovely!" he observed.

"You don't look too bad yourself. And you smell nice," she said, sniffing his neck playfully, pleased at the compliment which he had offered.

"Food'll be ready in about 40 minutes. Time for another drink before I serve up," he said, picking up an open bottle of wine, which had been breathing on the worktop.

"You're trying to get me drunk again!" Heelia declared.

"You can have a soft drink or water if you prefer?" Mosse offered.

"I'll drink the wine slowly," Heelia responded, her eyes smiling.

Retiring to the terrace table again, they sat close together on the bench, tasting tongues between tasting wine sips. Occasionally making conversation, they talked a little about the lake, the beach, the food, and the chalet. However, both were more interested in the intimate contact of kissing, which they frequently practised as they waited for the approaching meal.

Once the cooking time was complete, Mosse set two places with cutlery and placemats at a table in an indoor room adjacent to the kitchen. The dining room window looked out over the terrace and to the cross-valley vista of the White Mountain massif beyond.

"It's getting cooler now. Better to eat indoors," he said, as he set soft music playing in the background. He placed the dinner plates in the oven for a short time to warm them before serving the casserole and roast potatoes.

He placed additional glasses and a jug of water containing ice cubes and slices of a yellow acidic fruit on the table.

"Why don't you sit here, Heelia?" Mosse indicated a seat with the best view of the mountain panorama, inviting Heelia to sit down to dinner. He topped up their wine glasses and poured the chilled water into the additional glasses.

Heelia tasted the rich meat and wine sauce, enjoying the soft texture of the slowly cooked meat, which crumbled in her mouth. "This is delicious! I knew you made a good sandwich, Mosse, but you can cook too. This is better than the hotel food. I definitely made the right decision to come here. And I've saved on my hotel bill, too!"

"You haven't seen my bill yet," joked Mosse, as he instantly reddened in embarrassment, realising Heelia might have misunderstood him. "Don't take that the wrong way!" he added, realising his gaffe.

Heelia raised her eyebrows and glanced up playfully. "I don't know what you could possibly mean," she replied, giggling.

Mosse's embarrassment waned. Heelia had a sense of humour and was a mature, sensual lady who was not afraid of innuendo, despite being alone in the home of a virtual stranger. She was enjoying his company and felt relaxed, confident that he was trustworthy. They had both gone to efforts to present themselves well tonight, and the attraction between them was strong. Mosse felt his desire to know Heelia better growing ever stronger. Not simply lust, but a genuine wish to discover more about her background and personality.

When they had finished eating and placed their cutlery on the plates, Mosse offered, "I have some options for dessert, or we could just let dinner settle and chat for a while if you prefer?"

"I'm pretty full for now. We could have something later if you like. I don't mind; you chose," she replied.

Topping up the wine glasses, Mosse responded, "Ok, I know there is an awful lot for us to talk about, and I bored you today with my science ideas, so maybe we should know more about each other. What's such a beautiful lady doing up in the mountains all by herself? Why didn't you have a companion with you?"

"Well, as you know, I'm a language translator in my 30s and single. Most of my colleagues, friends and acquaintances are married and would drive me crazy if I went on holiday with them. I enjoy my own company, and I just wanted to explore this region because I've never been here before. It's cooler and wetter on this side of the mountains than in Perali, so it's greener and prettier."

"And were you expecting to find romance in the mountains?"

"You can't be serious! If I wanted to find romance, I'd have gone somewhere with lots of people, clubs and dancing – that sort of thing. Most of the people I've seen in the mountains are middle-aged couples out walking!"

"You seemed to be happy to talk to me when we first met two days ago," Mosse observed.

"I was, but you started the conversation. I would have been happy to continue the holiday on my own, but you were kind and nice to talk to, and it was like meeting a local guide. And you are good-looking with a sexy body! How could I resist?"

Slightly taken aback, Mosse laughed. "Thanks for the compliment, but if you're serious, then that's something we've got in common. You're beautiful with a lovely body too! What I don't understand is why you are single. Do all the males in Perali have bad eyesight? I would have thought they'd be queuing up to take you out."

"Thank you for flattering me. I have been married in the past, and I've had a few partners since, but never the right person. Maybe I'm very fussy, or maybe I'm just better on my own."

"I don't believe that. Every time we touch, it feels like you want us to be closer, to melt into each other. That wouldn't happen if there was no chemistry between us or if you just wanted to be on your own."

"Yes, I do feel that there is a connection between us; otherwise, I wouldn't be here now. But I'm also worried about that. Maybe I should explain to you that I wasn't born in Perali. I come from an Eastern culture, where marriage partners are chosen by village elders and extended families. My family went to Perali to escape that, but there are many other refugees and migrants there, many of whom want to choose who I should marry. In Perali, among my relatives and their countrymen, we wouldn't be having this

121

conversation. They would see our mere association as a betrayal of their culture."

Mosse was shocked at this revelation. "Surely you are free to make your own choices. Perali is a free country."

"But I live among a sub-community. Many of them would agree with you. We can make our own choices, but there are fundamentalists who would prefer to kill you than let you be my partner. Maybe I shouldn't have said this to you, but you wanted to know more about me."

"No, if that's who you are, then you should tell me, but it worries me. It sounds like somebody should set you free from that oppression."

"Maybe I've just got used to it, but I'm not trying to escape. I like my life. I like my job. I like my colleagues, and if I need to get away sometimes, then I can do, like this week, for example."

Mosse felt saddened and concerned for Heelia's easy acceptance of an oppressive environment. He was also unhappy that this suggested their current interaction would be no more than a holiday fling that would be over in a few days! The attraction between them was mutual, but they lived in different worlds.

Heelia sensed Mosse's uneasiness. Clutching his hand, she looked deep into his eyes. "Let's talk about you. Why would a handsome, intelligent man who can cook and is so passionate about the world around him be stuck on his own in a house up a mountainside?"

"Well, I split with a partner last year, so I moved out from where we'd been living. I normally do freelance IT network support, most of which can be done online, so I decided to move out to what had previously been just a holiday home in the mountains. The studies are really more an interesting hobby than a career. Like you, I can enjoy my own company, but sometimes it would be nice to have somebody to share it with, especially living in this environment. Having you with me the last few days made a big difference. It's one thing to have access to and appreciate nature, but sharing it with somebody else who also appreciates it adds another dimension."

"So, you didn't come here looking for romance either, but you found me very easily," she smiled.

"How could I miss you?" Mosse responded. "You lit up the lodge when you came in panting and dripping wet from the storm."

Heelia laughed, "Hah! So, you were leering at my wet body!"

Mosse reddened again. "Not consciously, although you were difficult not to notice, but truly, I just felt sorry for you at that moment. We were both on our own and at adjacent tables, so I started a conversation, but at that time, it was more out of curiosity than lust."

"So now you look at me with lust?" Heelia teased.

"You're twisting my words, but the truth is the more I see of you, talk to you and kiss you, the more I want to."

Heelia stretched across the table and kissed Mosse firmly on the lips. "Maybe we should have dessert now," she suggested.

Mosse returned to the kitchen and filled two bowls with chopped fruit, frozen, flavoured cream, and a sweet fruit sauce. He placed these on the dining table, and Heelia sampled hers.

Who Writes the Rules

"Mmmm, very yummy," she said, savouring the textures and sweetness.

When they had finished the desserts, Mosse filled their wine glasses once more, and they moved to a lounge sofa, where they resumed kissing and chatting, occasionally sipping their drinks until the glasses were empty again.

"Some more wine, Heelia?" Mosse enquired again.

"No, I shouldn't, or I'll be drunk. We should clear up after dinner before we go to bed."

They shared the task of washing and clearing away the items they had used for dinner, chatting and resisting the growing sexual tension, which threatened to pull them into another embrace.

After they had cleared up, they moved from the kitchen to the passage between their adjacent bedrooms, where they stopped and shared deep, passionate kisses for several more minutes.

Finally, Mosse said quietly, "I could do this all night, but I should let you go off to bed."

They slowly released their grips on each other and began to turn their respective door handles.

Heelia looked deeply into Mosse's eyes and said softly, "Thank you for a lovely day and a very tasty dinner. Goodnight, Mosse."

She entered the guestroom, smiling towards Mosse, and then closed the door behind her. She leaned back against it while an internal battle raged between her instincts and her inhibitions.

Mosse entered his room, also closing the door. He had wanted to invite Heelia to join him, but his principles prevented him from taking advantage of his guest. As he removed his shoes and socks, there was a gentle tap on the bedroom door. He opened it to find Heelia looking up at him affectionately.

"I knew you would be too much of a gentleman to ask, so I decided I had to take the initiative!"

She threw her arms around his neck and resumed the kissing embrace that they had shared shortly before. After a minute or two, she asked, "Aren't you going to invite me in?"

Mosse took Heelia's hand, guiding her into the bedroom as he closed the door behind them. Succumbing at last to the growing desire and attraction, they sensually undressed each other and lay on the bed. The mounting sexual energy was released over the next few hours. They explored each other's bodies, sharing the passion and instincts that nature bestowed on them to cement their relationship, making love until contentedly exhausted.

Finally, they relaxed, intertwined, arms holding firmly, legs locked together, two jigsaw pieces fitting perfectly together, breathing synchronously, hearts beating in unison. Two strangers from different cultures, united by nature. Their desires, instincts and chemistry had rapidly pulled them into the close togetherness of lovers. Perhaps too soon to know love, they had much to learn about each other's deeper thoughts, personalities and lifestyles. However, nature had poised them to consolidate what promised to be a happy relationship.

Who Writes the Rules

They lay close, occasionally kissing, stroking each other's skin and hair, gazing eye-to-eye with warm affection that wanted to be true love. Mosse desired the closeness to last a lifetime. Heelia blocked out all thoughts of the cultural differences between them. For now, they were inseparable. They both sank quickly into a contented sleep.

Chapter 9. Who Do You Think You Are?

Above the garden, the sky had lightened to a pale blue-grey as the first bars of the dawn chorus began to herald the approaching sunrise. Mosse stirred semiconsciously. About to drift back into sleep, memories of the night before came flooding back, arousing him into a new awareness of the warmth of Heelia's body next to his. He moved closer, delicately putting an arm around her, not intending to wake her. Heelia stirred, shuffling closer to Mosse, and purred gently. Instinctively, they kissed each other softly on the lips, then slowly found their passions rising again.

Within minutes they had resumed the love-making, which had subsided into sleep the night before. At first, gently and sensitively, then with all the energy they could sustain, until both were physically, emotionally and sexually fulfilled once more. Merging their bodies in a unified embrace, they slipped back into sleep until Sol was high above the horizon.

Falling out of a dream, Heelia became aware of Mosse stroking her hair. A sweet, slightly bitter, nutty aroma emanated from a cup that had been placed on a bedside cabinet beside her.

"I've made you some coffee," said Mosse as he climbed back into bed. "Did you sleep ok?"

"I slept like a baby. But I dreamt we made love again around dawn," she smiled. "Are you ready to do it again?" she joked.

"I'd love to, but I think a little rest might be needed

first. It's a beautiful sunny day outside, and you're supposed to be here to enjoy the mountain trails."

"The mountain trails are spectacular, but what we did here last night was even better," she teased.

"Then you should have both. Life needs variety," Mosse responded.

"So maybe today we should find another scenic trail then? Another picnic?" Heelia suggested.

They stayed in bed discussing options until they'd finished their coffee.

Snuggling close to Mosse, Heelia added, "It's so nice being together here that I almost wish it would rain, just so we had a reason to stay in bed all day. But I suppose we should make the most of this sunny weather."

Eventually, emerging from bed, they both showered and dressed, ready to tackle another mountain walk. Together, they selected the items they wanted for breakfast, which they ate outside on the terrace, and then they chose what they would take with them for their picnic.

They drove to the bakery, picking up fresh bread and cakes for lunch, then continued several kilometres to a cable car that would carry them from an entry point to the local winter sports arena. They parked at the base of the cable car, taking their walking sticks and backpacks with them to the ticket office, where they paid for return tickets.

The cable lift consisted of a loop of thick wire from which a series of cabins were suspended, each with a capacity for up to eight passengers. As the cable looped clockwise around the stations at the top and bottom, the cabins were switched onto a slower-moving loop through each station. The lower speed enabled passengers to step in on the departing side or off at the arriving side.

Mosse and Heelia passed their tickets under a scanning machine, which opened a turnstile gate into the station. They stepped into a cabin that was moving slowly through the left side of the station. As they sat down inside, the doors closed, and the cabin switched to the fast-moving cable that would carry it for three kilometres, elevating them from 1,100 up to 1,800 metres altitude in about ten minutes. They had the cabin to themselves, as there were few passengers in the early summer season. In the low season, a reduced number of lifts operated to provide a service for walkers to access the mountain trails.

The cabin passed over scattered chalets and apartments, crossing sports pistes, passing restaurants and an intermediate station, and then slipping quietly into a dark green forest. It ascended along a narrow clearing, which had been cut between the trees to allow the passage of the lift cabins. Looking backwards towards the base station, a panorama opened up behind them as they ascended – mountains, ridges, mountainside villages, plus the lower valley containing the lake and beach where they had spent the previous afternoon. The local terrain presented itself like a relief map stretching into the distance behind them.

The top station resembled a large concrete bunker set into the forest above them, rushing closer as the cable carried them upwards. Rolling into the bunker, the cabin decelerated rapidly. Several loud metallic clanking noises registered its transfer onto the geared system, which reduced the cabin movement to a slow walking pace. The doors opened automatically, allowing the passengers to exit. Mosse and Heelia stepped out of their cabin onto the station platform and exited the bunker.

They had arrived at a plateau at 1,800 metres altitude, from which a series of footpaths radiated to surrounding valleys and ridges. Beyond them stood a series of low peaks, interlinked by meadows and broad ridges, stretching out for about five kilometres towards a 2,500-metre peak to the southeast. Three-quarters of the way along the trail was the ridge from which they had both descended rapidly three days earlier, escaping the storm and finding each other. The series of ridges and the meadows, which descended from the plateau, formed a winter arena used for snow sports. Green and covered with flowers in the early summer, the mountain trails provided relatively easy walking at altitude, with multiple viewpoints from which to appreciate the surroundings. No snow remained in the arena, even on the 2,500-metre highest summit.

Further along the ridge and in some of the adjoining meadows there was a handful of mountain refuges and restaurants, including the one to which they had hurried to escape from the thunderstorm. The peaks acted as upper stations for ski lifts. A few of these hosted mountain restaurants that offered panoramic views over the ski arena and were suitable for refreshment stops.

The couple followed a trail along the edge of a ski piste, ascending slowly towards the next peak along the ridge. As they walked, they chatted.

"You should come here in winter, Heelia. It's totally different from this. A winter wonderland, but lots more people, especially during school holiday periods. Have you tried skiing?"

"No, I haven't. I'm not sure I'd like it. It would be

too cold, and I'd probably just fall over and injure myself."

"You dress for the weather. That keeps out the cold. The sun can be strong and warming up here, even if the air temperature is below freezing. And if you learn properly, you don't have to fall. You just start slowly and progress as your ability improves. It's all about developing your confidence to keep your centre of gravity above the skis and control your speed and direction. It's a magnificent feeling when you know you can confidently glide down a winter wonderland."

"Maybe it would be fun. I can't really imagine it without trying it," replied Heelia.

Mosse continued, "I suppose I'm a hypocrite, really. I want to do things to improve the environment, but skiing and mountain sport is bad for mountain ecosystems. The piste machines that flatten the snow damage the ground, compressing the soil underneath and delaying the normal melting of spring snow. That reduces plant diversity and density."

"Does it really?" asked Heelia. "You can see the meadows where the ski tracks are, but they're covered in flowers, too, aren't they?"

Mosse responded, "If you sample the plants on ski pistes and compare them with similar meadows which haven't been pisted for skiing, you find that there are fewer species growing on the pisted areas. It's not obvious when you look because you can see lots of flowers, but there is an impact."

"It's a shame. It seems wherever we Majans go, we have a bad effect on the environment," Heelia noted.

"Snow sports also mean more development on

mountain slopes, more roads, more buildings, more people, more pollution. The people travel a long way to get here, burning transport fuel in the process. When you combine all that with climate warming, that is bad for nature. There are lots of species living in unusual niches here, all at different altitudes, aspects and weather exposure. They've adapted to those niches and may not cope with rapid changes or loss of their local habitats. Many of the meadows you see have been cleared of forest in the past, originally for summer grazing pasture and small farming communities, but more recently for sports infrastructure."

"But you still ski!" Heelia observed.

"Yes, and I've just suggested you should try it too. That's why I'm a hypocrite. We all know what's best for the environment, but we aren't prepared to sacrifice our lifestyles and luxuries. It's always somebody else's problem to solve. But no serious attempts are made to fix environmental problems if that costs money."

"That's sad. This is such beautiful scenery, and it feels clean, not polluted."

"I suppose, like everything on the planet, it's all transient. Here today, gone tomorrow. But as a species, we accelerate processes by causing rapid environmental changes. Natural changes which should have taken thousands of years may now happen in decades, like the retreating glaciers you saw two days ago. The main cause is the rapidly increasing population of our own species. As our populations grow, we displace other species from the global ecosystem. And we have found lots of unnatural ways to change the environment for our own benefit, usually to the detriment of other species."

"But we are different," Heelia interjected. "We are special, not like other species."

"Do you really believe that?" Mosse responded. "We are exactly like any other biological organism on the planet. We have evolved to what we are now, but that's not special, just dangerous for the existence of all species, including our own."

"I've always been taught that we're not animals. We were put here by our Creator for a special purpose. You talked about evolution yesterday. Does that mean you think we've all evolved from monkeys?"

"I thought you accepted evolution as fact," replied Mosse. "Yesterday, we were talking about natural selection and adaptation to change."

"Yes, that's easy to see for animals. But aren't we different?"

Mosse hesitated before answering. In his experience, he had found that it's best not to get into discussing religion with anybody who strongly believes in it. However, he wanted Heelia to accept his view of the Majan's place in nature as an animal species.

"There is no species alive today that evolved from any other currently living species. But, if you trace our ancestry backwards, we come to moments when different species have diverged from a common ancestor. So yes, monkeys, apes and Majans have evolved from common ancestors in the last ten million or so years. That makes those species our closest relatives. All life is related; connected in a big tree of diverging branches. Our own species is just one of those branches."

Heelia responded, "I was taught that the Creator

133

made one male and one female who are the ancestors of all Majans. Maybe all the other animals evolved from common ancestors, not including us. Or maybe the first male and first female evolved from something else but became the source of all the Majans."

Mosse was relieved a little by Heelia's curiosity. Perhaps she was not so blinded by faith that she couldn't think about the logic of genetic evolution.

"Have you ever watched those entertainment programmes where somebody investigates the ancestry of a celebrity? They always find one or two distant ancestors who have interesting backgrounds – a genius, murderer, famous artist, or something like that. Those programmes annoy me. Their presentation is misleading," Mosse stated.

"But I like those programmes; they're interesting. It's nice to see that these people have some history," Heelia objected.

"Usually, the interesting ancestor story is five or six generations back – somebody's great-great-great-grandparent, for example. You have two parents, from each of whom you get half of your DNA. Agreed?"

"Yes, of course," answered Heelia.

"And each of your parents has two parents from each of whom you get one-quarter of your DNA?"

"Yes, I can see that," Heelia replied.

"If you go back six generations, then you have 64 great-great-great-great-grandparents, from each of whom you get just over 1.5% of your DNA. For an entertainment programme, there must be at least one or two people in that generation with interesting stories to tell, but you're not exactly closely related to them!"

"I hadn't thought about that, but don't you still have a direct family line you're descended from? A bloodline?" Heelia suggested.

"If you follow your paternal line, then your father's, father's, father's, father's father still only provided 1.5% of the DNA that you have inherited. He was one of a group of 64 ancestors in that generation. There are a couple of small exceptions. All males inherit their Y chromosome via the paternal line, so if you were a male, there would be just one of those 64 who provided your Y chromosome."

"So, if you're a male, then you're directly descended from a line of males! Like a king!" Heelia exclaimed.

"The Y chromosome is just a little one. It's only about two per cent of a male's DNA, so it doesn't really work like that. There is also a female line of sorts. Whether you are male or female, all the mitochondria in your cells came from your mother's ovum before it was fertilised, so just one of the 64 in that generation provided all your mitochondrial DNA. But mitochondrial DNA is only a very small proportion of your total genes. These things are pretty insignificant with respect to the total DNA in your cells. And as for the idea of a bloodline, it's not blood that passes your genes on; it's sperm and egg cells. That's just a sentimental idea from before we learned how genetics and evolution actually work."

"That all makes family trees a bit misleading!" Heelia noted. "They should get wider going backwards as well as going forwards."

"Indeed! It gets more interesting as you go back in time. If the average generation time is 25 years, then 500 years ago, I had one million ancestors. And 600 years ago, I had 16 million ancestors. But the population of my country between 500 and 600 years ago was between one and two million people."

"They couldn't possibly all be your ancestors! Could they?" asked Heelia.

"No. People have always lived in communities of different sizes, from small villages to towns and cities. Until the last hundred years or so, most people stayed in the community where they were born, so although they weren't exactly incestuous, there would be marriages between fairly distant relatives. The actual number of ancestors comes down significantly below the exponential calculation."

"Then you don't have quite so many ancestors?"

"That's correct. But lines of descent are totally mixed up. In fact, we aren't really descended from individuals. We are descended from gene pools. Every population has its own pool of each of the different genes in the species' genetic complement. Your own particular set of genes was filtered down to your parents from a large number of people who provided the overall gene pool. Does that make sense?"

"Yes, I think so. But you still haven't answered whether you think we're descended from monkeys," Heelia observed.

Mosse continued, "If you trace the ancestry of our species back about five million years, or about 200,000 generations, assuming 25 years per generation, then you come to a population living in the forests of the dark continent straddling the equator. Probably it's more generations, maybe 3-400,000, as our early ancestors are likely to have had shorter generation gaps. Do you accept that, Heelia?"

"I know that's where they *say* our ancestors first came from, so I suppose I can accept that."

"If you then take our closest ape relatives today and trace their ancestry back five million years, you find a population of small animals living in the forests of the dark continent, which don't look much like either us or today's apes. That population shared a gene pool. At some point, the population was separated into two groups, maybe by a large river or by environmental changes due to changing climate."

"So, you think that our ancestors and ape's ancestors were once the same species?"

"Exactly!" replied Mosse. "One group stayed in the forest and evolved into today's apes. The other moved onto savannah and became better at hunting other animals for food. This second group evolved into today's Majans. It was so successful as a species that they spread all over the planet, with its gene pools diverging between different regions and tribal areas. So, you can see that there was no first Majan male and female, just a transient population that went off in at least two different directions."

Heelia followed Mosse's logic but felt uneasy. Somehow this contradicted her worldview, which had been based on teachings she had never questioned. How could she be just an animal?

Mosse added, "So you see, all life is interconnected. If you trace any population alive today back half a billion years, you will come to a time when their ancestral populations were totally different creatures living in the oceans. These creatures had evolved from single-celled

137

Who Writes the Rules

organisms over the previous billion years. All life is related."

Heelia pondered what Mosse had said to her. She had always considered herself to be non-religious. She had been taught the religion of her family as a child, the principles, the prayers, the rules, the creation stories, etc. Her parents went through the rituals, but were not strict believers. She had been non-practising since her family took refuge in Perali when she was twelve years old. However, there was an element that had remained in her subconscious. An acceptance of a deity who had created the Majan species and provided a set of instructions. A moral guide by which to live. She had never questioned this. A simple faith provided answers to all the questions she couldn't explain. Why are we here? How did we get here? What happens when we die? Mosse's reasoning was somehow at odds with this – a threat to that faith.

The trail had taken them to a mountain restaurant on the next peak along the ridge.

"This conversation is a bit too heavy. Let's stop here and have a drink," Heelia said, taking a seat at an outside table on a sunny terrace overlooking the ski runs, which descended through forest tracks and meadows to the base resort towns down the mountainside.

"Sorry, but you did ask if I thought we had evolved from monkeys, so I was just trying to answer that," Mosse responded. "What we believe in is a part of who we are. If we want to get to know each other, then we need to discuss our life views, don't you think?" Mosse asked.

"I suppose so. But if the things that are important to us are different, we might decide we don't like each other."

"I don't see why," Mosse answered. "My parents voted for different political parties, but they didn't fight because of that. People can have different opinions on some subjects, especially with respect to religion and politics. They may both be right in some ways and wrong in others. You can accept that somebody's beliefs are different from your own and not argue about it."

Heelia looked around the valley, seeking to lighten the conversation. "Look down the meadow to the right of the next peak," she said, pointing a finger off down the mountainside. "There's the tree where I nearly died a few days ago."

Mosse followed her gaze to the broken tree near the entrance to the refuge where they had met during the storm.

"It seems so long ago now," Heelia observed. "Just a few days, but we've done so much together. I want it to go on and on, but in two days, I have to leave to go back to my life in Perali. That will make me sad," she said, moving her hand to hold Mosse's, which was resting on the table.

"Perhaps you can come back again. I'm not going anywhere. Come in the winter, and I'll teach you to ski. Or any time of the year. It's beautiful here all year round."

Mosse was also only too aware that even though they had only been together a few days, he would miss Heelia terribly when she went home.

When they finished their drinks, they continued their stroll along the trail. Occasionally descending, but mainly climbing along the undulating path as it took them up towards the distant summit. They met a few dozen other walkers along the course of the trail, all greeting each other as they passed. It was early afternoon when they reached the top of the highest ski lift. Above it was a rough, scree slope of crumbled limestone and mudstone debris, which had broken off from the underlying layers of rock.

As they followed a track up the scree, Mosse picked up a bullet-shaped piece of rock with a smooth surface and a banded pattern along its length. Showing it to Heelia, he explained, "This is a belemnite fossil. These little creatures swam around in the oceans about 150 million years ago."

"Oh, look!" Heelia exclaimed. "Another one, and here another one. How did they get here?"

"The rock we're walking on was formed from minerals deposited on the ocean bed more than 100 million years ago. The sea was full of belemnites at that time. When they died, their skeletons fell into the calcium carbonate deposits, from which these rocks were eventually formed. They were buried deep, compressed and solidified as they were covered in more deposit layers."

"They were buried under the sea? But we're 2,500 metres above that!"

"Yes. The surface of Thera has moved a bit since then. In the past 30 million years, those layers of rock have been pushed upwards and tilted by tectonic forces. This pushed up the White Mountain and lifted the layers that had previously covered it, twisting them into the mountain ridges that we're now walking on."

Fascinated by this story, Heelia collected a pocket full of belemnites as they climbed to the summit of the scree slope. They had arrived on top of the 2,500-metre peak. The panorama included the ski slopes and resorts below to the south and west, and the massif of the White Mountain dominated the landscape across a deep valley to the east.

Heelia pointed to a flat meadow stretching upwards to a series of glaciers on the massif across to the east.

"Look, Mosse. It's our glacial paradise valley, where we had our first kiss."

"Yes, you can look down into it from here. It's peaceful there. No skiers, no settlements, no infrastructure. Just wild mountain terrain, but easy to access."

At the top of the peak stood a panorama map carved into a metal plate. It was fixed to a stone platform and engraved with all the points of interest around the 360° circle visible from the peak. They spent several minutes studying the panorama map and locating the marked points in the surrounding mountains. Heelia drank in the panorama once more, trying to imagine the mountains rising and folding as the planet's crustal plates crumbled together. They had one more long embrace and kiss on the mountaintop before beginning their descent back along the trail for about a kilometre. Finding a bench overlooking a wide vista, they settled to eat their picnic lunch.

"Every time we stop, everywhere you look around here is just so stunning," said Heelia.

Mosse smiled, and they instinctively leaned their faces together, locking into a passionate kiss.

"You're going to get me excited again if you're not careful," Mosse declared.

"I don't mind that," Heelia answered. "That makes two of us," she said softly, smiling.

They sat for some minutes after finishing their lunch, kissing occasionally and content again in each other's company.

Eventually, Mosse suggested that they continue

their descent. The trail was steep in places, and they needed support from their walking sticks as they descended.

However, going downhill was easier and quicker than the uphill climb had been. They arrived back at the lift station late afternoon and stepped into a cabin returning to the station in the car park below.

When they arrived back at the chalet, they poured drinks and sat on the outside terrace, enjoying the vista once more.

"We can go out for dinner this evening if you like?" Mosse suggested.

"That might be nice, Mosse, but we have lots of food here that we can eat on the terrace. I'd rather just watch the stars light up over the mountains. I love it here."

"Whatever you prefer. You're the guest."

As the evening progressed, they snacked on bread and various cold items, readily at hand in the fridge. Sipping wine, they watched the colour changes on the White Mountain ice cap and glaciers, reflecting the light from Sol as it sank in the west.

Once the sky had darkened, they fell again into the amorous embraces they had enjoyed the previous evening, going to bed early to make the most of their short time together. All thoughts of faith, religion and personal difference were forgotten as instinct, passion, mutual attraction and sexual arousal took over.

Chapter 10. Doldrum

A bearded figure strode across a road bridge. The
bridge spanned 250 metres across a wide river in the centre
of the business sector of Doldrum. Constant traffic crawled
slowly in both directions. Tourists and business people
passed on the adjacent pavements. The man arrived at a
conference centre at the end of the bridge, where an event
was about to begin. He entered the conference centre,
accompanied by two fellow attendees. Like the tourists and
the drivers, his fellow attendees were totally oblivious to the
bearded man's deadly intentions.

Before moving to the mountain chalet, Mosse had
worked in Doldrum, the capital city of Wiseland, a
neighbouring country nearly 1,000 km to the north of
Carina. Doldrum was an old city with more than 2,000
years of history. Wiseland had become increasingly
important as a geopolitical power. At one time, it had been
the centre of a global empire, and it was now liberal and
democratic. An affluent country where, at least in principle,
everybody had equal opportunities to improve their lives.
For hundreds of years, it had attracted large numbers of
migrants. They sought a better life in Doldrum; a city
apparently paved with gold. People believed that here they
would be free from oppression. Free from the corruption
and war or violence, which too frequently prevented their
progress in their motherlands. Doldrum was a large city
with a diverse, multicultural population of more than nine
million people. They shared more than 250 languages, more
than 250 nationalities and a dozen or so religions.

Who Writes the Rules

Doldrum had the potential to be a perfect cultural melting pot. Many of its people recognised their commonality. Some helped others, regardless of background, features, skin colour, language or religion. In difficult times, many provided voluntary support and charity; they respected all people of all cultures as fellow citizens with equal rights. Others, however, only seemed to notice the differences between themselves and others. Languages, nationalities, cultural differences and religions created barriers. In good times, these were easy to surmount. However, the differences could become significant and unsettling in response to some event, local or otherwise.

On a number of occasions in Doldrum, individuals or groups carried deadly weapons in public places. They had used them to commit murder. They justified their actions in the name of religion, nationality or politics. Sometimes weapons were used between gangs belonging to the same cultural group – usually between youths trying to assert themselves in the stupid and naïve belief that this would somehow raise their status among their peers.

Mosse had moved to Doldrum after he had finished his initial education. In Doldrum, he had better opportunities for further education and work. He had chosen to leave again for his own personal reasons, not because of the potential for violence.

He had been born and schooled in an affiliated country – part of an island that had been politically split in two by civil war a century earlier. After the national split, the cultural divisions remained. These were usually defined by membership in different branches of one of the major religions.

During his early school years, Mosse had been sent to religious classes once per week. He was taught the beliefs and rituals of a church on one side of the cultural divide. Before he was old enough to understand anything about faith or religion, he was made aware that children attending a school a few hundred metres from his own were apparently different. Even though they looked just like any of his classmates, the children from the two schools avoided each other. They walked on opposite sides of the road in fear of each other. They came from opposite sides of the political and religious divide. They had been told by their peers or elder siblings that the children across the road were a threat.

Mosse had been a member of a youth group associated with the church his family attended. He enjoyed some of the activities offered by the group, but there were aspects that he couldn't agree with. For example, members were expected to attend church gatherings and religious classes; otherwise, they would not be selected for sports teams.

Mosse saw the religious education within his community as a form of indoctrination. As soon as he was mature enough to think seriously about the dogma and doctrines upon which his religion was based, he knew that he could not take it seriously. Part of the stated intention of the church was to offer moral guidance in the community. However, this was mixed with theological legends and supernatural stories, which he regarded as nonsensical. Within his society, religion was a label with which everybody was tagged, regardless of whether they believed in it or not. It served to create cultural barriers. It caused polarisation of the population into groups that became increasingly antagonistic towards each other.

As he progressed through school, Mosse had been increasingly interested in evolution and life. From his mid-teenage years onwards, he knew he could never have faith in supernatural phenomena or deities. Everything had a scientific explanation, even if that was yet to be determined.

It had been nearly 200 years since the processes underlying evolution had been explained by science. That, coupled with advances in genetics and life sciences, seemed to remove the need for supernatural explanations. The reasons why such explanations continued to drive people, often to war or murder in the name of a faith, frustrated and fascinated Mosse.

All of the Majans, with their different languages, cultures and religious beliefs, were one species – all descendants of those small, ape-like creatures that had lived in the forests of the dark continent. Today they all shared the same gene pool. They could all interbreed, which defined them as members of the same species. Any individual taken from their native culture at birth and placed in a different culture would grow up speaking the language and following the doctrines of their adoptive culture. Racial features or skin colour might reflect their biological origin, but otherwise, they were just another Majan individual. Similar to all of the other Majans on the planet.

So why did all the differences persist? The five-million-year-old common ancestor of Majan and ape could not be the same species as the modern Majan. Separated by hundreds of thousands of generations, they would have been genetically different. Interbreeding between the two, if physically possible, would almost certainly not have resulted in viable offspring. It's not possible to know exactly when, in the line of descendants, the modern Majan crossed the threshold that defined it as such. The earliest population that could have interbred with Mosse's generation successfully was thought to have lived about 300,000 years ago.

During that five-million-year period, the ancestral gene pool evolved through many changing populations. Fossils from various different time periods are regarded as different biological species. These included diverging branches, some of which became extinct. Climate changes over long time periods meant gradual changes in terrain, water and food availability. These changes affected the regions where the ancestral populations were evolving.

The lifestyle and biology of the small ape-like ancestor had to adapt to changing requirements. The individuals most able to survive and reproduce were the ones whose genes coded for the ancestry of the modern Majans. They had lived in small, extended family tribes, eating berries and nuts, and hunting other animals.

Adapting to this lifestyle resulted in modifications to physical, developmental and social characteristics. Their ability to stand and walk upright improved, freeing their upper limbs to become better at manipulation. Hands became better at producing and using tools and weapons. As they cooperated in hunting and tool-making, their communication improved. This was aided by the ability to vocalise familiar sounds, and speech developed as a result. Eventually, languages enabled conversation and discussion of ideas and abstract thoughts.

147

Who Writes the Rules

The development in a child of a large, complex brain was a long process. It took time to become capable of significant learning, reasoning and communication. As a consequence of that, despite a long gestation period, the newly born were highly dependent. They needed support from parents and extended family throughout a lengthy childhood.

Experiences and learning during childhood years would prepare them for adulthood. This meant that a mother could be raising several children of different ages concurrently. A mother would require support from a partner and other family members. Improvements in communication and language were necessary adaptations for the success of this lifestyle.

The first Majans, 300,000 years or roughly 12,000 generations before Mosse, were genetically and biologically similar to him. There may have been some minor differences in metabolism and features. Otherwise, they were the same species. Until that time, they had remained on the dark continent, close to the planet's equator. Their populations were very small – extended family tribes, likely to be between a few dozen and 200 individuals in size.

Communities were limited by their ability to find food, water and protection for a group of mixed ages. They lived a nomadic lifestyle, following seasonal and climate-driven migration of animal herds. The regions in which they lived 200-300,000 years ago supported a total population of fewer than 100,000 individuals. In lean periods, this could have dropped below 10,000 Majans on the planet.

The northern part of the dark continent was dry and barren through much of the past million years. However, occasional wetter periods meant that water sources and vegetation were able to spread into its north-eastern corner. Paths opened for grazing animals and their hunters to find a route to the adjacent, vast continental landmass to the north.

On just a few occasions since their emergence as a species, one or more tribes of Majans had taken this route. They found migration trails along river valleys, coastlines, and verdant terrain where food was sometimes abundant. They migrated into new valleys and floodplains. They were able to exploit new food sources, and their populations were able to expand. Terrain, food and water were plentiful. Tribal communities laid claim to new hunting grounds.

However, weather patterns could be cyclical, sometimes within fairly short timeframes. A few years when food and water were plentiful might be followed by lean years, possibly with cold winters.

The weather patterns in the northern landmass had greater temperature extremes than in the equatorial region where the species had evolved. They were a hairless species, needing to find shelter and keep warm in adverse weather conditions. Shortages of food, water and shelter, or animal pelts for warmth and protection would result in deaths from starvation, hypothermia and disease.

Occasionally, tribes in their hunting grounds would meet others. These were distant relatives who might generally be friendly, but could pose a threat in times of shortage. Competition for resources would result in conflict. Sometimes this was brutal, resulting in injuries and deaths.

There had been several migrations of tribes into the northern continent. These were separated by as much as 100,000 years. The earlier migrants, who had established

Who Writes the Rules

hunting grounds and settlements, faced invasion from distant relatives. Invading tribes were usually different in features, having been biologically separated for many generations. When they clashed, the consequences were invariably violent and destructive. The victors of battle either wiped out the earlier tribes or absorbed the few individuals who survived by interbreeding.

Since the time of the first Majan migrations into the northern landmass, there had been several ice ages where temperatures had dropped for thousands of years. The ice ages were separated by warmer periods.

Majan populations would grow during times when there was more vegetation and abundant herbivore prey. When the temperature dropped significantly, they would suffer from starvation and cold. The populations would be knocked back to smaller numbers. Northerly populations were pushed southward into conflict with other tribes.

Grasslands and grazing areas dropped in both latitude and altitude. Sea-level fell as a result of more water being held in ice caps and glaciers. Grazing areas stretched onto continental shelves as the coastline dropped to a lower level.

The last ice age had ended 12,000 years ago. Earlier northern settlements had been destroyed by the ice sheet and weather impacts. Coastal settlements dating from the last ice age were submerged again as ice melted and sea levels rose.

The recorded history of the Majan migration around the planet dated mainly from 12,000 years ago. Then, there were less than two million Majans on the planet. In Mosse's generation today, the global population had risen to eight billion. In just the last 100 years alone, the population increased by 300%, from two billion to eight billion.

The average Majan needed 1.75 kilograms of food per day in order to sustain a healthy life. That meant about 1,300,000 (1.3 million) tonnes of food was needed per year 12,000 years ago. This had now risen to 5,000,000,000 (5 billion) tonnes per year and was still rising exponentially. Forests and wilderness were turned into farmland to feed the growing numbers.

In a balanced ecosystem, populations are limited by the availability of food, water, space, etc. Populations of hunter-gatherer tribes at the end of an ice age were restricted by the resources they could obtain. As the climate warmed and ice melted, there was an increase in habitable terrain and more resources for exploitation. This allowed the Majans to expand their hunting grounds to higher latitudes and altitudes. However, some of their coastal territory, including earlier settlements, would be lost to rising sea levels.

Intelligence, reasoning and problem-solving skills offered new possibilities to the hunter-gatherer tribes. They gradually learned to exploit these in new ways during the millennia after the end of the ice ages. They enclosed and domesticated some animals. They learned how to grow food plant species. Irrigation of arid land increased the yield of food plants. Clearing of forests provided grazing terrain. This increased the available food supply.

Previously nomadic tribes, which had followed prey herds, became more likely to settle in fixed locations. They built shelters from which they could manage their enclosed animals. The shelters gradually expanded into

Who Writes the Rules

villages. Settlements supported communities as large as their farmed food supply could nourish.

Settlements provided targets for aggressors who could steal food supplies. In response, they became more fortified. Since not all inhabitants were required to work as full-time farmers, some developed other skills. Some became guards or soldiers to protect the settlement.

Adjacent settlements that were often culturally related would form alliances to ward off and protect against aggressors. New skills, such as metal exploitation, were used to produce both farming tools and weapons.

Neighbouring settlements grew into towns that required governance by strong leaders. Sometimes, the leaders were elected; other times, they were despots who took control by force.

Fortresses and citadels were built. Communities expanded around these, developing into cities: civilisation had arrived. Cities and their protectorates grew into empires.

The Majans could not have evolved their intelligence and reasoning ability without one key trait: curiosity. They needed explanations. Who am I? Why am I here? What happens when I die? Will I meet dead people again? What is the warm light in the sky that I can't look at directly?

When simple explanations couldn't be provided, mythology was created. Deities were assigned to explain natural phenomena. Stories that passed across multiple generations by spoken word became blurred. The actions of strong, ancestral leaders were transformed over time into the miraculous deeds of supernatural beings.

The best storytellers became the representatives of the deities. Sometimes they would claim their own special enlightenment. They defined rules that other individuals should follow.

These rules might be moral. Respect others. Don't steal. Don't kill other members of our tribe. Do kill anybody who threatens us!

Some of the rules became authoritarian demands. Worship the Deity. Pray to the Deity. Obey the Deity's representative. Give your life when the Deity's representative commands it!

Curiosity had been satisfied. It had all been done by the Deity. The Deity will look after us when we're dead as long as we obey his representative. All that was required in order to accept this was faith and obedience. Enforced by religious police and threats of punishment.

Social control had been established; control which could be applied from small tribes to empires.

Shelters turned into settlements, then towns, cities and empires. The nature of the rules to which the common Majans had to adhere became increasingly authoritarian. They demanded allegiance and submission to emperors and high priests. Sometimes on pain of death for disobedience or even for doubt. With the advent of writing, different empires produced their own version of an instructive holy rule book. This was invariably dictated by a creator deity to one of his representatives. The high priests wrote the rules.

The past 5,000 years of Majan history was a catalogue of conflicts, wars and alliances. Empires and nations fought for control of resources; expanding populations of Majans spread around the planet. Nations

Who Writes the Rules

explored new terrain, taking control, often killing, subduing or enslaving earlier occupants. They would claim resources in order to enhance their geopolitical power, usually in the name of a specific religion.

The curiosity, imagination and inventiveness of individuals led to discoveries in the working of natural sciences. These discoveries enabled new technologies. Discoveries were sometimes used to enhance the comfort of life. They might increase food production or produce new machinery and industrial capabilities. Unfortunately, technological developments were also applied to the production of ever more deadly weapons of war.

During recent decades, the Majans had experienced proliferation of weapons so deadly that to use them would probably lead to the extinction of their species. Wars continued without resorting to the use of the deadliest weapons. These were invariably conflicts between cultural groups. The divisions were often defined by the religious beliefs that the adversaries followed.

In natural ecosystems, species evolve in response to the changing environment. Since migrating out of the dark continent, the Majans had learned to change the environment to suit themselves. Their populations had increased from less than 100,000 to eight billion individuals. They had sculpted the planet to provide food and resources to support this population growth. To provide them with the products of industrial, technological and military advancement.

They had massively changed the global biosphere. They devastated landscapes, polluted rivers, lakes, seas and atmosphere, and caused the extinction of many other species. However, biologically and psychologically, they were still the same primitive hunter-gatherers who had occupied equatorial savannahs 300,000 years earlier.

Two psychological driving forces directed the behaviour of every individual Mayan: selfishness and altruism. These could be described as opposite sides of the same coin. They influenced individuals to behave in defence of what they believed to be their territory.

All of the impulses and instinctive actions that animals display in response to external stimuli are directed towards self-preservation. Protection of the individual was necessary if it were to survive long enough to pass its genes to the next generation. However, the Majan is a social animal needing to protect the extended family or tribe, who share a gene pool. The Majans had evolved to protect the group instinctively, even if that meant self-sacrifice.

Altruism drove Majans to protect the tribal territory to ensure continuity of the tribal gene pool through subsequent generations. Among modern Majans, territorial behaviour meant much more than protecting tribal hunting grounds. Every individual had a sense of identity – a concept of self or ego that defined different levels of territory. All of these levels needed to be defended.

At the simplest level was self-preservation: survival of the individual. Immediate family was usually the next most important unit in need of protection, followed by extended family. All of the cultural groupings to which the individual belonged were also territories to be defended.

The primitive association with a tribe had been superseded by membership of a social or cultural group. This could mean nationality, language, religion, sports

Who Writes the Rules

team, cult or gang. Anything evoking strong emotional ties might arouse the instinctive passions calling for self-sacrifice to protect the territory. To protect the family. To protect the nation. To protect the gang!

In modern Majan society, wars were fought, and murders were committed in the name of cultural divisions. Violent actions were driven by instinctive territorial behaviour. Perceived barriers incited mobs and created unjustifiable hatred in the name of protecting the territory.

When the bearded man arrived at the conference, security was insufficient. On production of an invitation and proof of identity, he was permitted entry. Under his closed jacket, he was carrying knives that hadn't been detected. He was wearing a fake suicide vest. He visited a toilet where he strapped a knife to each wrist. He opened his jacket, exposing what appeared to be a vest packed with explosives and shrapnel.

The focus of the conference was the rehabilitation of offenders and helping to integrate them into society. The bearded man had been one of those offenders. He had apparently repented and was considered ready for reintegration into a free society. The organisers of the conference included people who devoted their lives to trying to help others. The territory that their altruism strove to protect was the entire species, regardless of social and cultural differences. They recognised only the commonality between individuals. They held no hatred or contempt for the offenders, just a genuine desire to help them to lead normal lives.

The bearded man left the toilet. He immediately and indiscriminately attacked a number of the conference organisers. He killed two of them and injured others. He was chased from the building by several people, including other ex-offenders. He ran back along the bridge but was tackled by his chasers and other members of the public. They held him on the bridge until armed police arrived. Fearing that the suicide vest might be genuine, the police ordered the pursuers to back off and warned the bearded man to stay down. When he moved, he was shot a number of times. He was eventually confirmed to have died.

The bearded man had been told that if he died a martyr to his religion, he would immediately go to paradise, where he would be rewarded by the company of dozens of virgins. He murdered the people who had been trying to help improve his life. He died believing he had murdered good people and that he was a martyr. It didn't matter that they were good people; they were not of his religion. They symbolised the society that he had been taught to hate. His Deity would be pleased with that and reward him for eternity.

Were the bearded man's actions selfish or altruistic?

He had done it in the belief that he would be rewarded with virgins for eternity. Selfish!

He had sacrificed himself in the name of his religion. Altruistic!

He had been sufficiently brainwashed to direct hatred at and murder innocent people, justifying it by imagining that his Creator wanted this to happen!

Who Writes the Rules

Chapter 11. Avalanche Thunder

Awakening early, Mosse and Heelia were once more engulfed in the passion that had united them for the past few days. Exploring each other's bodies, gazing eye to eye, occasionally speaking but saying little, they kissed and caressed, longing only to continue their close contact. Making love, then slipping back into relaxed sleep once more, wrapped together, until mid-morning.

Lifting her head, Heelia muttered sadly, "It's our last full day together, Mosse."

"Last? Only if you don't come back to me," Mosse responded.

"Let's not think about the future today. I don't know whether we should just stay in bed all day or go hiking again."

"You'll burn me out. I think hiking up mountains is probably the easier option," Mosse said, smiling.

"I didn't say have sex all day; just stay in bed," Heelia laughed.

"Fine. But you still haven't seen a glacier up close, just the valley below them. I thought I would take you to another spectacular setting where you can walk on the glacier."

"Ok, let's do that. I *am* supposed to be on a walking holiday!"

"I'll sort out some breakfast, then we can get ourselves organised," replied Mosse.

Donning a bathrobe, Mosse went to the kitchen,

where he prepared a breakfast of bread, eggs and fried, processed meats. He set coffee brewing and poured glasses of fruit juice. Heelia found a second bathrobe and joined him in the kitchen.

"Let's eat outside again in the sunshine," she suggested, picking up plates and cutlery, which she carried to the terrace table.

As they sat on the terrace eating breakfast, Mosse pointed across the valley to the White Mountain massif.

"Look towards the glacier valley where we went on the first day out, then look to the left of that. There is a peak in the foreground from which a high ridge runs from about 2,500 metres, right up to about 4,000 metres to meet the ice sheet at the top. To the left of that ridge is a long glacier descending all the way from the top of the ridge down to about 1,800 metres, like an extended dragon's tongue. The top half is glowing bright white in the sun as it drops down quite steeply from the ice cap, but it gradually darkens to a pale grey-blue colour at the bottom."

"Yes, I can see that clearly. It looks very steep, with lots of dark lines cutting across it. I guess those are crevasses?"

"That's it. It's about eight kilometres from here as you look at it. We can drive to a parking place at about 1,400 metres altitude. From there, it takes about an hour and a half to walk up to the bottom of the glacier. We can head over there as soon as we get ourselves organised."

"That sounds like a nice plan. It looks very dramatic from here."

"It is. I'm sure you'll love it up there."

They finished breakfast, showered and gathered

Who Writes the Rules

snacks and drinks into backpacks as before, stopping once more at the bakery on the way to Carina. Mosse followed the same road as on their first day together, but on reaching the junction where the valley roads diverged, he took a different route that ascended to the left side valley. The road climbed steeply for a few hundred metres, turned a sharp hairpin bend, and then climbed gently for about three kilometres, following the contours along a steep mountainside. They ascended through coniferous forest and scrubby clearings until they reached open meadows. After driving through a small hamlet of chalets, they arrived at a car park a little above 1,400 metres.

Stepping out of the car, Heelia scanned the surrounding scene. The parking area was located in a broad corrie about one kilometre wide. It had been cut in the shape of a horseshoe by ancient glacial erosion. From the base of the corrie, forested slopes curved upwards on three sides to about 1,800 metres. The open side behind them dropped down through a gorge carved into the mountainside over millennia by a torrent of glacial meltwater. They had entered the corrie by driving up one side of the gorge from the junction below.

Above the 1,800-metre tree line, the glacier stood majestic, reaching up to a bright blue sky, towering above them while releasing a torrent of meltwater, which cascaded down through the centre of the horseshoe. As it poured downwards, the torrent cut a trough across the middle of the corrie, then tumbled on down through the lower gorge to Carina and beyond.

Mosse took the backpacks and walking sticks from the car and joined Heelia.

"There are a number of different paths we can take from here," he explained. "There is a circular route, going up the corrie slope on one side of the torrent and then coming down on the other side."

"But how do you get across the torrent?" asked Heelia.

"There's a bridge at the top. It's a series of wooden pieces held up by wires suspended above the torrent. It's about 20 metres across, but it wobbles when you walk across it," Mosse warned Heelia.

"Sounds a bit scary. I hope I don't panic."

"You'll be fine. It's fun. If we take the path up the left side of the corrie, it's mainly through open meadow, and it's longer, so not as steep as the other side. It's easier to go up that way, cross the bridge and then come down the right side, which is a steep path through the forest. After we go across the bridge, we can walk up to the bottom part of the glacier."

From the car park, there were several paths, all signposted to various destinations, with distances and average walking times marked. The car park, which had capacity for several dozen vehicles, was nearly full.

"It's busy here," remarked Heelia.

"Yes, it's very popular. In peak season, we would have needed to get up early to be sure of a parking space." Mosse pointed to a well-trodden, wide path, which climbed gently away from the car park. "That's our path."

They set off at a steady pace, their walking sticks lending a little support on the steeper parts of the path but hardly needed. They ascended past a few farm sheds, through meadows adjacent to forest, occasionally passing

Who Writes the Rules

fellow walkers. After about an hour, just below the snout of the glacier, the path entered a forest of conifers. They proceeded along a relatively flat trail that traversed the hillside under the trees.

Within five minutes of entering the forest, they could clearly hear the roar of cascading water, getting louder and louder as they approached it. As they proceeded, the path emerged into a clearing where the sound of rushing water rose to a crescendo. Posts on either side of the path held the cables from which the wooden steps of the bridge were suspended. There were several walkers in front of them starting to cross the bridge.

Heelia watched as they crossed the span of 20 metres. The bridge bounced slightly to the rhythm of their footsteps, but all were clearly enjoying the experience, stopping in the middle to look down at the torrent while shouting to each other to be heard above the crashing of the water on the rocks below.

"It does look exciting!" Heelia shouted back to Mosse, who was close behind her.

When the group in front had left the bridge, Heelia and Mosse followed to its centre, which rocked gently up and down in synchrony with their footsteps. Heelia turned to Mosse, reaching her arms around his neck and kissing him passionately as the bridge oscillated gently under their movements.

"Did you feel the ground move then?" Heelia yelled above the din of the torrent.

Mosse laughed. "I always feel the ground move when you do that."

The bridge crossed the torrent about 30 metres

below the top of the cascade, which obscured the view of the glacier above. However, in the opposite direction, they had an unobstructed view across the valleys to the southwest.

"Look, Heelia. About seven or eight kilometres over there is the peak where we found the belemnites and the place where we had our picnic yesterday."

"Yes. You can see so much from up here. I could just stand here listening to the water and enjoying the view, but we shouldn't block the bridge for the next walkers," she said, glancing at some people who were waiting to come back across the bridge.

They continued to the other side of the cascade, then took a path uphill towards the base of the glacier. The path climbed steeply through forest, emerging after 100 metres to open space. Before them was a flattened area of rock debris about 400 metres square, as if a huge fist had pulverised the mountain, leaving broken pieces of various sizes scattered across the terrain. Above the rocky devastation, a lake of cloudy, blue-grey water about 50 metres in diameter lapped against the bottom reaches of the glacier ice. The lake was constantly being filled with meltwater and feeding the torrent that raced across the broken rocks towards the top of the cascade before dropping down the mountainside under the bridge.

The pair carefully made their way down from the edge of the forest onto the square of broken rock fragments.

"This is all debris that the glacier has carried down from the higher parts of the massif and then dropped here as the ice has melted."

Heelia picked up some rock pieces. Crystalline,

with white and black layers, and some pink crystals mixed in.

"This is gneiss or migmatite," Mosse explained. "The centre of the massif has been pushed up from the bottom of the planet's crust by continental plates being forced together. The layers of rock above were compressed and heated until they were almost melting, and the crystal structures were changed into the layers that you can see here."

"The crystals are pretty. A bit like granite, but in layers," Heelia observed.

"They're metamorphic rocks formed by the immense pressures and temperatures deep within the planet's crust. These mountains are fairly recent and are still being lifted by the same forces of nature."

"You mean the White Mountain is getting taller?" asked Heelia.

"Yes, but it's also being eroded by ice and water, so I don't think you'll notice in the next few days. These mountains have been growing during the last 50 million years as the plates have been pushing together. Most of the uplift has been in the last 10-20 million years. Remember I said the belemnites were under the sea 150 million years ago?"

"Yes, and now they're at the top of a mountain!"

"You've got it! The layers that were at the bottom of the sea 150 million years ago have been buried under more layers of sediment, compressed, and then gradually raised and tilted under the pressure of tectonic plate movement, mainly in the last 50 million years. Where the layers have been exposed up the mountain, you can see the fossils of what was at the bottom of the sea 100 million years earlier."

"That's fascinating. I'm going to treasure my little collection of belemnites!"

At that moment, a distant rumbling noise suggested thunder.

"Are we going to have another storm?" Heelia remarked, concerned that they may get caught in a downpour.

"It's not thunder; it's the glacier."

"The glacier? It was thunder!"

Mosse directed Heelia to the glacier, which dropped from the ice cap 2,000 metres above them to the dark-grey, debris-covered mass adjacent to the square where they stood. The lower section nearest to them had a gentle gradient, but the upper two-thirds descended steeply and was split extensively by transverse crevasses.

"If you keep watching the upper parts of the glacier, every now and again, a chunk will break away and cause a local avalanche on that part of the glacier. The chunks are called seracs. They're a bit like icebergs and break off as the glacier creeps downhill. The thunder you hear is the noise of that avalanche."

While Heelia stared up at the deeply crevassed part of the glacier, she noticed movement as a serac broke away from the glacier and tumbled, disappearing into a white cloud of snow and ice thrown up by the avalanche. "I see it, but there's no thunder!"

As she finished speaking, a distant crack followed by deep, thunderous rumbling, lasting at least ten seconds before fading, echoed down the mountainsides adjacent to the glacier.

Who Writes the Rules

"Oh, now I can hear the thunder. You can almost feel the power of the avalanche!"

"The glacier is continually moving downwards, like a very slow river, being topped up by new snowfall forming the ice sheet at the top, while the bottom end melts. The movement causes pieces to break off, especially where the gradient is steep. What you're looking at is about two to three km away and more than 1,000 metres above us. It's like thunder and lightning. You see it, and then you hear it seconds later, depending on how far away you are."

"Ah, yes, I see. That's amazing. I hope there isn't a chance an avalanche can reach down here."

"No, it's only happening on the steep part of the glacier, which is well away from us. I think it would take a serious earthquake to cause a large mass to fall as far down as here. "

"That's reassuring. I prefer to listen from a safe distance!"

"But the glaciers are melting more rapidly because of global warming, which causes water to build up underneath them," Mosse continued.

"Is that a problem?" Heelia asked, concerned.

"It can be. There was an incident about 130 years ago when over 200 people were killed. It was mid-summer after warm weather. There's a glacier in a valley above us, at about 3,200 metres altitude, which had a lake building up below it as it melted in the warm summer weather. Just like the little lake you can see here, but probably a lot bigger, with water accumulating under the ice. The lake was held back by a moraine wall, a bit like the debris zone you can see here.

"In the early hours of the morning, the wall collapsed, and the whole lake rapidly drained through where we're standing right now. It plummeted down through the valley where we've parked the car. It gathered mud, rock and tree debris as it swept down the mountainside and through the gorge below, eventually sweeping across the lower valley where we swam in the lake. It didn't hit the town of Carina, which sits above the river gorge, but at the bottom of the gorge is a hotel where there are thermal springs. The hotel was full because it was mid-summer. It was swept away, and most of the people who'd been sleeping peacefully there were killed in an avalanche of water, mud, rock and anything else that had been picked up."

"Oh, that's horrible. Poor people. But the thermal treatment centre is still there. Isn't there a risk this will happen again?"

"It's possible. The local administration and the electric company are aware of where any water can build up under the glaciers, and they monitor them continuously. But global warming must be a major concern for anybody living near the meltwater torrents."

"You live in a dangerous place! Is it safe for us to be standing here below the glacier?"

"I think your biggest risk just here is twisting your ankle walking on this terrain. Everywhere is dangerous if you don't pay attention to the risks. I don't take unnecessary risks, and I don't live near any potential avalanches."

"This is another beautiful place. And fascinating. The mountains are still rising; the glacier is alive, making thunder, crushing the rock, causing avalanches. And you're

Who Writes the Rules

right; there are risks everywhere in life. You just need to know how to limit them," observed Heelia.

"Do you know about 60 people die every year, on average, climbing the White Mountain?" Mosse asked.

"Really?" replied Heelia. "I've heard of some incidents, but that's a lot of people."

"Yes, it's surprising. They think it's an easy walk up known trails across the ice cap. But the air is thinner. It's harder to breathe, and you can get altitude sickness. In the summer, the snow and ice melt, and crevasses open up. Plus, you've seen how quickly the weather can change! If people aren't properly prepared, they can be in trouble easily. Even professional guides can be caught out by changing weather or crevasses!"

They picked their way through the field of stones and broken rock pieces of all sizes, moving towards the small lake. At the back of the lake, cloudy with silt particles, making the water look blue, there was a cavern where the lake disappeared under the melting ice. A wall of wet, pale blue ice several metres thick rose above the cavern, a layer of rock debris covering the upper surface of the ice. Seen from the forest, the bottom of the ice tongue had been completely grey, blanketed in dust, silt and broken rock. Very little ice was visible on the bottom kilometre of the glacier, but beneath the grey blanket, the ice was translucent blue and continually melting.

The pair walked along the edge of the covered glacier, then climbed carefully out onto the blanketed ice mass, picking their way through the debris blanket. In places, they could see holes in the ice, where it had melted, revealing small crevasses under which water could be heard flowing rapidly towards the lake.

"I think we should go back to the edge," Heelia suggested. "I wouldn't like to fall down one of these holes!"

"You're right. What was I saying about not taking risks?" muttered Mosse.

They made their way back to the edge of the forest, where they found a position facing the glacier. Here they could relax, have their picnic lunch and enjoy each other's company while watching avalanches falling from the upper reaches of the glacier, listening to the thunder, and counting the seconds between to estimate the distance.

They rested by the side of the glacier for nearly two hours before returning down the path that they had taken after crossing the bridge. The path through the forest was much steeper than the route they had climbed to reach the bridge. In places, steps were cut into the path, with handrails to help the descent. Their walking sticks were a necessary aide to the climb down the forest path, taking the strain off their knees as they negotiated the steep track.

The track descended parallel to the cascade, the surrounding forest opening in places to reveal dramatic waterfalls and deep pools. At times, the sound of the torrent drowned out the bird calls and made it necessary to shout or talk loudly in order to be heard as they descended.

After about 30 minutes, they arrived at the bottom of the slope, where a branch in the path was signposted for the car park. The branch took them to a second bridge, which took them back across the meltwater torrent, beyond the steep face of the corrie, at a point below the cascade. The torrent cut its way below the bridge, across the bottom

Who Writes the Rules

of the combe, and down into the lower gorge.

Following the path for another 30 minutes, they found themselves back at the car. It was late afternoon as they began the drive back down the mountainside.

"Are you hungry? Heelia," Mosse asked.

"A little. What are you planning?"

"I know it's a bit early for dinner, but I know a place that serves good crepes. If we have something now, then we can have a lazy evening at the chalet and just snack later if we need to."

"That sounds like a good idea," Heelia smiled, looking forward more to the lazy evening than the crepes.

Chapter 12. The Big Bang

After driving back down from the gorge, Mosse turned to the south, away from Carina, and drove five kilometres to a smaller, neighbouring town. It was a pretty town of golden-brown varnished chalets decorated by window boxes and displays of brightly coloured flowers. The centre was an accumulation of restaurants, cafes and shops selling mountain sports equipment and clothes. The local businesses catered primarily for the many tourists who visited the area. They found a suitable parking place then walked a few minutes to the restaurant that Mosse had suggested.

The restaurant was typical of the traditional buildings in the area. Everything was sculpted from natural wood. The walls were adorned with pictures of mountain scenes, in between a few pairs of wall-mounted, crossed, antique skis. A few stuffed animals watched from shelves, while red and white checked table clothes added colour to the golden-stained wooden furniture. Cooking odours crept through the restaurant. Hints of bacon, cheese, onions, coffee and slightly burnt butter pervaded the dining area, stimulating appetites. A dozen couples occupied tables, some eating, others engaged in conversation, sending a soft babble of unintelligible mixed-language sounds rippling across the room.

Greeting them as they entered, the patron led Mosse and Heelia to a free table in an exterior garden, leaving them with a menu to peruse. They each selected a savoury

Who Writes the Rules

crepe covered with slices of a local cheese melted over chopped pieces of ham. To follow, they had dessert crepes with sweet sauces, washed down by cold drinks and coffee.

"That was delicious, Mosse. A nice way to finish the afternoon," Heelia smiled.

"Glad you enjoyed it. That should fill the gap for a few hours," Mosse responded.

After settling the bill, they returned to the car and drove back to the chalet, where Mosse poured them both a cold alcoholic drink, which he took to the terrace. Heelia was leaning against the balcony rail, staring across the valley to the glacier where they had been earlier. Mosse put the drinks on the terrace table and stood behind Heelia, wrapping his arms around her waist and clasping his hands across her abdomen.

"It's sad now, Mosse, looking back at the places we've been to together. But I have to say thank you for being my guide. You've shown me places I would never have found on my own. And you've explained so much to me."

"Now I think you're making fun of me. You don't want to say how much I've been boring you."

"No, that's not true. You've been a great guide, and very interesting. I've learned lots of things about glaciers and belemnites, and mountains forming, and I've seen such beautiful places. I couldn't have done this without your help."

"I was hoping you might think I'd been more than a guide. Guides don't normally provide the services you've been receiving," Mosse noted jokingly.

"I'm sad because I have to go home tomorrow, and it's not just the mountains I'll miss. I'll miss you. I have to be careful how I say it, or I might cry, and then I'll feel stupid."

"Don't cry, or I might, too. Then I'll feel even more stupid than you!"

A tear formed in Heelia's eye as they laughed together, and she turned so that they could embrace in a kiss once more.

"Can we take the drinks to the bedroom?" Heelia suggested.

"I was just thinking that might be a nice idea," Mosse replied.

They spent the next hour as lovers, embracing forever, pushing away all thoughts of separation, merging their bodies, their emotions, eyes gazing into eyes, each wanting to fall deeply into the persona behind them.

Energy expended temporarily, they chatted softly, caressing each other gently. At length, Mosse suggested they return to the terrace as the sun would be setting soon. Heelia would have one last opportunity to watch the slow-motion repainting of the White Mountain and its glaciers by the changing light as Sol sank below the western horizon.

Donning their bathrobes, they returned to the terrace, where they sat tightly together on the cushioned bench, sipping drinks while watching the great tongues of ice across the valley change from white to cream to yellow, to orange to pink to grey. A slow-motion film of the massif sinking from the soft pastel hues of evening sunlight into the gloomy shadows of approaching darkness.

"It's such a wonderful sight. You're lucky to be able to see this any time," said Heelia.

Who Writes the Rules

"It's not always visible. Sometimes we have rain, as you know. Quite often, the cloud is low, so you can't see the glaciers."

"You know what I mean. Whatever the weather, everything here is spectacular. It's fascinating watching how the colours are continually changing on the ice. And the thunder of the avalanches. I can't see or hear them now, but I can almost feel the energy just by gazing across the valley. It was magnificent to see that today."

"You could stay here with me. Then you could see it all the time too."

"You know I can't do that, Mosse. I have a family and work to go back to."

"You could come back anytime you're free."

"I don't know when that would be or if it's the right thing to do."

"Why is it not the right thing to do?"

"You know what I mean. We come from different cultures. Here, it doesn't matter, but I don't know that I can. My family and friends wouldn't understand."

"But you're not a believer. You don't practise your religion. Don't they know that already?"

"Just because I don't practise doesn't mean I'm a non-believer. Maybe I believe there is something out there that guides us."

Mosse was a little shocked by Heelia's revelation. He was beginning to think that she accepted natural explanations for everything. However, there was a spiritual side to her – a fascination for which she didn't need or want scientific explanations.

"Are you telling me you believe in a deity?"

174

"I've always believed there is a Creator. Otherwise, where did everything come from, Mosse?"

"Have you heard of the Big Bang?"

"Yes, but I can't say I understand what that means."

"When astronomers look at the Universe with the latest telescopes, they learn a lot from their observations. One thing that has been known for decades is that all the stars and galaxies that they can see are moving apart. Can you visualise that?"

"Yes. I can see stars in the night sky, and I can imagine they're all moving apart. I've heard that said before."

"So, if they're moving away from each other as we go into the future, that means if you go back into the past, you have to reverse the process. They would all be moving closer to each other. You agree?" Mosse said.

"Yes. That would make sense."

"Then, if you go back far enough, the whole Universe will be in the same place."

"I understand that but can't see how it's possible. The Universe can't just disappear unless you get to the point when it was created."

"Never mind that. We can't demonstrate it; we can only predict it using maths. But if you can, imagine all of the mass of the Universe squeezed together into the smallest possible space that it will fit. You can't go back beyond that, but imagine there's a threshold where the pressure of all that mass squeezed together caused it all to be converted to energy and blasted outwards, like a massive nuclear explosion. All the energy of the Universe blasted out like a balloon, which keeps expanding outwards. That was the Big

Who Writes the Rules

Bang! Are you still with me, Heelia?"

"Yes, I'm listening. Don't suggest I don't understand; I'm not stupid! I can imagine the balloon getting bigger."

"Ok. As the balloon expands, much of the energy is converted to mass – first, sub-atomic particles, then atoms. Gravity causes masses to attract each other, eventually forming stars, in which heavier atoms are formed by the fusion of lighter atoms. Some nebular clouds of atoms begin to condense, with stars forming in the centre and planets forming in orbital belts around them. The planets are attracted to the star in the middle and fall towards it due to gravity, but they don't fall into it because it's also moving. The falling planets just keep orbiting the star in order to keep up with its trajectory. The star is in orbit around the centre of a galaxy, and all the galaxies have been moving away from the centre of the Universe ever since the Big Bang. Does that make sense?"

"That sounds like an amazing picture. It's not easy to visualise, but I'm trying. But how and where do we come into the picture?"

"Well, the Big Bang happened about 14 billion years ago. Our own star, Sol, and its planets formed less than five billion years ago. Life has been evolving on our planet Thera for the last four billion years. Our species, the Majans, has been around for the last few hundred thousand of those years, and we probably won't last much longer. We've only existed as civilisations more settled than hunter-gatherer tribes for a few thousand years, but during the last few hundred years, we've been increasingly destroying the planet. We're likely to have a nuclear war in the next couple of hundred years. We're occupying a very tiny slice of time, but soon we'll be extinct."

"Why do you believe this is how things happened?"

"Everything that has been observed in science supports this reasoning, especially the story of our own evolution as a species. If there were any evidence to suggest other explanations, scientists would examine that. That's what scientists do."

"Ok. But if I accept that what you have said is correct, that doesn't explain how and why everything is as it is. Where did it all come from? Why are we here? Maybe the Big Bang happened because the Creator wanted it to happen that way."

"Why do you need a creator? There is a simple paradox here. If you need to have a creator, then you need to ask where the creator came from. Was he created by a different creator? If so, then who created that one?"

"Well, if the Big Bang wasn't created by something, why did it happen? Did everything just materialise out of nothing?"

"I like to imagine it all happened in some sort of Big Bang/Big Crunch cycle. Nobody knows what happened before the Big Bang. We can only measure time since the Big Bang, so we can only guess what happened before that. There are different views on this, but we have no way of seeing before the Big Bang, and we can't see into the future either. Think of the balloon expanding outwards, then losing pressure and shrinking back again, then inflating again, then shrinking back again and so on forever. Can you visualise that?"

"I can visualise the balloon blowing up and

Who Writes the Rules

shrinking again. Not sure I can think of the Universe doing that, though!"

"Remember we said that at the time of the Big Bang, all the mass of the Universe was compressed so much that it crossed a threshold where there was a massive energy release that caused the expansion?"

"Yes. I've got that," Heelia replied.

"We've been expanding for about 14 billion years, but let's say the force of the expansion was running out of steam. Maybe over the following 15-20 billion years, everything starts to slow down, so gravity starts to pull moons into planets; planets into stars, stars into black holes in the centre of galaxies, and black holes into a supermassive black hole at the centre of the Universe. That's the Big Crunch. The balloon contracts back down to nothing." Mosse glanced at Heelia to gauge her reaction.

"And what next, then?" she asked.

"We're at the end of measurable time. The end of the Universe as we know it, but all of the mass is still there, locked into the supermassive black hole. But then, at a certain point, the pressure under gravity in the supermassive black hole hits a threshold where it triggers the next Big Bang. That's the start of a new, inflating Universe, and so on, ad infinitum. We don't need a creator because the Universe yoyos in and out forever, with a new Big Bang every 40 or 50 billion years."

"And is that what scientists believe, or is this just your theory Mosse?"

"I don't know. Ask a cosmologist or astronomer or a physicist. They might tell you I'm talking nonsense! I think the jury is still out on this." Mosse laughed.

"You're too clever for your own good! I was convinced you knew what you were talking about!"

"Well, you never know. I could be right. Anyway, I see no need for a creator. Especially one who created us as his playthings. We're stunningly insignificant in space and time, in comparison with the rest of the Universe. We're the creators in our over-fertile imaginations. Our ancestors have created many deities in their own image, and then indoctrinated children to believe in them."

Heelia was beginning to feel uncomfortable with the discussion. Regardless of whether she practised her religion or not, she had been brought up to believe that there was a superior force, which oversaw life, and that we should respect it. She did not normally think about it, but the questioning of her basic faith was starting to feel like a threat rather than an explanation.

What Mosse was saying might have been correct, but he sounded smug, like he knew better than her parents and teachers, and the people in her community. His explanations were unveiling a cultural barrier of which they were on opposite sides.

Heelia had thought she was falling in love with Mosse, but now she wasn't sure whether she was beginning to see a very fine line between love and hate. She wanted to go back to the chalet and rekindle their love-making, to stay with him and forget her outside life, but he was making her question her faith. As the thought flashed through her mind, she realised that it wasn't a threat to her own faithful belief in religious dogma that concerned her. That wasn't really important to her. What mattered was the blind faith observed by the people around her; her parents, friends and neighbours back in Perali. Any loss of her faith would be seen by them as a betrayal, which would lead to her being ostracised, or something even worse. Admission of her romantic association with Mosse would be disastrous; a heretic, a blasphemer, an atheist!

"I think we should change the subject, Mosse. This is making me feel uncomfortable."

"I'm sorry. As you've said, we come from different cultures and have different views about life. We've had a great time together the past few days, and I don't want to ruin that by saying something stupid."

Heelia was glad to accept an apology from Mosse. They hugged tightly and then kissed passionately once more. However, it felt like they had just had their first argument as a romantic couple. Until that discussion, they had been growing closer, falling in love even, but now there was a dent in their mutual trust. Heelia felt that her faith and, more importantly, that of her family had been demeaned.

Mosse was disappointed that Heelia couldn't simply accept his reasoning. But why should she? Did it really matter? She was entitled to her own opinions.

Mosse poured them another drink, and they stayed on the terrace, watching the sky darken and the stars beginning to peer through. They turned the bench around to face away from the artificial lights of Carina. To the south, they could clearly see the myriad of stars and their galaxy, which swept across the night sky.

"The sky is beautiful tonight," said Heelia. "Now, when I look at all those stars and galaxies, I'm going to think of expanding balloons and Big Bangs!"

Mosse laughed, glad that Heelia was still trying to show her sense of humour. Hopefully, by morning, the creation discussion would have been forgotten again.

"What time is your bus tomorrow?" Mosse asked.

Heelia had travelled from Rimano, a large city in the north of Perali. A coach service, which passed through a tunnel underneath the White Mountain, emerged at Partimix, a popular climbing resort on the north side of the massif. She had taken a taxi from there to Carina, but tomorrow, Mosse would take her on the 30-minute drive back to the station at Partimix.

"Three o'clock in the afternoon," she replied.

"That's good; we don't have to get up too early. We can go to Partimix during the morning, explore a bit and then have lunch there. It's a pretty town, but very touristy. Lots of people."

"That'll be nice, Mosse."

They sat on the terrace for some time, talking about Partimix and some of the other tourist centres in the region, until Heelia shivered slightly as the last warmth of the day was crushed under the dropping temperature of a cold, clear night sky.

"You're cold now." Let's go back inside," said Mosse.

They returned to the bedroom, dropping their bathrobes. They climbed back into bed, where they hugged and kissed each other firmly on the lips once more. Perhaps they had drained their energy earlier. Possibly they were tired from climbing mountains. Maybe their passion had waned following their discussion of the Big Bang on the terrace.

Who Writes the Rules

Whatever the reason, Heelia rested her head on Mosse's shoulder, kissed his cheek and said softly, "Thank you for another lovely day, Mosse. Goodnight."

Both were tired and a little saddened as they drifted off to sleep.

Chapter 13. Religion

When they woke on their last day together, Mosse and Heelia made an attempt at rekindling the passion of their previous love-making, but somehow the intensity had diminished. The emotion was less ecstatic, the connection loosening, their actions becoming more ritualised.

Heelia had been attracted and impressed by Mosse's knowledge and passion for nature, and his concerns about environmental damage. However, now, she was seeing something darker. He was arrogant and contemptuous of anybody who believed in a creator.

Mosse was disappointed and downhearted. He was aware that he had upset Heelia, but failed to appreciate why that should be. His only explanation was that she had been so indoctrinated in her childhood that, even though she didn't actively practise her family's religion, she was not open to rational discussion when it came to deities.

He felt angry with himself. He should have known from previous experience that this subject was best not approached with somebody who seriously believes in it without questioning it. How could he have a complete relationship with somebody who would not objectively debate with him at least?

They lay quietly for a while, both deep in streams of semiconscious thought. Eventually, Mosse kissed Heelia on the cheek and then raised his head.

"I'll go make some coffee."

"Thank you, that would be good."

Mosse levered himself off the bed and, donning his

Who Writes the Rules

bathrobe, strode through to the kitchen. After five minutes, he returned to the bedroom, placed a coffee cup on the cabinet next to Heelia, then climbed into bed, sitting up against the pillows with his hands wrapped around his coffee cup.

"You seem sad, Mosse. What's wrong?"

"Of course, I'm sad. You're leaving today."

"I think it's more than that. I can sense it. Tell me what you're thinking."

"Up until last night, we were making love at night and again in the morning. But today, we didn't make love; it was just sex. Physical relief. Going through the motions. What's happened to us?"

"We're very different, Mosse. And maybe we're just starting to realise that. Perhaps we can't be lovers because we're not in good harmony."

"That's not true. Up until now, we've had chemistry, and passion and emotion, but since our talk about creation, we've lost that. Why should we let that come between us?"

"It's true that until yesterday I just wanted to freeze the moment," Heelia said softly. When we were wrapped together, I didn't want to let go. But now we're getting to know each other. Maybe we're seeing things we don't like about each other?"

"The only thing that has changed since yesterday is that we had that talk about creation and the Big Bang. The belief in superstition!"

"But now you're showing me your true self. You're looking down at me for believing. That's condescending," Heelia replied.

"I don't look down at you. I'm just disappointed.

184

You're erecting a barrier between us."

Heelia felt the barrier rise again, but who was to blame? Why was Mosse being so smug? He was treating her like a child! He was right, and she was stupid! She protested, "Don't you see? You're blaming me again because I believe there is something more powerful than ourselves."

To Mosse, religious belief was like a brick wall. It wasn't based on reality. It was a nail which was usually hammered into the brains of young children, who then grew up unable to pull it out. How could he get that idea across to her? "I'm not blaming you. I'm blaming the culture that has indoctrinated you."

Heelia sensed anger stirring in her mind. Now he was blaming her family, her teachers and the society in which she lived – the territory she needed to protect. "I resent that. You're insulting my family and my community."

"I'm sorry. I don't want to offend you, but it hurts that I'm losing you to superstition and irrational beliefs."

"If the Creator is irrational, then why do so many people believe?"

"That's a long story. Do you really want my explanation?"

Heelia gritted her teeth. Maybe she had had enough of Mosse's explanations. They were beginning to hurt and drive a wedge between them. But she wanted to stop the argument. To fix the issue. Should she give him a chance?

She responded despondently, "I'm not sure that I do. Can you keep it brief?"

"I can try."

Heelia stared hard at Mosse, unsure whether she

wanted to consider his views any further. In some ways, it would make it easier for her to depart if they weren't on good terms, but when they had been so close, she ought to try to make up with him. It would be better to return with only the best memories of her visit to Carina.

"Ok, I'm listening," she replied.

"You have to think about our basic instincts and the history of the Majans as a species over the last 100,000 years or so. Our ancestors then were biologically similar to us but obviously didn't have the knowledge that we have today. In the early days, small groups or tribes migrated from the equatorial, dark continent to the northern temperature continents. Their natural instincts were to be altruistic in support of any members of their own tribe or cultural group. However, they could also be murderously aggressive towards any other group that they saw as a threat."

"Well, that bit hasn't changed much in the last 100,000 years, has it, Mosse?" she laughed.

"Not at all," Mosse responded. "They were also very curious. They had the same sort of reasoning capability as we have now. Their problem-solving and analytic prowess could not have evolved without them also having an innate curiosity. They needed answers to everything, such as, 'Where do we come from?' and 'Why are we here?'"

"Yet again, that hasn't changed! Just like we do today!" Heelia responded.

"They had the same awareness of self, ego, or consciousness that we do today, too: an internal persona that picks up the stimuli from the senses. It sees, hears, feels, smells, tastes, thinks and directs all the parts of the body to do its bidding."

"That's what I would call the immortal soul: the bit that transcends life, prays to the Creator for salvation and passes to either a perfect or horrendous eternity after death," Heelia added.

"Now, this is where we differ," said Mosse. "You recognise the description of the persona. It's familiar because it describes who you are. Capable of sensing the world around you but somehow floating on a different plane. The bit that dreams when we sleep and imagines itself outside the body. Am I right?"

"That sounds about right, but didn't you say this is where we differ?"

"You think it's immortal, whereas I would say that it's not immortal. The soul is your ego or self, which develops with the rest of your brain and intellect as you develop from foetus to infant to child to adult. The soul's view of the world is what is presented to the brain via the senses, but somehow it feels as if the ego is disconnected from the physical body. Why should this thing we call the soul or ego be immortal? It will die when the brain dies."

Heelia stated, "Anybody who believes in ghosts or spirits will tell you that the soul lives on after death!"

"There is no reason why that should be the case. Just like us, our ancestors in hunter-gatherer tribes could not accept that when we die, we die. They believed that their own ancestors, their parents, and eventually, they themselves must go somewhere when the body dies. So, they imagined their egos to be immortal souls. These two factors, the need for answers to unknown questions and the desire for immortality, were fundamental building blocks of religious belief."

"That doesn't explain why so many people believe in these things today unless there's a foundation that supports their beliefs! There are more believers than non-believers. So, why do you think you're right? Why should you know any better than everybody else? Maybe it's you who has been brainwashed into non-belief!"

Mosse felt a little bemused. Heelia could throw back a defensive wall. Why could she not listen to logic and reason? To what is accepted scientific knowledge? He tried to carry on with his reasoning. "Ok. Our ancestors believed that their ancestors existed beyond their world after death. They started to ask their "spirit" ancestors to help control weather, fertility, etc. They started to perform rituals. They buried items with dead relatives to accompany them to the afterlife. They also passed stories by word of mouth about strong individuals and heroes. The stories were exaggerated with each retelling until their ancestor heroes became the deities, controlling those aspects of nature they didn't understand. The sun, the moon, the stars, the seasons, rainfall, the sea, the weather. All of these things had deities assigned to them."

"But today, we know better. There's just one Creator deity," Heelia asserted.

"That depends on which religion you follow. Some still have multiple deities. The truth is that, as most of the natural world became understood by civilisations and philosophers, they didn't need multiple deities. Just one would do, to provide the answer to all the remaining unanswered questions."

"But what about the soul and life after death? You haven't explained why we believe in these things."

"As our ancestors began to adopt agriculture and settle in fixed locations, their communities got bigger and bigger, becoming ever less personal. People who were regarded as strong or knowledgeable would have been community leaders or tribal chiefs. Some of these people believed they could explain the supernatural: phenomena such as life after death or communication with deities. They developed rituals that their followers were obliged to obey, like praying for good harvest or victory in conquest, etc."

"Why would people follow rituals and pray if they didn't believe in it?" asked Heelia.

"They may not have had a choice. In early civilisations, they may have been too scared not to follow the rituals. As civilisations advanced, they were more and more indoctrinated into potentially offering their lives in holy wars as well as contributing money or goods for religious buildings and temples. But they were blackmailed with the promise of eternity in paradise against eternity in hellfire. Without evidence for any of these supernatural entities and afterlife, and no scientific evidence to the contrary, they were usually too terrified of the consequences to disobey."

"But all that's ancient history, holy wars etc. These things don't happen today, do they?"

"They certainly do. In the early days, religious stories were passed by word of mouth, but in the last few thousand years, the main religions have created their own rule books. These were supposed to define the basis of their theology and the rules that the Creator deity wants us to follow. Throughout history, right up until now, there have been many conflicts, which are sometimes described as political. However, even the political boundaries leading to conflict are a consequence of association with different religious groups."

"For example, your culture and mine and their respective religions?" noted Heelia.

"Yes, it seems we've had lots to fight about for more than a thousand years. And look at us. We should be lovers and soulmates, not enemies."

"How can we be soulmates when mine is immortal, and yours isn't?" joked Heelia.

"Actually, there is something a little bit spiritual about the soul. It does transcend the physical body," Mosse said, smiling.

"What? What am I hearing from you? Are you making a joke?"

"If you were to come back to me again this time next year, I would be looking at a different physical person, but you would still have the same ego, which would know me, even though I would also be a physically different person."

"What do you mean by that? That sounds like nonsense."

"You accept that in a year you will lose blood, skin cells peel off, nails and hair grow?"

"Yes, of course. But that doesn't make me a physically different person."

"Well, all of the rest of your tissue cells are continuously dying and being replaced, so in a year, you will be nearly completely different; different cells, different molecules, but still the same ego. Even the part of your brain that controls the consolidation of short-term into long-term memory is continually being replaced. Your body is like a complex ecosystem, with each tissue type behaving as if it were an individual species with a population of single cells, which die off and are regenerated throughout your life. And just like an ecosystem, if you remove one species, it could have a drastic effect on the rest of the system. But that bit of you, which is talking to me now and looking out through your eyes, transcends the physical replacement of your body cells. Even brain cells. That's quite spiritual, isn't it?"

"So, you have accepted that the soul transcends the physical body. So why not accept that the soul can be immortal, carrying on somewhere else when the body has died?"

"What we're referring to as the soul is actually a function of the brain. The processes of thinking and responding to sensory stimuli require living brain cells. Even if individual brain cells are replaced, the processes can continue, just as a muscle will continue to contract, even though the fibres are all replaced. If the brain dies, then those processes will cease. What use would an immortal soul be?"

"If you accept that the Creator exists and has a place for us in paradise, then maybe that's where the soul will go for eternity. Don't you see that?" Heelia argued.

"Ok. What about babies dying during childbirth who have no experience or learning? What value would their souls have in paradise? Or an elderly person who dies with serious dementia, such that they can't remember anything or think rationally? Or somebody who has a serious brain injury following a stroke and dies shortly afterwards? Do their souls all revert to some prime condition like that of a 25-year-old? If so, would that mean they'd forfeited any knowledge they learned in later life?"

"I guess that would be for the Creator to decide!"

"The reality is that there's no evidence for anything supernatural. People who believe there is do so because, for many generations, they've been told every day, from when they were old enough to listen, that they must follow these rules. Their parents aren't lying because that's what they believe, after being told it by the priests, who also believe it because they've had the same message passed to them through many generations of priests. Until the last few hundred years, ancient dogma was accepted, but modern science enlightens us to the extent that we can see that the supernatural is exactly that – against the rules of nature. Supernatural means unreal."

"But what about moral guidance? Doesn't religion make sure people are good?"

"People are intrinsically good, although obviously some more so than others. Unless they've got very bad character traits, people generally want to help each other, even laying down their lives for others in some cases. We're naturally altruistic. We know it's wrong to steal from or kill others. We know we should respect each other and treat others as we would expect to be treated ourselves. Religions claim to give moral guidance, but they've stolen that from our natural instincts. We are instinctively good with or without religion."

"If that's the case, then why have there always been

wars in the name of religion?"

"Remember the hunter-gatherer tribes? They are altruistic with respect to members of their tribe but can be murderously competitive against other tribes. The same applies to religion. In many cases, people behave altruistically or generously towards people of their own faith, but can be antagonistic to the point of intense distrust or even hatred towards other faiths."

"As I told you, some of my community would regard you as a blasphemer. Death penalty!"

"It's not just religion. There are many social divisions that evoke the same types of responses: nationality, skin colour, sports team, etc. They can all lead to conflict if allowed to. It's territorial behaviour. The animal instinct is to defend what it perceives to be its territory and will sometimes fight to the death for it."

"So, you're telling me that all religions will cause conflict if they come up against each other. Maybe everybody should just share one big religion, then," suggested Heelia.

"Or no religion. Just common moral values and a recognition that we're a single social group: the Majan species. Don't look at the colour differences or listen to the language differences. We're all just one species killing our planet!"

"That sounds a bit dramatic. How do you make everybody non-religious on a planet where most people have one?"

"It can't happen overnight. We need to re-educate the world. Today many children are indoctrinated before they're even old enough for school. They emerge from the womb as a blank sheet and begin by learning how to interpret the signals from their own sense organs. Then their curiosity grows with them. Teach them how to speak, and to read and to write. To ask questions and learn the truth. But don't teach them faith in the supernatural. Teach them what is right and what is wrong, but base it on instinct and observation, not on dogma and mythology. Teach them *how* to think, not what to think!"

"Who decides what is right and what is wrong? Do you have the authority to dictate these things?" asked Heelia.

"There are different meanings to right and wrong. Determining factual right and wrong is a function of scientific investigation and knowledge. Seek the truth and only the truth. Don't teach mythology as fact. Don't lie. Thy shalt not bear false witness. Deciding moral right and wrong is a social function that should be determined by consensus, following our altruistic instincts."

"Some people pray to help them cope with problems. Belief in a superior power or a dead relative going to paradise helps them to accept difficult situations. Praying helps ease their suffering. Would you deny them that?"

"But is it really necessary to lie to people, give them a false perception of life? If I were dying, I would prefer the doctors keep me informed rather than trying to comfort me by telling me I'll get better soon. At least that would give me a chance to prepare for the end of my life and to consider how my family might be affected. Why pray to something non-existent? It would be better to understand reality and focus on the best way of dealing with it."

"Did I ask you to keep it brief?" said Heelia.

"How can you cover something like this briefly? Do you still think I'm condescending?"

Heelia's anger had subsided. Maybe it was Mosse's suggestion that the soul transcends the body, even if he says it's not immortal. Or maybe she could agree with much of his logic.

"No. You mean well. I can't argue with you. Possibly everything you say is correct, but I can't change the way I feel. Having always felt there is something spiritual guiding us in life, I can't just drop that because you tell me it's not so."

"I'm not asking you to change yourself in any way. There's something very lovable about a lady who attracts a butterfly and sees it as the Spirit of the Ice," Mosse replied.

"You know what the real problem is, Mosse? I know we could be happy together, whether in bed or up a mountain. But we come from different societies, and I can't stay in yours. I really wish that wasn't the case. Maybe I resent the cultural difference between us because I would love to take you to meet my family in Perali, but that would probably destroy my life. Things would never be the same again."

"Ok. Perhaps we should move on from this conversation. I want us to enjoy the last few hours together."

Heelia leaned toward Mosse, kissing him on the lips. A tear blurred her eye. She wanted to return to the warmth – the connectedness which made her want to stay forever.

Who Writes the Rules

"I agree, Mosse," she said. "Let's make the most of what time we have left."

They finished their coffee, showered, dressed, and had a light breakfast on the terrace before setting off for Partimix.

Chapter 14. Separation

From Mosse's chalet terrace, the white, linear concrete structure of a road mounted on a viaduct was visible at about four kilometres distance and 400 metres lower in altitude. Mosse was immensely irritated by the almost constant, distant drone of heavy transport vehicles climbing the viaduct, which formed part of a major road route.

"Noise pollution!" he would regularly complain.

The rumble of traffic drifted on the wind, climbing the surrounding mountainsides. The secluded valleys to which he had taken Heelia offered some shelter and an escape from it. A return to tranquillity.

The viaduct climbed from 600 metres to 800 metres, suspended on massive, reinforced stilts up to 70 metres tall, as the road ascended along a section three kilometres in length. The viaduct linked the lower valley near the swimming lake with a road that climbed the north side of the massif into the Partimix valley.

Mosse saw the viaduct as a massive blot on the landscape, but it provided an important route to a tunnel that passed underneath the White Mountain, linking his region with the country of Perali on the other side of the massif.

Having loaded Heelia's bags into his car after a quick breakfast, the couple set off mid-morning, through Carina and then dropping further down the meandering route until they came to the slip road, which connected to the viaduct at the valley bottom.

"This is quite a spectacular bridge," Heelia commented as they drove along the stilted section with vertical drops on either side.

To one side was a wall of trees and rocky mountain slopes rising steeply above their heads. The other side was semi-urban, with industrial buildings, chalet communities, a railway line and rural roads scattered across flat meadows and woodland, through which a fast-flowing river carried away the meltwater from the glaciers above the Partimix Valley.

"Yes, but best if I keep my eyes on the road rather than admiring the view," Mosse replied as he passed a series of heavy lorries struggling slowly up the gradient of the viaduct. "Not the best place to have an accident!"

"Don't say that, Mosse. I'm scared now!"

Mosse smiled and added reassuringly, "Don't worry. I've driven here lots of times, and the route is easy from the end of the bridge all the way to Partimix."

The upper end of the bridge connected to a road, which wound gently up through forest for a few kilometres, then continued for several more kilometres along a wide, level valley at about 1,000 metres altitude. On both sides, chalet communities and meadows merged into forests that blanketed the slopes as they rose into the higher mountain massifs on either side.

They passed the snout of a large glacier on the north side of the White Mountain massif, which, receiving little sunshine, reached down to below 1,400 metres. A few minutes more driving took them into the town of Partimix, where Mosse turned immediately into a very crowded parking area but managed to find a free space quickly.

"I told you it was very touristy here. It's the main climbing base for the White Mountain. It's always crowded and sometimes impossible to park. The town is always buzzing. Lots of cafes and bars. Also quite picturesque, with an interesting climbing museum. But I want to take you to the Ice Grotto. We have to catch a train just beside the car park here. Luckily, there's one waiting to leave, so let's be quick."

As they walked towards the station just a hundred metres from where they were parked, they could see the two bright red carriages of a rack and pinion rail train waiting at the platform. Passing through the station entrance, Mosse walked quickly to a ticket machine and purchased two return tickets for the Ice Grotto. The pair walked out along the platform and opened a door in the middle of the front carriage. The train was already quite full of passengers, but Mosse found a single empty seat with a view on the left side of the train.

"You take this one," he offered to Heelia. "You're the tourist. The seat is on the valley side, so you'll have a good view of the ascent and the sea of ice from here. I can stand in the aisle."

Heelia smiled as she sat down, happily accepting the offer of a seat.

Within a few minutes, the train glided quietly out of the station, the sound of the electric engine camouflaged by the rhythmic clacking noises of the wheels crossing rail joints. For twenty minutes, the train climbed over meadows, through forests and up the mountainside, offering occasional glimpses of the town of Partimix stretching along the valley

199

below.

The train turned gradually out of the forest, slowing as it entered the station 100 metres above the debris-coated tongue of a long, relatively flat glacier, which curved down a long valley from the centre of the massif beyond, where it swept up into the ice cap above.

"Wow. Fantastic view of the glacier from up here!" Heelia exclaimed.

"What's left of it," muttered Mosse.

After descending from the train, the passengers followed a path from the platform to a telecabine lift system. A handful of cabins were strung along a steeply descending loop of strong steel wire, which carried them partway down to the glacier.

"We should walk quickly here," Mosse told Heelia. "The more people we pass, the less time we have to queue when we get down to the telecabine."

Historically, at the time of its construction, the telecabine had taken passengers to the top of the glacier. However, since then, the glacier had melted significantly, shrinking inwards and downwards, with its edge now more than 200 metres away from the bottom of the telecabine. A series of undulating paths, metal and concrete ramps and staircases formed a route over the rugged terrain of rocks and moraine debris, stretching from the base of the lift to the glacier grotto entrance.

Mosse and Heelia had been among the first passengers off the train and managed to stay in front of most of them as they walked to the telecabine. Within a few minutes, they were on board a descending cabin, gliding down to the path below. Exiting the telecabine, they negotiated their way along to the path of ramps and metal staircases, which took them to the grotto entrance.

"Wow. Amazing!" Heelia uttered as she arrived at the entrance to the grotto.

A tunnel of roughly three metres in diameter had been cut into the glacial mass. Non-slip matting covered the floor, and the interior was illuminated so that the smooth ice walls of the tunnel shone a translucent, pale grey-blue. They entered and passed through the tunnel, which stretched for about 100 metres into the heart of the glacier.

The air inside was cold but refreshing. They walked slowly forward in the iridescent blue twilight. After about 15 metres, they arrived at a recess cut into one side of the tunnel, illuminated in a rich, cerise pink. A large clock cabinet had been sculpted into the ice, displaying a working clock face.

As they continued along the tunnel, they came to other side recesses containing sculptures or displaying exhibits. Old pictures showed mountain climbers from the previous century. They wore clothes of traditional fabrics that were tough but not as weather resilient as modern garments. They carried old-style hooks and heavy ropes to help them ascend the White Mountain. Bearded faces, weather-beaten, wrinkled and as hard as the rockfaces they climbed. They were characterful images of the past when the glacier would have crept much further down the mountainside.

Chambers illuminated in bright kingfisher green, or rich red, offered their displays and exhibits to a slowly moving stream of passing tourists. Bright pinks, greens and blues added a mystical quality to the tunnel and its recesses.

Who Writes the Rules

"It's like a fairy palace. Maybe my little Spirit of the Ice lives in here!" said Heelia, reminiscing about the butterfly that rode on her hand a few days earlier.

"I don't think your little Spirit of the Ice would last long here. A bit too cold and dark. It would prefer warmth and sunshine."

"Ha! It's a spirit. It doesn't care about heat and cold or light and dark; it just likes magical places. The paradise valley was magical, and so is this grotto!"

"Ok; I can't argue with that," Mosse laughed. He loved her tongue-in-cheek, fantasy logic. For a moment, a feeling of desolation swept through him. A reminder that they only had a few hours left before Heelia's departure.

"Do you know that they have to re-carve this grotto every year?" he asked, trying to divert his thoughts back to the present and the final few hours in Heelia's company. "That's because of the movement of the glacier. And they have to keep adding new sections to the path, about 20 steps each year, to get to the grotto from the telecabine because the glacier is receding so quickly."

"Oh, Mosse! Why do you have to bring everything back to reality? Let's just enjoy the moment Heelia put her arms around Mosse's neck and kissed him firmly on the lips, ignoring the other tourists in the tunnel.

"Hey," said Mosse. "We need to go somewhere more private if you're going to do that!"

"Unfortunately, there's no ice bedroom in the tunnel," Heelia added, lips pouting.

"If there were, you'd get us arrested!" Mosse responded. "And it might be a bit cold!"

They both laughed and released their embrace,

turning to explore the remaining exhibits until they had reached the end of the tunnel.

"Time to head back, I think," said Mosse. "Hopefully, we'll have time for a quick bite to eat before your bus goes."

They walked slowly back along the tunnel, having a long look at each recess for the last time as they made their way to the entrance.

"I don't know how much longer they can keep this open," Mosse said. "Another few years and the ice will have receded too far."

"That's so sad. Where will the Spirit live when the ice palace has gone?" Heelia added.

Exiting the grotto, they climbed their way back along the path to the telecabine, in which they ascended to return to the station.

Sol had shone on them for several days, gracing them with warmth and clear skies. Today was becoming more humid, the sky less clear, darkening slowly from the west.

"I think we may have another thunderstorm later," Mosse observed. "Hopefully, it will stay away until you're on your bus."

They waited about 15 minutes for the next train, chatting about the exhibits and the extent of the glacier, marvelling at the effort that had gone into carving the tunnel and its recesses. Both felt a sadness that the glacier was disappearing and a deeper gloominess that the remaining time before Heelia's departure was also rapidly melting away.

When the train arrived, they waited for the next

group of passengers to exit, then quickly found seats together. After about ten minutes of waiting at the platform, the train slipped quietly out of the station, winding its way back down the mountainside towards Partimix. During the descent, Mosse pointed out peaks and features across the valley and details of the town centre as it came ever closer.

They arrived at the bottom station with just an hour to spare before the bus departure.

"Not a lot of time to go for lunch, I'm afraid," Mosse told Heelia. "We can get a takeaway from a kiosk at the bus station. That should keep you going for a few hours."

They walked from the glacier train station back to the car, collected Heelia's bags and then headed to the main station from where the bus would depart. There were several kiosks at the station forecourt, some selling food and drinks, others selling confectionary or books and newspapers. A rack on the pavement displayed the front pages of a variety of newspapers, some of which came from other countries and were printed in the language of their origin.

The front page of several journals showed the smiling faces of two young adults – one male, the other female – alongside a picture of another adult male being held down on a pavement by several people. The headlines included: **Terrorist Attack on Doldrum Bridge.**

Mosse picked up a journal and scanned the front page. Apparently, the two smiling faces were those of people who had been helping rehabilitate the bearded man who was being held down on the bridge. It seems his response to their selfless actions was to murder them. In his desire to be a martyr, he had destroyed innocence and invited his own execution, which was achieved when the police shot him dead on the bridge.

"Why?" Mosse muttered aloud in disbelief.

Heelia shuddered as she briefly examined what had provoked Mosse's reaction.

"He's not from my culture, Mosse. He may have claimed to be, but he was a misguided fanatic. People will look at the religion of my family and associate us with these actions, but it's not fair. These people use the name of our religion falsely. We're peace lovers; we only want what is good for everybody."

"You don't have to explain, Heelia. There are misguided people in all cultures. They're driven by hatred. They may use the name of a religion and claim that what they do is in that name, but they do these things out of a fanatical hatred. If it weren't religion then the same maniacs would have some other cause that they would want to fight for. Sadly, where religion fails is by promoting the idea of an afterlife and the glory of martyrdom. Without that, this killer would not have done what he did."

"Please don't get back to the subject of religion and the afterlife. I have to go soon. Let's just remember what we have had together these last few days."

Mosse put his arm around Heelia's shoulder and pulled her towards him, squeezing her gently.

"Yes, you're right, Heelia. But if it wasn't for these crazy cultural barriers, then what we have had could have lasted much longer. I can't go to where you live, and you can't tell your family about me. Ask yourself why. I know it's only been a few days. We don't know each other well enough to say we're in love, but right now, you're on a very high pedestal and I think you always will be because if I can never really get to know you, I'll never have a reason to stop being infatuated."

"Please stop, Mosse. I don't want to get emotional in the bus station, but you're going to make me cry if you keep talking like that."

"Ok. Let's get something to eat."

They found a kiosk selling a range of sandwiches, plus hot and cold drinks. Heelia selected two different sandwiches, one to eat now with a coffee to wash it down. A second, with a bottle of water, would be fine for her bus journey. Mosse also selected a sandwich and a coffee. They found a free bench in a green area nearby and sat down for their last meal together.

"Hardly gourmet cuisine," Mosse observed as they ate their sandwiches. "I thought we'd have more time to have a proper lunch together."

"That's not required. Just something to fill the empty stomach for a while," Heelia added. "I enjoyed seeing the ice cave today. That, and your company, of course, was more important than what I have for lunch."

"Remember, you can keep in touch with me. Maybe come back again, in the winter, for skiing? Or any other time of the year. Just let me know in advance. Don't just turn up dripping wet at a mountain restaurant."

"Warn you in advance of coming? So that I don't find you with another lady?" Heelia joked.

"No. So that you don't come here when I'm somewhere else, and we miss each other!"

"You know I was joking, Mosse. I can't promise to come back, and I can't expect you to wait for me. Maybe you'll meet somebody nicer than me and fall madly in love, and I'll be jealous from a distance."

"Right now, I can't imagine meeting anybody nicer than you, Heelia. I will always relive these last few days with you until you come back and give me some more great times to remember."

They hugged tightly again on the bench and kissed passionately, oblivious to any observers in their vicinity. The atmosphere was increasingly humid, and the sky was slowly darkening; a distant rumbling of thunder announcing the approaching storm.

"I should go for the bus now; before it starts to rain," Heelia said sadly after several minutes of embracing. "We met in a thunderstorm, and now we part in the next one."

Mosse checked his watch. The bus was due to leave in 15 minutes, but they had a few minutes to walk to the bay where the bus was parked and waiting to leave.

"Ok," said Mosse with resignation as he stooped to pick up Heelia's case. "Let's go."

They walked to the parked bus and placed Heelia's suitcase in the baggage locker. At the door of the bus, they hugged tightly once more for a good half minute before both relaxed and sighed, peering into each other's eyes. For the last time?

Leaning forward, Heelia briefly kissed Mosse on the lips as the first large splashes of rain formed dark spots on the pavement.

"Goodbye, Mosse. Don't stand near any trees!" she said, eyes watering slightly as she fought to suppress the emotion she was feeling.

Mosse looked directly into her eyes and opened his

mouth, seemingly unsure of what to say.

"Don't say it!" Heelia instructed. "Better that we just remember."

Mosse nodded as she stepped onto the bus, glancing back with a smile, then walking down the aisle to find a seat by a window. Mosse stood on the pavement just beyond, waiting the last few minutes for the bus to depart. The engine was already running as the driver made announcements about the route, the timings, safety, and food and drink services available on board.

Heelia didn't hear any of it. Her mind raced as she tried to maintain a smiling composure while Mosse waited to wave goodbye. The rain was now falling steadily, large droplets beginning to run down the window, obscuring the eye contact between them.

Finally, the bus began to pull slowly forward. Heelia waved and blew a kiss to Mosse as he waved back, beginning to soak under the increasing rainfall, slowly sinking into the background as the driver accelerated and pulled clear of the bus station. The tears Heelia had fought to hide from Mosse now began to well up in her eyes.

A lady sitting across the aisle smiled and said, "Just let it go, dear. He can't see you now."

Heelia smiled back at her, then turned away as her lip quivered, and she gave up trying to suppress an escaping sob. She knew what Mosse had wanted to say to her, and she had wanted to say the same. Pointless now, holding back the emotion. It was better to let it out and confine it to her memories when she arrived home.

Chapter 15. Reflections

Flashes of lightning cut vivid gashes in the sky, belching out booms of thunder, which rolled and echoed along the sides of the long, deep Partimix valley. The rain came in torrential bursts, bouncing off pavements and rattling on rooftops. Mosse stepped back into the station doorway, sheltering from the downpour as he watched the bus pull away from the forecourt, turn a corner and then disappear from sight.

In a dispirited mood, Mosse did not intend to wait for the rain to stop. He trotted quickly through the downpour back to his car and climbed into the driver's seat as wet as Heelia had been on the day they had met. He sat stationary for some time while the rain drummed heavily on the roof and windscreen. Eventually, the rainfall eased, and the sky seemed to lighten once more. He started the engine and headed back down the valley to Carina and his chalet.

The drive back was difficult. Not because of the rain; Mosse was used to driving in all conditions thrown at him by the mountain climate. It was difficult because he found it hard to concentrate on the road. The events of the past few days raced through his mind. The empty passenger seat beside him reminded him that he was on his own again. He had been used to being on his own, which had never been a problem, but now he felt as if he had lost a limb.

Heelia was special. Beautiful, intelligent, happy, humorous, sexy; a perfect companion. And now she was gone.

Who Writes the Rules

When he got back to the chalet, Mosse took off his wet clothes, showered and dressed in clean, dry garments. Everywhere he looked, he could see Heelia: her bright eyes smiling, her laughter haunting every room in the chalet. He considered going to bed and trying to sleep off his sadness, but knew only too well that the bed would be far too empty for him to relax in it.

He went to the kitchen and poured himself a beer. The rain was still falling intermittently, sometimes heavily. Lightning flashed within a few kilometres, but the terrace table was sheltered by the chalet roof, and it was still warm enough to sit outside under cover.

He took his beer to the terrace, sipping slowly, counting the delay between lightning and thunder. His mind wandered back to yesterday's visit to the glacier and Heelia counting the delay between avalanches and the thundering sound they produced.

This evening the view across the valley was obscured by low cloud and rain, but Mosse could see right through it in his imagination. He could see the track where the butterfly had alighted on Heelia's hand. He could see the paradise valley, where they had their first kiss. He could see the moraine they climbed together. He could see down to the lake in the lower valley. He could feel the warmth of her body as they swam in an embrace at the lake's surface. He could taste her tongue and lips as they had kissed. He could feel the passion in their embrace as they made love. Heelia was everywhere. Mosse sighed, finished his beer and returned to the kitchen, where he poured another.

Returning to the terrace table, Mosse knew he

couldn't shut Heelia out. Nature had intended their relationship to happen. Pheromones? Mutual attraction? Circumstances? He couldn't explain why things worked for them, but the reasons for their relationship failing were of society's making, not nature's.

What were the things that separated him and Heelia? Although he had been raised in a society where religious identity was strong, he had been disillusioned by the conflicts and hypocrisy that he had witnessed in his youth. He was a non-believer, rejecting his society's attempt at brainwashing him into acceptance of mythological dogma.

Heelia didn't consider herself religious, yet she had been taught to believe in a family religion with a different set of dogmatic mythologies. The teachers of all their societies' religions would claim that their philosophies were correct and necessary for moral instruction in their respective cultures. In Mosse's opinion, morality was natural and instinctive. It was not necessary to believe in religious dogma in order to distinguish between right and wrong.

The pair were strongly attracted to each other, physically, intellectually and emotionally, and could have formed a long-lasting, solid, romantic relationship. However, their different cultural backgrounds would mean that neither would be respected by the other's families and peers.

The fact that Heelia was more open to religious ideology and the idea of spirituality than Mosse would not have weakened their relationship. To Mosse, it was better for a couple to have some differences of opinion than

211

simply to agree about everything. If she chose to believe in a creator, to have faith in something supernatural, then that was her free choice. It was not for him to deny or ridicule this. However, it should be equally acceptable for him to be totally atheistic, seeking natural explanations for life and the Universe.

Heelia could have accepted Mosse's views while retaining her own spirituality and opinions. However, the society in which she lived would not have permitted their relationship. Within her community, the relationship would be considered heretical and dangerous for them to pursue.

In questions of life and nature, Mosse preferred to determine the fundamental scientific truth. However, he also asked himself:

Is faith harmful?
Does it matter if people believe in invisible spirits?
Does it matter if people pray?

Perhaps the answers are No, No and No, if the beliefs of an individual don't have an impact on the lives of others.

But what about childhood indoctrination?

To Mosse, it was completely unacceptable to teach mythological dogma as fact. A child at birth has a unique DNA blueprint, which determines his or her development and metabolism. The child's brain starts as a blank canvas that will become painted with a worldview, learning to interpret the input from sense organs and developing ideas about how the world works. Let the child learn. Encourage it to think. Explain what you know to be true. When it is old enough it may seek answers to fundamental questions. If one of these answers is to assign everything to a deity, then let the individual make that decision freely. To repeatedly state to a developing child that mythological beliefs are true will potentially brainwash that child into believing in a false picture of reality.

Surely it is better to see the truth in black and white and to appreciate the glory of nature in all the colours of the rainbow than to exist in an imaginary Universe painted many shades of grey? Do not teach as fact what cannot be demonstrated to be true. That may simply be perpetuating a lie.

And what about hatred and murder in the name of a religion?

Surely all religions state that it is wrong to kill others? The image of two smiling, happy faces on a newsstand flashed through Mosse's head.

Why?! How could this possibly be justified?

It is not nature that turns people into killers; it's nurture. The blank DNA blueprint designs an individual with a unique metabolism, fingerprints, iris pattern, etc. Nurture kills that individual. Nurture decides which tribe, which territory, which deities, which language, which rules to follow.

Who writes the rules?

They teach us who to love and who to hate; who is friend and who is foe; who to help and who to fight; who to kill and who to die for!

We are all the same colour on the inside. If you cut us, we all bleed red. When will the political and moral leaders of all our societies grasp that we are one species, destroying the planet we share? When will we learn to direct our energy, effort and resources into fixing the problems

213

Who Writes the Rules

we've created rather than seeking new targets for exploitation?

By the time Mosse poured his third beer, the rain had stopped and clouds were parting, beginning to reveal stars in the evening sky. He began to think about the majesty of the night sky, especially seen through the clear air of the mountains, away from the light pollution around community settlements.

Sol was just one star in a galaxy of 100 million others. There were trillions of galaxies in the Universe. There were likely to be millions of planets just like Thera. Could some of these planets support intelligent life?

The Big Bang was more than 14 billion years ago. Looking out into the night sky, much of the history of the Universe was revealed. But all of the light images of the stars and galaxies were old. The light from something a million light years away took a million years to reach Thera. Mosse could only see it as it was a million years ago. Even the light from Sol was over eight minutes old by the time it reached Thera.

The laws of physics and thermodynamics are fixed throughout the Universe. The evolution of life on Thera had been driven by these laws. All the galaxies throughout the Universe appeared to be of different ages. However, they were, in fact, all 14 billion years away from the Big Bang. The apparent age difference was a consequence of the time taken for light from distant galaxies to reach Thera.

The Big Bang kicked off the evolution of several generations of stars. Sol and its planets formed in the wake of a supernova explosion five billion years ago. This cycle of star generations was a prerequisite for the formation of the metals and heavy elements needed in order for a rocky planet like Thera to emerge.

All of the other galaxies had been evolving since the Big Bang. Therefore, it's likely that most star systems with Thera-like planets also formed around four or five billion years ago. The Majans were a consequence of roughly four billion years of carbon-based, biological evolution. Following the same laws of nature, it was very likely that functionally similar, intelligent life evolved on some other rocky planets within the same time frame.

However, for the first three billion years of evolution on Thera, life consisted of very simple cells. Only after the evolution of sexual reproduction could adaptation accelerate. Only then would more complex lifeforms appear. It was in the last 500 million years that plants and animals emerged from the oceans to evolve on continental landmasses. During that time, some groups of creatures dominated ecosystems for long periods. Between these eras were mass extinctions. These were caused by meteorite collisions, large-scale volcanic eruptions or significant changes in atmospheric chemistry and climate. The atmospheric chemistry and climate changed due to variations in tectonic plate position or other factors.

In other words, the evolution of intelligent life was not a predetermined sequence of events but a consequence of many unpredictable factors. Creatures like the Majans, capable of manipulating their environment, may have emerged on one Thera-like planet after three billion years. On another, it may have taken ten billion years, or possibly not at all, depending on many variables.

The Majans had existed as a biological species for

about 300,000 years. However, it was only in the last 20,000 years that their populations had expanded extensively around the globe. It was only in the last 5000 years that their populations had begun to increase exponentially, as agricultural production advanced. It was only in the past 100 years that their populations skyrocketed due to increasing technological and medical developments. These kept more and more people alive for longer while turning Thera's ecosystems into agricultural and industrial wastelands.

The Majan's existence as a species capable of space exploration and communication with life on other planets had spanned less than 100 years. The planetary system of Sol was close to five billion years old. That meant that the period during which there was technologically advanced life in that system was 100/5,000,000,000 or about two millionths of one per cent of the lifetime of Thera.

Whatever amount of four to five-billion-year-old rocky planets there were in the Universe, they would need to have liquid water for biological life, as known to the Therans, to evolve. If evolution followed similar paths to that on Thera, then the chance of intelligent life capable of developing space travel and advanced communications technology existing at precisely the same time as the current Majan society was extremely slim.

If such a species existed somewhere on another rocky planet, then it was likely to be at least hundreds of light years away. This would mean that if a Majan researcher projected a communications signal into space, it would take hundreds of years to arrive. If the recipients could receive, analyse and respond to the signal, it would take hundreds of years more for the response to be received by the Majans.

Coincident with the development of communication and space travel by the Majans was the proliferation of weapons of mass destruction. Given the political, religious and cultural divisions in Majan society, Mosse reckoned that his species would have blown each other to oblivion long before receiving any communication response from a different planet.

If, perchance, there was another intelligent species out there, would they view the Majans as food? Or as an existential threat? They were hardly likely to welcome the Majans, who were forever at war with each other, with open tentacles!

In any case, the existence of an intelligent species on any rocky planet would be brief and transient – a tiny eddy in the flow of life. Their intelligence would likely permit them to develop weapons of mass destruction, just as the Majans had. This would surely lead to their own extinction within hundreds of years.

They would be so far away that no transport technology could reach them within the lifetime of a Majan space crew. Travel close to the speed of light was not possible. A journey to the nearest habitable planets could take thousands of years. There was no known technology that would suspend the animation of the crew members.

Mosse poured his fourth beer and gazed at the sky. He assured himself that, whatever alien species were out there, the Majans could never possibly make contact with them. They were too far away to ever reach Thera. The Majans should not concern themselves with jumping planets when they've finished with their destruction of Thera. There were more important problems to address at home.

The Theran biosphere was like an island ecosystem. The energy flowing into the biosphere from Sol was constant. Some was absorbed by the primary production photosynthesisers, which were then consumed by other species.

The Majan population was exploding exponentially thanks to medicine and technology that kept an ever-ageing population alive for as long as possible while live birth rates also shot up. They consumed more and more of the primary production, leaving less and less for other species.

They lamented the extinction of many species, for which they were responsible through the destruction of natural habitats. They knew they were causing rapid climate change, but political indifference and competition meant that they procrastinated. They took too little action to address the causes and reverse the changes.

The Majans had too many cultural divisions, political and religious differences. Global leaders were constantly at odds, each with their own set of life's philosophies. Too many already had nuclear weapons, while others sought to develop them.

Who writes the rules for living in an over-populated, multi-cultural, dying society?

The rules followed by each culture were usually different ways of saying the same thing. They were rules intended for social control. Maybe it was time for global leaders to acknowledge that moral guidance doesn't need the supernatural. Instead of looking to the sky for deities and other life forms, Majans needed to look at the undeniable truth of their origins and fate. They needed to fix the problems they'd caused or give way to the next phase of evolution after their own extinction.

Mosse poured his fifth beer, or was it his sixth?

Does it matter if people pray?

Possibly some people gained hope or comfort from praying. To Mosse, it was just wishful thinking. With nothing out there to respond to a prayer, it was more important to grasp reality and take whatever responsibility you can for whatever it is you are hoping for.

However, Mosse could still imagine a few things worth praying for.

- Controlling and reversing the Majan population explosion.
- Dismantling and removing all weapons of mass destruction.
- Repairing the damage that the Majans had done to Thera's ecosystems.
- The return of Heelia to his arms.

Who Writes the Rules

Epilogue:
And Now for Something Completely Different

Two hundred years after Mosse's brief encounters with Heelia, the species had still managed to avoid extinction. Despots had withheld their fingers from the red button that fired the nuclear weapons. The population had more than doubled to nearly 20 billion in the first hundred years, during which they continued to burn fossil fuels and cut down forests much faster than they could possibly recover or be replanted. The consequent runaway global warming had made much of the landscape uninhabitable and destroyed food crops.

During the second hundred years, a pandemic had wiped out half the population, while famine and starvation took three-quarters of the survivors.

There were also some positive changes. The development of nuclear fusion as an energy source meant that carbon-based fuels were no longer required. The one-time food production lands of the Majans returned to forests, which removed carbon dioxide from the atmosphere and stored it as biomass. The global warming of the previous two centuries was slowly reversed. By the end of the second hundred years after Mosse's death, the planet's ecosystems were recovering, largely due to the decimation of the Majan population.

Mosse had been wrong about the possibility of the Majan species travelling to other planets. They had managed to confound the laws of physics and biology. Somehow or other, spacecraft propulsion had been developed, which enabled travel at two per cent of the speed of light.

Astronomers believed that a star just 22 light years away from Thera had several planets that were similar in characteristics and might support Majan life. That meant that if a spacecraft could avoid technical problems for 1,100 years, plus a century or two for acceleration and deceleration, then it might just reach one of these planets and hopefully find a safe landing place.

Cryogenic technology had been developed, capable of freezing individual Majans until the system woke them up again at some time in the future. Although this had not been successfully tested for more than one year, it was assumed that, once frozen, a subject could be recovered again several thousand years later.

Due to the vast distances involved, there was no opportunity for the Majans to send unmanned exploration probes. However, it was decided that the need to establish a colony before the nuclear arsenal was finally used justified the launch of a deep-frozen colonisation team of 20 males and 20 females.

A team of incredibly brave, healthy, young adult volunteers was assembled, trained, frozen and encapsulated in a very high-velocity experimental spaceship. The craft contained an array of the most powerful computers ever constructed. It carried a database of the accumulated knowledge of the Majan species about life, the Universe and everything (*). It had enough fuel in its fusion energy generators for a 1,500-year journey across the galaxy.

It had been estimated that any advanced species that had developed nuclear weapons would not survive for more

Who Writes the Rules

than 1,000 years. The weapons would proliferate until, sooner or later, a despot or fanatic would gain sufficient control to use them in anger and stupidity. Even if this didn't lead to the immediate extinction of the species, it would normalise the concept of nuclear war. Nuclear weapons would be used in follow-up conflicts, in which the combatants would rapidly wipe each other out.

Unfortunately, this prediction turned out to be correct. A mere 300 years after launching the colonisation craft, the Majans on the planet Thera began an escalating nuclear war. The result was the extinction of their own and nearly every other species on the planet. A despot thought he had the right to control the destiny of other people and impose his political system on them. When they objected, he obliterated everybody, himself included.

While the nuclear holocaust destroyed the planet and wiped out the Majans, the sleeping, frozen colonisers were travelling at more than 6,000km/sec across the galaxy. Miraculously, the spaceship's computers had been brilliantly programmed to use machine learning and artificial intelligence algorithms. This enabled it to think better in nanoseconds than a flight crew could have done in weeks. It performed perfectly.

A planet was detected with a similar mass, chemical and atmospheric constitution as Thera. Its distance from its sun was also nearly identical to that of Thera from Sol. The computers set the controls for the heart of the planet Gore.

Life on the planet Gore had been evolving for nearly four billion years. It now comprised a wide variety of plant and animal species. One particular species, the Gorimen, had escaped the constraints of natural ecosystems.

They had learned to use tools and technology to modify their environment for their own purposes.

The Gorimen were an arrogant species who believed they had been created by a supreme commander in order to dominate all other species in the Universe. However, they lived in many different kingdoms across the planet. They directed their domination instincts against their neighbours, with whom they were typically either at war or trying to maintain an uneasy truce. The Gorimen had civilisation, but their technological development was several hundred years behind that of the Majans.

As the spaceship decelerated towards Gore, the control system thawed and awakened the colonisation team. They gradually recovered consciousness, oblivious to the nuclear holocaust on Thera. They felt as if they'd just had a very good night's sleep.

The craft had scanned the ground and detected a large flat area that was covered in a soft golden-yellow, grass-like plant about half a metre deep. The Gorien wheatfield looked like the perfect landing spot.

The chosen landing spot was in farmland in the Kingdom of the Cannabubbles. They were suspicious people who could be remarkably charming but were totally untrustworthy. The Cannabubbles had been observing the approach of what they thought was a comet. They were surprised and impressed when it gradually slowed down, orbited the planet a few times, and then descended onto a rural wheat field. The farmer was less impressed that an alien spacecraft had flattened large circular patterns into his wheat crop.

Sergo, the regional special police commandant,

Who Writes the Rules

instructed the local farmers to approach the alien spacecraft slowly, armed only with pitchforks. The police snatch squad, armed with more deadly weapons, would stay a safe distance behind them, out of sight.

"Stay well back from the craft, but stand your ground. If anybody comes out, then pretend you think they're superheroes. Drop to your knees and kiss the ground as if you're worshipping them. They'll have a false sense of security, and we can trap them," Sergo told the farmers.

"What if they attack us?" One farmer responded.

"Then we'll call in the army and shell them from behind cover."

"I'm not going near them; they'll shoot us!" said another farmer.

"If you don't, then we'll shoot you," replied Sergo.

The farmer knew Sergo was serious and did as he was instructed.

The bridge crew of the spacecraft watched their monitors. A large group of people were standing a hundred metres away.

"They look just like us but a bit primitive," said the captain. "They only have pitchforks as weapons. We'll go outside." Turning to the second lieutenant, he instructed, "Take a party of three. If they try anything, shoot in the air. If they don't back off, start shooting the leaders."

A door at the side of the craft slid upwards, and a staircase folded down to the ground. As the landing party stepped slowly down into the field of wheat, the Cannabubbles fell to the ground, bowing before them.

"They think we're superheroes," said the second lieutenant as he approached the Cannabubbles. Raising his hands, he smiled at the Cannabubbles and gestured to them to stand up. "We come in peace, brothers."

The farmers stood, smiling, guessing that the meaning of the sound coming from the alien was a message of peace.

"We've fooled them. They think we're friendly," said a farmer.

"Offer them some water," said another.

A leading farmer took a drink from a bottle of water and then held it out to the second lieutenant, who cautiously accepted and took a drink.

Turning to his colleagues, he said, "It's ok. Just water. They're friendly."

The two groups smiled and muttered to each other, unable to understand their respective languages. Gradually the other coloniser crew members came down to join them, all with side-holstered guns but assured that the locals were friendly.

Sergo arranged for food and beer to be sent forward. One lot of bottles went to the farmers, another to the aliens, who all lost consciousness within a few minutes of drinking it. The special police squad collected the sleeping colonisers and drove them to holding cells in a nearby town. Then they were taken to a 'research lab.'

The Majan colonisers were held for several weeks while the police linguists learned how to communicate with them. Then a couple were probed to find the most sensitive parts of their bodies. The whole party were then interrogated for any useful information, or simply because the Cannabubble police enjoyed inflicting pain. The Majan IT support team very quickly revealed the workings of the ship's computer system and database.

A couple of them were killed and dissected by an anatomy research team. A few were sent to the kitchen butcher, who quickly established the location of the tenderest cuts. These were forwarded to the Masterchef team to investigate the best way to flavour and cook their new meat source. The others were selected, one by one, to be served at banquets for the police and political dignitaries.

As the supply of Majan meat dwindled, a banquet was arranged in honour of their King, Vladiput, the mighty-hungry, Grand Master of the Cannabubbles.

"Are you telling me we're down to the last one?" demanded Vladiput.

"I'm afraid so, your almightiness," replied Sergo, who'd been promoted to national security chief after capturing the aliens.

"We should have kept some for further interrogation until we know all about them!"

"No need to, your majesty. We've broken into their database, which has all the knowledge their species ever gathered. It explains how to build some very powerful weapons, which will be great for putting our unruly neighbours in their place."

"Couldn't we have farmed them as a food supply?"

"It seems they take too long to mature. We'd have to eat them small and just keep a few for breeding. Not worth the effort, your excellence."

"Where did they come from? Can't we go and get some for special occasions?"

"Too far away. We don't know how to get there, so

it would take too long, your mightiness."

"Pity," said Vladiput as he swallowed the last mouthful of the last Majan. "It's very tasty. Just like pork!"

Within fifty years, all life on the planet Gore was extinct as a result of the Cannabubbles' discovery of how to make nuclear weapons.

* A small tribute to the great Douglas Adams, author of *Life, the Universe and Everything*, who, hopefully, would have found this epilogue amusing.

Who Writes the Rules

Sources

Although *Who Writes the Rules* has been presented as if it were a science fiction novel, the embedded scientific and anthropological content, however contentious, has been assembled from a wide range of reference sources. It is regarded by the author as being factual, based on life on the Planet Earth. The most significant of the sources are listed below.

Energy and Life
Schneider, E.D. and Sagan, D. (2005). Into the Cool: Energy Flow, Thermodynamics and Life.

Evolution, Ecology and Anthropology
Archibald, Herbert L. 2014. The Enigma of the Wildlife Population Cycle Solved? Evidence that the Periodicity and Regularity of the Cycle are Driven by a Lunar Zeitgeber. Canadian Field Naturalist 128(4): 327-340.

Begon, M., Townsend, C. R. and Harper, J. L. (2006). Ecology. From Individuals to Ecosystems.

Bennett, K. D. (1997). Evolution and Ecology. The Pace of Life.

Clutton-Brock, T. H. and Pemberton, J.M. (2004). Soay Sheep. Dynamics and Selection in an Island Population.

Dartnell, Lewis. (2019). Origins. How Earth's History Shaped Human History.

Dawkins, R. (2004). The Ancestor's Tale. A Pilgrimage to

the Dawn of Life.

Diamond, J. (1993). The Third Chimpanzee. The Evolution and Future of the Human Animal.

Diamond, J. (1998). Guns Germs and Steel. A short history of everybody for the last 13,000 years.

Diamond, J. (2005). Collapse. How societies choose to fail or survive. Harari, Y. N. (2011. Sapiens. A Brief History of Humankind.

Manco, J. (2013). Ancestral Journeys. The Peopling of Europe from the First Adventurers to the Vikings.

Mithen, S. (2003). After The Ice. A Global Human History, 20,000-5,000 BC.

Nurse, Paul. (2021). What is Life?

Owen-Smith, N. (2002). Adaptive Herbivore Ecology. From Resources to Populations in Variable Environments.

Rutherford, A. (2018). The Book of Humans. A Brief History of Culture, Sex, War and the Evolution of Us.

Turchin, P. (2003). Complex Population Dynamics. A Theoretical Empirical Synthesis.

Turchin, P. (2016). Ultrasociety. How 10,000 Years of War Made Humans the Greatest Cooperators on Earth.

Wilson, R. C. L., Drury, S. A. and Chapman, J. L. (2001). The Great Ice Age. Climate Change and Life.

Yasuda, I. (2018). Impact of the astronomical lunar 18.6-yr tidal cycle on El-Niño and Southern Oscillation. *Sci Rep* **8**, 15206.

229

Religion

Bellah, R.N. (2011). Religion in Human Evolution: From the Palaeolithic to the Axial Age.

Boyer, Pascal. (2001). Religion Explained: The Evolutionary Origins of Religious Thought

Dawkins, R. (2006). The God Delusion.

Harris, S. (2006). The End of Faith: Religion, Terror and the Future of Reason

Shelby, A. (2014). The Evolution of Religion. How Religions Originate, Change and Die … And Why It Affects Us All.

Toorpakai, M. (2016). A Different Kind of Daughter.